PRAISE FOR *THE ABANDONED GENERATION*

"I was listening to the radio the other day. An 'expert' was asking how we can expect people in Pakistan to believe in democracy when millions can't afford to feed their children (some men are driven to suicide by the shame, he said) while many others live the life of millionaires? And I thought, who is saying this same thing about the United States. In *The Abandoned Generation*, Henry Giroux demonstrates once again why he is one of our most important social and political critics. As our economic fortunes ride the roller coaster of neo-liberal short-sightedness, and our political freedoms disappear into yet another invisible war, it is the children of this country (and the world) who suffer the most. As he has for decades, Giroux brings his intellectual acumen, his critical insight, and his passion for justice together in a book that everyone who cares about the future should read!"

—Lawrence Grossberg, University of North Carolina-Chapel Hill

"In *The Abandoned Generation* Henry Giroux documents how the U.S. is at war with its youth. Responding to recent events like 9–11 and the war on terror, Giroux argues that creating a better future for our youth and fellow citizens will require a struggle for democracy and creating critical citizens rather than unthinking patriots. In these important and insightful studies, Giroux challenges us to become critical analysts of contemporary discourse and politics and to participate in strengthening and enriching our democracy in the face of threats from within and without."

—Douglas Kellner, George F. Kneller Chair
in the Philosophy of Education, UCLA.

"Henry Giroux's provocative book, *The Abandoned Generation*, is not only a condemnation of the way we neglect the young in America, but it is also a passionate call for radical social change. Instead of the exploitive policies and strategies of corporate America that target young people as consumers and bring about the maltreatment of children as objects, Giroux demonstrates convincingly that there are still possibilities to close the gap between rich and poor and to create a more democratic means of education and acculturation for the young. His book is a major contribution for all those already engaged in collective struggle, and it will certainly stimulate all readers to become more socially aware of the intolerable conditions that young people must presently endure in America—and not only in America."

—Professor Jack Zipes, Professor of German and Comparative Literature at
the University of Minnesota and author of *Sticks and Stones:
The Troublesome Success of Children's Literature from Slovenly Peter to Harry Potter*

ALSO BY HENRY GIROUX

Public Spaces/Private Lives: Democracy Beyond 9–11 (2003)

Breaking in to the Movies: Film and the Culture of Politics (2002)

Beyond the Corporate University: Pedagogy, Culture, and Literary Studies in the New Millennium, edited with Kostas Myrsiades (2001)

Kriitten Pedagogiikka, co-authored with Peter McLaren (2001)

Stealing Innocence: Corporate Culture's War on Children (2001)

Theory and Resistance in Education (Revised edition, 2001)

Impure Acts: The Practical Politics of Cultural Studies (2000)

Critical Education in the New Information Age, co-authored with Manuel Castells, Ramon Flecha, Paulo Freire, Donaldo Macedo, and Paul Willis (1999)

The Mouse That Roared: Disney and the End of Innocence (1999)

Sociedad, Cultura Y Educacion, co-authored with Peter McLaren (1999)

Channel Surfing: Racism, the Media, and the Destruction of Today's Youth(1998)

Cultural Studies and Education: Towards a Performative Practice, edited with Patrick Shannon (1997)

Pedagogy and the Politics of Hope: Theory, Culture, and Schooling (1997)

Counternarratives, co-authored with Peter McLaren, Colin Lankshear, and Mike Cole (1996)

Fugitive Cultures: Race, Violence, and Youth (1996)

Between Borders: Pedagogy and Politics in Cultural Studies, edited with Peter McLaren (1994)

Disturbing Pleasures: Learning Popular Culture (1994)

Education Still Under Siege, co-authored with Stanley Aronowitz (Second Edition, 1994)

Living Dangerously: Multiculturalism and the Politics of Culture, (1993)

Border Crossings: Cultural Workers and the Politics of Education, (1992)

Igualdad Educativa Y Differencia Cultural, co-authored with Ramon Flecha (1992)

Postmodern Education: Politics, Culture, and Social Criticism , co-authored with Stanley Aronowitz(1991)

Postmodernism, Feminism and Cultural Politics: Rethinking Educational Boundaries, edited (1991)

Critical Pedagogy, the State, and the Struggle for Culture, edited with Peter McLaren (1989)

Popular Culture, Schooling & Everyday Life, edited with Roger Simon (1989)

Schooling and the Struggle for Public Life (1988)

Teachers as Intellectuals: Toward a Critical Pedagogy of Learning (1988)

Escola Critica E Politica Cultural (1987)

Education Under Siege: The Conservative, Liberal, and Radical Debate Over Schooling, co-authored with Stanley Aronowitz (1985)

The Hidden Curriculum and Moral Education, edited with David Purpel (1983)

Theory and Resistance in Education (1983)

Pedagogia Radical: Subsidius (1983)

Curriculum and Instruction: Alternatives in Education, edited with Anthony Penna, and William Pinar (1981)

Ideology, Culture and the Process of Schooling (1981)

THE ABANDONED GENERATION

Democracy Beyond the Culture of Fear

Henry A. Giroux

First published 2003 by PALGRAVE MACMILLAN™
175 Fifth Avenue, New York, N.Y. 10010 and
Houndmills, Basingstoke, Hampshire, England RG21 6XS.
Companies and representatives throughout the world.

PALGRAVE MACMILLAN is the global academic imprint of the Palgrave Macmillan division of St. Martin's Press, LLC and of Palgrave Macmillan Ltd. Macmillan® is a registered trademark in the United States, United Kingdom and other countries. Palgrave is a registered trademark in the European Union and other countries.

ISBN 1-4039-6138-7

Library of Congress Cataloging-in-Publication Data
Giroux, Henry A.
     The abandoned generation : democracy beyond the culture of fear / by Henry A. Giroux.
          p.   cm.
     Includes bibliographical reference and index.
     ISBN 1-4039-6138-7
     1. Critical pedagogy—United States.   2. Youth—United States—Social conditions.   3. Politics and education—United States.   4. Education—United States—Curricula.   5. Social justice—United States.   6. Mass media and youth—United States.   I. Title.
LC196.5.U6 G56   2003
370.11'5—dc21

2002035514

A catalogue record for this book is available from the British Library.

Design by Letra Libre.

First edition: April 2003
10 9 8 7 6 5 4 3 2 1

Printed in the United States of America.

For Susan, again and again

CONTENTS

ACKNOWLEDGMENTS

One of the most serious, yet unspoken and unrecognized, tragedies in the United States is the condition of its children. We live in a society in which too many young people are poor, lack decent housing and health care, attend decrepit schools filled with overworked and under-paid teachers, and who, by all standards, deserve more in a country that prides itself on its level of democracy, liberty, and alleged equality for all citizens. We also live at a time when politicians are far more will-ing to cut taxes for the rich than provide social provisions for children who are marginalized by virtue of class and race. Dietrich Bonhoeffer, the Protestant theologian, believed that the ultimate test of morality resided in what a society does for its children. If we take this standard seriously, American society has deeply failed its children and its com-mitment to democracy. For many young people, the future looks bleak, filled with the promise of low-paying, low-skilled jobs, the collapse of the welfare state, and, if you are a person of color and poor, the threat of either unemployment or incarceration. But power as a form of dom-ination is never absolute and oppression always produces some form of resistance. Fortunately, more and more young people nationally and internationally are mobilizing in order to fight a world dominated by corporate interests, and they are struggling to construct an alternative future in which their voices can be heard as part of a broader move-ment to make democracy and social justice realizable.

This book was inspired by both the political passion and courage of this generation of youth, many of whom recognize that the world stands at a critical juncture, if the future is not simply going to repeat a present in which corporate interests and power shape much of the social, political, cultural, and economic landscape. For many young people, social injustices—from class oppression to racial violence to the ongoing destruction of public life and the environment—can no longer be tolerated. One of the central messages coming from those youthful demonstrators who have taken to the streets in cities such as Seattle and Genoa is that we all live in a historical moment in which corporate power not only defines political culture, but debases democracy as it collapses under the weight of market relations that neoliberals define as empowering and transformative. At the same time, public education, which is one of the few spheres left not governed by the language of commercialism, is under assault by the advocates of the alleged free market; under the leadership of a deeply conservative government inextricably tied to business interests, learning appears to have no relationship whatsoever to providing the knowledge and skills necessary for students to participate in and shape public life. But most importantly, according to hundreds of thousands who have gathered in various cities throughout the globe, the gap between the rich and the poor, particularly among children, is growing wider and can no longer be accepted. In the midst of the current expressions of resistance and demonstrations of political hope, in spite of the seeming disparities of interests, the message that appears to unite this generation of youthful protesters is that a more democratic and just world is possible. Such a world, however, can only be realized through the collective struggles of many people willing to unite in their efforts to make real the possibilities and promises of a truly democratic world order. This book is dedicated to those who believe that it is not only possible to think against the grain, but crucial to act in ways that demonstrate political conviction, civic courage, and collective responsibility.

I want to thank a number of friends who take seriously their role as engaged intellectuals and in doing so take a stand and address the major social issues that affect children every day. I particularly want to thank Susan Searls Giroux, who once again in our conversations touched upon many of the ideas which animate this book. She is not only my best friend and partner, she also models for me what it means to struggle courageously against a world deeply in need of compassion, social justice, and hope. I also want to thank Panayota Gounari, my former graduate assistant, for the tireless help she provided while I was writing this book. Thanks also to Christopher Robbins for his research and editorial skills. And then there are countless friends who read drafts and in some cases made numerous comments. These include: Arif Dirlik, Imre Szeman, Paul Youngquist, Ralph Rodriguez, Jackie Edmundson, Stanley Aronowitz, Doug Kellner, Roger Simon, Ken Saltman, Jeff Nealon, Lynn Worsham, Barry Kanpol, David Theo Goldberg, Lawrence Grossberg, Sut Jhally, Donaldo Macedo, Kostas Myrsiades, Lee Quinby, Robin D. G. Kelley, Carol Becker, Norman Denzin, Nick Couldry, Peter Trifanos, Ted Striphas, Micaela Amato, Don Schule, Gary Olson, Dean Birkenkamp, and Jayne Fargnoli. Needless to say, I alone have to bear the responsibility for the final outcome. I also want to thank my children, Brett, Chris, and Jack, for their great sense of humor, insight, and love. I am deeply appreciative of the support provided by my editor, Michael Flamini, who supported this book right from the beginning. He is a wonderful friend and courageous editor. I also want to thank, Sue Stewart, my assistant, who has provided invaluable help in a range of administrative matters. I am enormously grateful to Dr. "Chip" Davis at the Hershey Medical Center for successfully operating on my knees and giving me the opportunity to be able to walk, skip, dance, and sometimes run again. Once again, I am appreciative for having Grizz around, my aging canine companion. While writing this book, earlier versions of some of these chapters were published in *JAC, Teachers College Record, Harvard Educational Review, Arena, Cultural Studies/Critical Methodologies, Tikkun,* and *Against the Current*.

INTRODUCTION

The War Against Youth
in the Post-9/11 Era

> *There is now within the social and political order a specific problem of child-hood. A problem inseparable from those of sexuality, drugs, violence, hatred and all the insoluble problems posed by social exclusion. Like so many other areas, childhood and adolescence are today becoming spaces doomed by the abandonment to marginality and delinquency. . . . Today, the general quick-ening of the pace of life condemns childhood to accelerated obsolescence.*
> —Jean Baudrillard[1]

Already imperiled before the terrorists attacks on September 11, democracy appears even more fragile in the United States in this time of civic and political crisis. This is especially true for young people. A great deal has been written critically about the passing of new antiter-rorist laws that, in the name of "homeland security," make it easier to undermine basic civil liberties that protect individuals against invasive and potentially repressive government actions. Yet, at the same time, there is a thunderous silence on the part of many critics and academ-ics regarding the ongoing insecurity and injustice experienced by young people in this country, which is now being intensified as a result of the state's increasing resort to repression and punitive social poli-cies.[2] Concerns about terrorism and security almost completely ignore what these terms mean beyond a violent attack against property and persons. There is a sense of moral and political indifference, if not cynicism, about the forms of domestic terrorism suffered by children who are poor, hungry, homeless, neglected, lacking medical care, or suffering physical abuse by adults.

Increasingly, children seem to have no standing in the public sphere as citizens, and thus are denied any sense of entitlement and agency. Children have fewer rights than almost any other group and fewer institutions protecting these rights. Consequently, their voices and needs are almost completely absent from the debates, policies, and legislative practices that are constructed in terms of their needs. This is not to suggest that adults do not care about youth, but most of those concerns are framed within the realm of the private sphere of the family and can be seen most clearly in the moral panics mobilized in the dominant media around children being abducted or preyed upon by pedophiles or other evil assailants. The response to such events, tellingly, is more "get tough on crime" policies, never condemnation of the systemic failure to provide safety and security for children. Children seem absent from any public discourse about the future and the responsibilities this implies for adult society; rather, children appear as objects, defined through the debasing language of advertising and consumerism. If not represented as a symbol of fashion or hailed as a hot niche, youth are often portrayed as a problem, a danger to adult society or, even worse, irrelevant to the future. This is particularly evident in the slew of Hollywood films about youth that have emerged in the last 20 years, such as *187, Black and White, Gummo, Jawbreakers, Bully, Traffic,* and *Murder by Numbers.* Young people in these films are seen as either dangerous, mindless, addicted to drugs, or socially irresponsible, and almost always crassly immature.

In recent times, a whole generation of youth have been labeled as superpredators, spiraling out of control—rather than corporate culture, corrupt government institutions, and the church. In 1997, Congressmen William McCollum of Florida captured this sentiment, however crudely, by claiming that contemporary youth "are the most dangerous criminals on the face of the earth."[3] Shortly after the school shootings at Columbine High School in Littleton, Colorado, Barbara Kantrowitz and Pat Wingert in *Newsweek* described youth as having a dark side and claimed that youth culture in general represents "'Lord of the Flies' on a vast scale."[4] *Time* magazine ran a cover story in August of 2001 proclaiming that "Kids Have Too Much Power," and in a January 2002 article, made it clear that kids can't expect any help or support from adults by running a picture of a baby on the cover with the large caption "You're On Your Own, Baby."

In the first *Time* cover, the power of adult society is projected onto youth, releasing adults from any responsibility for how they use their own power. According to this article, young people are spoiled rotten, baby-boomer children who are almost entirely defined by an inflated sense of self-importance and the urge to shop. Of course, the cure for this problem is for their parents and other adults to exercise more control and authority. In the second cover story, the overriding message is that adult society shoulders no responsibility for shaping children's future, thus affirming both the irrelevance of children and the future itself. This story suggests that in the age of Enron, risk is now the overriding fact of adult life, so much so that the next generation will have to take care of itself since adults have too much to worry about already (given that their 401K retirement funds no longer provide the necessary safety net for the future). Both stories make it clear that in this society, children are one of the lowest priorities.

Lawrence Grossberg argues that what is new about the plight of children is that, until recently, they always served as a "kind of symbolic guarantee that America still had a future, that it still believed in a future, and that it was crucial to America to invest in that future." And that "The [current] rejection of childhood as the core of our social identity is, at the same time, a rejection of the future as an affective investment."[5] Grossberg correctly suggests that the war being waged against youth cannot be separated from the needs of many adults to discount their own responsibilities as engaged citizens and to erase the obligations of the future.[6] This battle is waged by adults laboring under the logic of an allegedly pure market system that, in reality, only pays lip service to individual freedom while undermining the bonds of social life and social obligations.[7] Against the claim that youth have always been the scorn of older generations is the brute fact that in the age of deregulation, there are fewer institutions and organizations willing to champion children's rights or protect them from corporate predators. And, as Manuel Castells has noted, the consequences for children have been dreadful. Castells is worth quoting at length:

What is different is that we are witnessing a dramatic reversal of social conquests and children's rights obtained by social reform in mature industrial societies, in the wake of large-scale deregulation, and the bypassing of governments by global networks. What is different is the disintegration of traditional societies throughout the world, exposing children to the unprotected lands of mega-cities' slums. . . . What is new is mass, global tourism organized around pedophilia. What is new is electronic child pornography on the net, worldwide. What is new is the disintegration of patriarchalism, without being replaced by a system of protection of children provided by new families or the state. What is new is the weakening of institutions of support for children's rights, such as labor unions or the politics of social reform, to be replaced by moral admonitions to family values which often blame the victims for their plight.[8]

The Abandoned Generation argues that the United States is at war with young people. All youth are targets, especially those marginalized by class and color. This is a war waged by liberals, conservatives, corporate interests, and religious fundamentalists against those public spaces, goods, and laws that view children and youth as an important social investment, and includes a full-scale attack on children's rights, social services, the welfare state, and the public schools. Youth have become the all important group onto which class and racial anxieties are projected. Their very presence represents *both* the broken promises of capitalism in the age of deregulation and downsizing and a collective fear of the consequences wrought by systemic class inequalities, racism, and a culture of "infectious greed" that has created a generation of unskilled and displaced youth expelled from shrinking markets, blue collar jobs, and any viable hope in the future. Youth occupy a degraded borderland within the economic and cultural geography of neoliberal capitalism, in which the spectacle of commodification exists side by side with the imposing threat of the prison-industrial complex. The war against youth can, in part, be understood as part of the fundamental values and practices of a rapacious, neoliberal capitalism; moreover, the consequences of this complex cultural and economic assault can no longer be ignored by educators, parents, and other concerned citizens. Jean and John Comaroff are helpful here and observe:

As the expansion of the free market runs up against the demise of the welfare state, the modernist ideal in which each generation does better than its predecessor is mocked by conditions that disenfranchise the unskilled young of the inner city and the countryside. Denied full, waged citizenship in the nation-state, many of them take to the streets, often the only place where, in an era of privatization, a lumpen public can be seen and heard. The profile of these populations reflects also the feminization of post-Fordist labor, which further disrupts gender relations and domestic reproduction among working people, creating a concomitant "crisis of masculinity"; a crisis as audible in U.S. Gangsta rap as in the South African gang rape, as visible in the parodic castration of "The Full Monty" as in the deadly machismo of soccer violence or the echoing corridors of Columbine High. This is not confined to youth or workers, of course . . . but it is magnified among them.[9]

No longer seen as a crucial social investment for the future of a democratic society, youth are now demonized in the popular media and derided by politicians looking for quick-fix solutions to crime. In a society deeply troubled by their presence, youth prompts in the public imagination a rhetoric of fear, control, and surveillance—made all the more visible with the 2002 Supreme Court decision upholding the widespread use of random drug testing of public school students. Such testing of all junior and senior high school students who desire to participate in extra-curricular activities shows a deep distrust of students and furthers the notion that youth have become a generation of suspects. Schools increasingly resemble prisons, and students begin to look more like criminal suspects who need to be searched, tested, and observed under the watchful eye of administrators who appear to be less concerned with educating them than with policing their every move. Trust and respect now give way to fear, disdain, and suspicion. Moreover, this perception of fear and disdain is increasingly being translated into social policies that signal the shrinking of democratic public spheres, the hijacking of civic culture, and the increasing militarization of public space. Police and drug-sniffing dogs now are a common fixture in public schools. In many suburban malls, young people (especially youth of color) cannot even shop or walk around without either appropriate identification cards or in the company of their parents. Excluded from public spaces outside of schools that once offered young people the opportunity to learn a sport, play music, hang out in a youth club, attend alternative educational clubs, and develop their own talents and sense of self-worth, young people are now forced to hang out in the streets, and at the same time are increasingly subject to police surveillance, anti-gang statutes, and curfew laws, especially in poor, urban neighborhoods.

Instead of providing a decent education to poor young people, we serve them more standardized tests. Instead of guaranteeing them food, decent health care, and shelter, we increase their rates of incarceration, evidenced by the fact that the United States is the only industrialized country that sentences minors to death and spends "three times more on each incarcerated citizen than on each public school pupil."[10] Instead of providing them with vibrant public spheres, we offer them a commercialized culture in which consumerism is the only obligation of citizenship. But the hard currency of human suffering as it impacts on children can also be seen in some of the astounding statistics that suggest a profound moral and political contradiction at the heart of the United States, of one the richest democracies in the world: 20 percent of children are poor during the first 3 years of life and over 13.3 million live in poverty; 9.2 million children lack health insurance; millions lack affordable child care and decent early childhood education; in many states, more money is being spent on prison construction than on education; and the infant mortality rate in the United States is the highest of any industrialized nation. When broken down along racial categories, the figures become even more deplorable. For example, "In 1998, 36 percent of black and 34 percent of Hispanic children lived in poverty, compared with 14 percent of white children."[11] In some cities, such as the District of Columbia, the child poverty rate is as high as 45 percent.[12] While the United States ranks first in military technology, military exports, defense expenditures, and the number of millionaires and billionaires, it is ranked eighteenth in the gap between rich and poor children, twelfth in the percent of children in poverty, seventeenth in the efforts to lift children out of poverty, and twenty-third in infant mortality.[13] One of the most shameful figures on youth, reported by Jennifer Egan in the *New York Times,* is that "1.4 million children are homeless in America for a time in any given year . . . and these children make up 40 percent of the nation's homeless population."[14] In short, economically, politically, and culturally, the situation of youth in the United States is intolerable and unforgivable. It is all the more unforgivable because President Bush insisted during the 2000 presidential campaign that "the biggest percentage of our budget should go to children's education." He then passed a 2002 budget in which 40 times more money went for tax cuts for the wealthy than for education.[15] But Bush's insensitivity to American children represents more than a paean to the rich since he also passed a punitive welfare reform bill that requires poor, young mothers to work a 40-hour week while at the same time it cuts low-income childcare programs.

For many young people and adults today, the private sphere has become the only space in which to imagine any hope, pleasure, or possibility. Neoliberalism, with its emphasis on market forces, narrows the legitimacy of the public sphere by redefining it around the related issues of privatism, consumption, and safety. Big government, recalled from exile after September 11, is now popularly presented as a guardian of security—security not in terms of providing adequate health care or a social safety net, but with increasing the state's role as a police force—resulting in the ongoing abridgement of basic freedoms and dissent, the criminalization of social problems, and the prioritizing of penal methods over social investments. Ardent consumers and disengaged citizens provide fodder for a growing cynicism and depoliticization of public life at a time when there is an increasing awareness not just of corporate corruption, financial mismanagement, and systemic greed, but also of the recognition that a democracy of critical citizens is being replaced quickly by a democracy of consumers. The desire to protect market freedoms and wage a war against terrorism, ironically, has not only ushered in a culture of fear but is also dealing a lethal blow to civil freedoms. At the heart of this contradiction is both the fate of democracy and the civic health and future of a generation of children and young people.

In this insufferable climate of increased repression and unabated exploitation, young people and communities of color become collateral damage in an ongoing war against justice, freedom, citizenship, and democracy. As the foundations of the national in-security state are solidified through zero-tolerance policies, antiterrorist laws, soaring incarceration rates, the criminalization of homelessness, racial profiling, and anti-immigration policies, the forces of repression become more integrated, marked by an increasing combination of various elements of federal and local law enforcement agencies. *The Abandoned Generation* argues that as desperate as these conditions appear at present, they have become the basis for a surge of political resistance on the part of many youth, intellectuals, labor unions, educators, and social activists all over the world. This book suggests that under such circumstances it is time for intellectuals, parents, young people, and others to take a stand and remind themselves that collective problems deserve collective solutions and that what is at risk is not only a generation of young people and adults now considered to be either a generation of suspects or a threat to national security, but the very promise of democracy itself.

Against the culture of fear and its emphasis on emergency time, which appeals to short-term efficacy and removes the application of governmental power from public deliberation, *The Abandoned Generation* calls for a notion of public time, one that fosters civic engagement and public intelligence. This means at the very least creating the conditions for making government accountable for its actions while also mobilizing citizens to reclaim the power necessary to shape the institutions, values, and social practices that influence their lives on a daily basis.

The greatest challenge Americans face does not come from crazed terrorists, but in the ongoing battle to expand and deepen the principles of justice, freedom, and equality on behalf of all citizens—especially young people, who are quickly becoming an abandoned generation. This is not going to take place, as President Bush's policies tragically demonstrate, by shutting down democracy, eliminating its most cherished rights and freedoms, and deriding communities of dissent. On the contrary, any attempt to enact real patriotism—if the pledge to "liberty and justice for all" is to mean anything at all—must begin with the current state of crisis among youth rather than devolve into the jingoistic posturing currently fashionable among many U.S. congressmen and the acolytes in the press who have spent the last decade pandering to crass commercialism and the values it projects. The struggle for democracy has to be understood and engaged through politics, not vacuous moralism. If politics is to be reclaimed as the center of individual and social agency, civil life will have to be motivated not by a culture of fear but by a passion for civic engagement, ethical responsibility, and the promise of a substantive democracy. As cultural critic Noreena Hertz observes, "The political state has become the corporate state," and the implicit contract between the state and the citizen, which is fundamental to a strong democratic society, has been broken.[16] If corporate power has awarded economics and participation in the market greater respect than those forms of political agency that are central to creating vibrant democratic public spheres, citizenship becomes reduced to market rituals, while democracy is hijacked in order to reproduce vast inequalities of power, influence, and wealth. The situation has become all the more dangerous with the post–September 11 increased push toward national security, the widening militarization of everyday life, and the relentless marginalization of all the non-market values central to an inclusive democracy.[17]

This book is divided into two sections. In the first, I focus on the varied ways in which the post–September 11 climate has created a culture of fear that raises serious questions about the meaning of patriotism, democracy, education, and the emergence of a repressive state. This section provides a theoretical framework for understanding and engaging the emerging culture of fear in the United States and its effects both domestically and globally. In the second section, I address how the culture of fear is both impacting youth and creating a crisis at the very heart of a democratic society. In this section, I focus specifically on the assault on public schools, Hollywood images of the nation's most vulnerable youth, and the ongoing commercialization of higher education. In this book, I employ a language of criticism as well as a language of hope. In doing so, I focus not merely on the destruction of civil liberties and the growing attack on the bodies and rights of young people but also on the opportunities for developing new vocabularies, resources, and modes of collective struggle—which are emerging in the global justice and anti-corporate movements being waged by young people all over the world. Such struggles provide new models and diverse strategies for addressing the problem of unaccountable global power matched by growing attempts to "enrich and enliven, educate and animate democratic practice."[18]

We live in dangerous times, and the American public should not underestimate the degree to which its civil liberties and public resources are at risk. But rather than being an occasion for despair, the problems we face offer an opportunity for organizing our passions and energies in order to reaffirm the democratic commitments to equality, liberty, justice, and critical citizenship. Now more than ever the time has come for adults and young people to organize together, to cross national borders, to create the conditions necessary to reject cynicism, and to struggle collectively for a more just world and the possibility of a realizable democracy.

CHAPTER I

Public Time versus Emergency Time

Politics, Terrorism, and the Culture of Fear

Five months after the horrific terrorist attacks on the Pentagon and the World Trade Center, President George Bush announced in his State of the Union Address on January 29, 2002, that the "war against terror is only just beginning" and that if other governments exhibit timidity in the face of terror, America will act without them. Claiming that the security of the nation was his first priority, Bush proclaimed a war without end and suggested that the United States would act unilaterally throughout the world to enforce what he called "our responsibility to fight freedom's fight." Appealing to what he described as a resurgent sense of unity and community in the country, Bush announced that American citizens were no longer willing simply to live their lives devoted to material pursuits and a "feel good" attitude. According to Bush, in the aftermath of the events of September 11, America had been reborn with a renewed sense of patriotism, community, and public spiritedness. Painting the United States as a beacon of civilization, Bush urged Americans to perform voluntary acts of public service, be alert for signs of potential terrorism at home, support massive increases in the military budget, endorse an energy policy that involves more drilling for oil, accept a huge tax cut for the rich and major corporations, and tolerate the suspensions of some basic civil liberties and freedoms that would grant more power to the police, Federal Bureau of Investigation (FBI), Central Intelligence Agency (CIA), and other security forces.

While Bush and his associates are quick to remind the American people that much has changed in the United States since September 11, almost nothing has been said about what has not changed. I am referring to the aggressive attempts on the part of many liberal and conservative politicians to undermine informed debate, promote a remorseless drive to privatization, and invoke patriotism as a cloak for carrying out a reactionary economic and political agenda on the domestic front, while simultaneously cultivating an arrogant self-righteousness in foreign affairs in which the United States portrays itself uncritically as the epitome of purity, goodness, and freedom, while its opposition is equated with the forces of absolute evil.

As a wartime president, Bush enjoys incredibly high popular ratings, but beneath the ratings and the president's call for unity, there is a disturbing appeal to modes of community and patriotism buttressed by moral absolutes in which the discourses of evil, terrorism, and security work to stifle dissent, empty democracy of any substance, and exile politics to a realm of power no longer subject to criticism or public debate.[1] Shamelessly pandering to the fever of emergency and the economy of fear, President Bush and his administration are rewriting the rhetoric of community so as to remove it from the realm of politics and democracy. In doing so, they are not only concentrating their political power, but pushing through harsh policies and regressive measures that cut basic services and public assistance for the poor, offer school children more standardized testing but do not guarantee them decent health care and adequate food, sacrifice American democracy and individual autonomy for the promise of domestic security, and allocate resources and tax breaks to the rich through the airline bail-out and retroactive tax cuts. Under the auspices of a belligerent nationalism and militarism, community is constructed "through shared fears rather than shared responsibilities," and the strongest appeals to civic discourse are focused on military defense, civil order, and domestic security.[2] Within the rhetoric and culture of shared fears, patriotism becomes synonymous with an uncritical acceptance of governmental authority and a discourse "that encourages ignorance as it overrides real politics, real history, and moral issues."[3]

The United States has a desperate, unfulfilled longing for community, steeped as it is in the ethic of neoliberalism with its attempts to subordinate all human needs to the dictates of the market and the bottom line, while simultaneously demonizing "not only government but the very idea of public service and public goods."[4] Allowing a handful of private interests to control all aspects of the larger social order, neoliberalism defines society exclusively through the privileging of market relations, deregulation, privatization, and consumerism. Under the reign of neoliberalism, the social collapses into the private, part-time labor replaces full-time work, trade unions are weakened, everybody becomes a customer, and the exchange of money takes precedence over social justice, socially responsible citizens, and the building of democratic communities. In such ruthless times any invocation of community seems nourishing, even when the term is invoked to demand an "unconditional loyalty and treats everything short of such loyalty as an act of unforgivable treason."[5] How can any notion of democratic community or critical citizenship be embraced through the rhetoric of a debased patriotism that is outraged by dissent in the streets? What notion of community allows Peter Beinart, editor of *The New Republic,* to wrap himself in the flag of patriotism and moral absolutism while excoriating those who are critical of Bush policies? He writes: "This nation is now at war. And in such an environment, domestic political dissent is immoral without a prior statement of national solidarity, a choosing of sides."[6] Charges of unpatriotic dissent are not restricted to either protesters in the streets or to those academics who incurred the wrath of Lynne Cheney's American Council of Trustees and Alumni for not responding with due Americanist fervor to the terrorist attacks of September 11.[7] It was also applied to former Senate majority leader Tom Daschle when he offered a mild critique of President Bush's plan to launch what appears to be a never-ending war against terrorism. Trent Lott, the Republican leader at the time, responded with a crude rebuke, suggesting that Daschle had no right to criticize President Bush "while we are fighting our war on terrorism."[8] It appears that the leadership of the Republican Party and its supporters have no qualms about dismissing critics by impugning their patriotism. Tom Davis of Virginia, the head of the G.O.P.'s House campaign committee, branded those who criticize Bush's policies as "giving aid and comfort to our enemies."[9] The Family Research Council went even further by running ads in South Dakota "likening Tom Daschle to Saddam Hussein because he opposed oil drilling in the Arctic National Wildlife Refuge."[10] "Community" in this version of public discourse demands not courage, dialogue, and responsibility, but silence and complicity.

Eric Hobsbawm has observed that "never was the word 'community' used more indiscriminately and emptily than in the decades when communities in the sociological sense became hard to find in real life."[11] Maybe it is the absence of viable communities organized around democratic values and basic freedoms that accounts for the way in which the language of community has currently "degraded into the currency of propaganda."[12] How else can one explain the outrage exhibited by the dominant media against anyone who seems to question, among other things, the United States's support of friendly dictatorships, including Afghanistan and Saudi Arabia, the USA Patriot act with its suppression of civil liberties, or those who suggest the need for a serious discussion about how United States foreign policy contributes to the widespread poverty, despair, and hopelessness throughout the world, offering terrorist nihilism the opportunity "to thrive in the rich soil of exclusion and victimhood."[13] Actual democratic communities are completely at odds with a smug self-righteousness that refuses to make a distinction between explaining events and justifying them. As Judith Butler points out:

> to ask how certain political and social actions come into being, such as the recent terrorist attack on the U. S., and even to identify a set of causes, is not the same as locating the source of the responsibility for those actions, or indeed, paralyzing our capacity to make ethical judgments on what is right or wrong. . . . but it does ask the U.S. to assume a different kind of responsibility for producing more egalitarian global conditions for equality, sovereignty, and the egalitarian redistribution of resources.[14]

Such questions do not suggest that the United States is responsible for the acts of terrorism that took place on September 11. On the contrary, they perform the obligatory work of politics by attempting to situate individual acts within those broader sets of conditions that give rise to individual acts of terrorism, while simultaneously asking how the United States can intervene more productively in global politics to produce conditions that undercut rather than reinforce terrorism. At the same time, such questions suggest that the exercise of massive power cannot be removed from the practice of politics and ethics, and such a recognition demands a measure of accountability for the consequences of our actions as one of the most powerful countries in the world. As Lewis Lapham observes, "[I]t is precisely at the moments of our greatest peril that we stand in need of as many questions as anybody can think to ask."[15]

The rhetoric of terrorism is important because it operates on many registers to both address and inflict human misery. Moreover, such rhetoric is often used to redefine the delicate balance of freedom and security crucial to any democratic society, and it carries with it an enormous sense of urgency that often redefines community against its most democratic possibilities and realized forms. Rising from the ashes of impoverishment, human suffering, and religious fundamentalism, terrorism, at its worst, evokes a culture of fear, unquestioning loyalty, and a military definition of security from those who treat it as a pathology rather than as a politics. In part, this is evident in Bush's "war against terrorism," which, fueled by calls for public sacrifice, exhausts itself in a discourse of moral absolutes and public acts of denunciation. This all-embracing policy of anti-terrorism depoliticizes politics by always locating it outside of the realm of power, and strips community of democratic values by defining it almost exclusively through attempts to stamp out what Michael Leeden, a former counter-terror expert in the Reagan administration, calls, "corrupt habits of mind that are still lingering around, somewhere."[16] The narrowing of community and the ongoing appeal to jingoistic forms of patriotism divert the public from addressing a number of pressing domestic and foreign issues; it also contributes to the increasing suppression of dissent and what Anthony Lewis has rightly called the growing escalation of concentrated, unaccountable political power that threatens the very foundation of democracy in the United States.[17] This is evident in Attorney General John Ashcroft's decision to relax restrictions on the FBI's ability to conduct domestic spying as part of its stepped-up counter-terrorism campaign, overturning restrictions that were adopted after disclosures of abuse in the 1960s and 1970s by the FBI under Cointelpro, an FBI domestic spying program aimed at disrupting oppositional political groups. Dispensing with probable cause restrictions in order to begin counter-terrorism investigations, the new FBI regulations allow federal agents to search commercial data bases, monitor the World Wide Web, and compile dossiers on people and groups without the need to show that a crime has been committed. According to officials at the American Civil Liberties Union, the new guidelines "say to the American people that you no longer have to be doing something wrong in order to get that FBI knock at your door."[18]

With the passage of the Homeland Security Act, a further threat to civil liberties is underway in the development of the Total Information Awareness System. This is a giant government computer system being set up to spy on Americans. The giant computer system will allow government intelligence agencies and law enforcement to gain instant access to information from e-mail, internet use, travel, credit card purchases, banking transactions, phone records, and medical fines; all without a search warrant. Marc Rotenberg, executive director of the Electronic Privacy Information Center, a group that is concerned with civil liberties, claims that the new computer system represents "the most sweeping plan to conduct surveillance on the public since at least the 1960s."[19]

The Bush administration's contempt for law and due process applies not only to non-citizens and foreign terrorists but to American citizens as well. For instance, Jose Padilla, a former gang member, was labeled by Attorney General John Ashcroft as an "enemy combatant" and locked in a Navy brig in South Carolina, accused of planning to detonate a radioactive bomb in New York or Washington, D.C. The administration later issued an embarrassing correction, admitting that there was no hard evidence that Padilla was actually involved in such a plot, but he was still being held without charges. Here is an American citizen whom the government argues was involved in a plan to explode a "dirty bomb" in the United States, though it provides no evidence or legally sound reason for incarcerating him. Bob Herbert, a columnist for the *New York Times*, compared the action of the U.S. government in the Padilla case to behavior fitting of tyrannical societies. But he goes further:

> Today it may be Padilla. Tomorrow it might be you.... The war against terror is not merely a fight for survival. It's a fight for the survival of a free and democratic way of life. If that's not the case, then we're just blowing stale smoke rings of hypocrisy when we place our hands over our hearts and recite pledges about liberty and justice, or sing about the free and the brave.[20]

Herbert may be right. Another American citizen, Yaser Esam Hamdi, a 21 year old who was captured in Afghanistan and eventually imprisoned as an "enemy combatant" at the Guantanamo naval base in Cuba, is also being detained without charges and denied his constitutional rights; he is currently imprisoned on a Navy brig in Norfolk, Virginia. At the same time, Attorney General Ashcroft announced, according to Jonathan Turley, a writer for the *Los Angeles Times*, a desire for camps for U.S. citizens he deems to be "enemy combatants."[21] If this conjures up images of the Japanese internment camps set up during World War II, Ashcroft's Terrorism Information and Prevention System (Operation TIPS) suggested the workings of the KGB under Stalin. Operation Tips, which had been scheduled to start in August 2002 but has since been abandoned, planned on recruiting millions of American workers, including meter readers, utility workers, cable technicians, and postal carriers, who have access to private homes as informants to report to the Justice Department any activities they believed suspicious, unusual, and potentially terrorist-related. President Bush's web site described the program, without irony, as "a national system" that "will involve the millions of American workers who, in the daily course of their work, are in a unique position to see potentially unusual or suspicious activity in public places."[22] For Bush and Ashcroft, the culture of fear fueled by emergency time provides the conditions in which Americans can be asked to spy on each other, dissent can be viewed as un-American, and dissenters can be subjected to possible internment.

At the core of Bush's notion of community and hyper-patriotism is a notion of temporality detached from a sense of public deliberation, critical citizenship, and civic engagement. Jerome Binde refers to this view of temporality as "emergency time," and describes it as a "world governed by short-term efficacy," which under the imperatives of utter necessity and pragmatism eschews long-term appraisals and gives precedence to the "logic of 'just in time' at the expense of any forward-looking deliberation."[23] According to Binde, emergency time opens the way for what he calls "the tyranny of emergency." He explains:

> Emergency is a direct means of response which leaves no time for either analysis, forecasting, or prevention. It is an immediate protective reflex rather than a sober quest for long-term solutions. It neglects the fact that situations have to be put in perspective and that future events need to be anticipated. Devising any durable response to human problems . . . requires looking at a situation from a distance and thinking in terms of the future.[24]

Lacking any reference to democratic collective aims, the appeal to emergency time both shrinks the horizon of meanings and removes the application of governmental power from the fields of ethical and political responsibility. Emergency time defines community against its democratic possibilities, detaching it from those conditions that prepare citizens to deliberate collectively about the future and the role they must play in creating and shaping it. Thus, cynical reason replaces reasoned debate with the one-way gaze of power, and popular resistance to the war is dismissed as "a demagoguery of the streets, while dictators are offered up to us as responsible representatives of their countries."[25] But emergency time in the context of Bush's "war against terrorism" also rejects the radical secularism at the heart of substantive democracies in favor of a religious vocabulary. The metaphysics of religious discourse dispenses with the task of critically engaging the elaborate web of historical, social, and political factors that underscore and give meaning to the broader explanations for terrorism. Instead, the complexity of politics dissolves into the language of "crusades," "infidels," "goodness," and "evil." As Steven Lukes and Nadia Urbinati point out: "A rhetoric of emergency has arisen in which a Manichean impulse is given free range, in which 'our' (American? Western?) values are seen as threatened by an enemy that is seen as the incarnation of evil and variously identified as 'fundamentalist' and 'Islamist' as embodied in Al Qaeda and personified by Osama bin Laden," and once again Saddam Hussein.[26]

It is the displacement of politics and the weakening of democratic public spaces that allows for religious fundamentalists increasingly to define the basis of community, civic engagement, and the realm of the social. Against this notion of emergency time, educators, cultural workers, and others need to posit a notion of public time. According to democratic theorist Cornelius Castoriadis, public time represents "the emergence of a dimension where the collectivity can inspect its own past as the result of *its own actions,* and where an indeterminate future opens up as a domain for its activities."[27] For Castoriadis, public time puts into question established institutions and dominant authority. Rather than encouraging a passive attitude towards power, the idea of public time demands forms of political agency based on a passion for self-governing, actions informed by critical judgment, and a commitment to linking social responsibility and social transformation. Public time legitimates those pedagogical practices that form the basis for a culture of questioning—one that provides the knowledge, skills, and social practices that encourage an opportunity for resistance and a proliferation of discourses. Public time unsettles common sense and disturbs authority while encouraging critical and responsible leadership. As Roger Simon observes, public time "presents the question of the social—not as a space for the articulation of pre-formed visions through which to mobilize action, but as the movement in which the very question of the possibility of democracy becomes the frame within which a necessary radical learning (and questioning) is enabled."[28] Put differently, public time affirms a politics without guarantees and a notion of the social that is open and contingent. Public time provides a conception of democracy that is never complete and determinate but constantly open to different understandings of the contingency of its decisions, mechanisms of exclusions, and operations of power.[29] At its best, public time renders governmental power explicit, and in doing so rejects the language of religious rituals and the abrogation of the conditions necessary for the assumption of basic freedoms and rights. Moreover, public time considers civic education the basis of justice because it provides individuals with the skills, knowledge, and passions to talk back to power, while simultaneously emphasizing both the necessity to question that accompanies viable forms of political agency and the assumption of public responsibility through active participation in the process of governing.

Against Bush's disregard for public discussion of his policies, his fetish for secrecy, his clamoring for a notion of patriotism that is synonymous with mindless conformity, and his flaunting of presidential power, public time gives credence to a notion of democracy that calls for the establishment of unbounded interrogation in all domains of public life. Democratic politics and viable notions of community are affirmed when public spaces are created that enable individuals and movements to exercise power over the institutions and forces that govern their lives. Under such conditions, politics is not viewed as a form of pathology, but is central to what it means to build vibrant public spheres and democratic communities.[30]

What has become clear both in Bush's State of the Union Address and in the policies of his administration is that there is no discourse for recognizing the obligation of a democratic society to pay its debts to past generations and fulfill its obligations to future generations, and especially to the young, who are being increasingly abandoned at all levels of government. His tax cuts privilege the commercial interests of the rich over public responsibilities to the poor, the elderly, the environment, and to children. His call for military tribunals for trying non-citizens, his initial detaining of over 1,200 Arabs and Muslims for extended periods in secrecy, and his willingness to undermine basic constitutional freedoms and rights by enhancing the power of the police and other law enforcement groups pose a grave threat to those civil liberties that are fundamental to a democracy.[31] Edward Said argues more specifically that

> Bush and his compliant Congress have suppressed or abrogated or abridged whole sections of the First, Fourth, Fifth and Eighth Amendments, instituted legal procedures that give individuals no recourse either to a proper defense or a fair trail, that allow secret searches, eavesdropping, detention without limit, and, given the treatment of the prisoners at Guantanamo Bay, that allow the US executive branch to abduct prisoners, detain them indefinitely, decide unilaterally whether or not they are prisoners of war and whether or not the Geneva Conventions apply to them—which is not a decision to be taken by individual countries.[32]

Most importantly, Bush's "war against terrorism" camouflages how democracy is being undermined through an anti-terrorist campaign that relentlessly attempts to depoliticize politics itself. What began as the demonization of political Islam has now been extended to the demonization of politics itself as Bush and his cohorts put forth policies that attempt to erase the possibility of imagining a democratic future, the democratic space of the social, the meaning of democratic community, or the practices that anchor democratic life. As Barnor Hesse and S. Sayyid insightfully observe:

> Through such processes, politics seems exiled. While the centre is re-occupied by a naturalized world order, politics is proscribed from the domain of order itself. Paradoxically, cynical reason becomes a dominant ideology within an apparently post-ideological West. In a Western world apparently deprived of political alternatives to corporate capitalism, neoliberalism and global social inequalities, what once passed for politics has been exclusively transposed to the space occupied by those discontented with the West, and dispossessed by it.[33]

By depoliticizing politics, the "war on terrorism" becomes both an empty abstraction and a strategic diversion—empty because terrorism cannot be either understood or addressed through the discourse of moral absolutes and religious fervor. Militarism does not get at the root of terrorism, it simply expands the breeding grounds for the conditions that give rise to it. Military intervention may overthrow governments controlled by radical fanatics such as the Taliban, but it does not address those global conditions in which poverty thrives and thousands of children die every day from starvation or preventable diseases; where 250 million children of all ages are compelled to work under harsh conditions; and where some 840 million adults are without adequate shelter and access to health care.[34] As long as such inequalities exist, resistance will emerge and terrorism will be the order of the day. Not only is this a problem that will not be solved by dropping thousands of bombs on poor countries (with or without accompanying packets of food), it also suggests rethinking how U.S. policies actually contribute to these conditions through the country's support of military dictatorships, unilateral disregard for international coalitions, and ongoing support for the ruthless policies of global neoliberalism. The rhetoric of "anti-terrorism" cleanses Bush and his cohorts of the obligations of political and ethical responsibility on a global level by ignoring the complex bonds that tie the rich and the powerful to the poor and the powerless. Such ties cannot be explained through the language of a rabid nationalism, hyped-up patriotism, or religious zeal. As Judith Butler points out, fatuous moralism is no substitute for assuming responsibility for one's actions in the world. She writes:

> ... moralistic denunciation provides immediate gratification, and even has the effect of temporarily cleansing the speaker of all proximity to guilt through the act of self-righteous denunciation itself. But is this the same as responsibility, understood as taking stock of our world, and participating in its social transformation in such a way that non-violent, cooperative, egalitarian international relations remain the guiding ideal?[35]

Moralism may offer Bush and his cohorts the mantle of innocence, but it does nothing to further the dynamics of democracy or civic engagement and may, as the novelist John Edgar Wideman suggests, even serve to "terrorize" those Americans it claims it is benefiting:

> By launching a phony war [Bush] is managing to avoid the scrutiny a first-term, skin-of its teeth presidency deserves. Instead, he's terrorizing Americans into believing that we require a wartime leader wielding unquestioned emergency powers. Beneath the drumbeat belligerence of his demands for national unity, if you listen you'll hear the bullying, the self-serving, the hollowness, of his appeals to patriotism. Listen carefully and you'll also hear what he's not saying: that we need, in a democracy full of contradictions and unresolved divisions, opposition voices.[36]

If Wideman is correct, and I think he is, then Bush's "innocent" posturing and his righteous rhetoric of anti-terrorism also provide a massive diversion from addressing those political issues at the heart of a real, inclusive democracy. Bush commits us to the dark world of emergency time, a world divided between good and evil, one in which "issues of democracy, civil comity and social justice—let alone nuance, complexity and interdependence simply vanish."[37] In this world of emergency time, politics assumes a purity that posits only one right answer, one side to choose. Not only does emergency time provide Bush with a political identity that closely resembles a kind of martyrdom, it certifies him as the proper authority for speaking the only admissible language and holding down the only acceptable position.[38] The ideology of emergency time not only refuses to question its own assumptions, it also refuses to acknowledge its glaring absences—those issues or points of view it either ignores or marginalizes. Hence, in the name of "fighting freedom's fight," Bush constructs a worldview in which the growing gap between the rich and the poor is ignored, massive unemployment is disregarded, the war against youth marginalized by class and color does not exist, poverty and racial injustice become invisible, the shameful growth of the prison-industrial complex is overlooked, Enron is easily forgotten, and threats to the environment evaporate.

Bush's notion of security and freedom depoliticizes politics and makes a sham of civic complexity and responsibility. If we are to challenge his policies, educators, parents, and other concerned citizens need to reclaim a notion of politics and pedagogy that embraces a notion of public time and that fosters civic engagement and public intelligence. This means at the very least making governmental authority accountable for its actions while also mobilizing citizens to reclaim the power necessary to shape the regimes of power and politics that influence their lives. A vibrant democracy recognizes that national security cannot be limited to military security and terrorism cannot be reduced to attacks by religious and political fanatics. Security also means "healthy, educated, and safe children and strong families and communities,"[39] and terrorism also includes what can be called the "terrorism of everyday life," manifest, in part, through the suffering and hardships experienced by millions of adults and children who lack adequate food, health care, jobs, child care, retirement funds, and basic living quarters.

One classic example of how Bush's anti-terrorist campaign is driven by a dead-end moralism, a culture of fear, and a politics of emergency time that punishes youth and prevents any analysis of the causes of terrorism is a provocative advertising campaign that was sponsored by the White House drug control office in 2002 and run extensively both in print media and on television. Shot in stark black and white, the ads begin with close-ups of the faces of exclusively dark-haired teenagers (no blond, suburban kids in this group). Their faces appear in rapid succession on the television screen. Each teenager admits matter-of-factly in short staccato sentences a litany of horrendous crimes they allegedly helped people commit. The mantra includes: "I helped murder families in Columbia," "I helped kids learn how to kill," "I helped a bomber get a fake passport," and "I helped blow up buildings." After each admission, a different youthful face repeats any one of the following refrains: "It was just innocent fun," "Hey, some harmless fun," or "All the kids do it." The ad ends with the message: "Drug money supports terror. If you buy drugs you might too." More recent anti-drug ads are even more offensive. Using the same signature message, "Drug money supports terror. If you buy drugs you might too," they demonize youth in more extreme fashion. One example from an ad titled "Timmy" features a young boy facing the camera, who says matter-of-factly "I kill mothers, I kill fathers, I kill grandmothers, I kill grandpas, I kill sons, I kill daughters, I kill fireman, I kill policeman. [pause] Technically, I didn't kill these people; I just kind of helped." It is difficult to tell if the qualification is for added effect or if the insanity of the charges has become clear, if only as an afterthought.

Ostensibly a blow against the war on drugs, but framed as part of the war against terrorism, the ad campaign suggests that children are, in part, responsible for promoting terrorist campaigns being waged all over the world, including those directed at the United States on September 11. The goal of the campaign is to shame young, casual drug users by leading them to believe that the drugs they purchase help pay for terrorist activities, especially those acts engaged in by the Al Qaeda terrorists who attacked the World Trade Center and the Pentagon. What is so disturbing about these ads is not only the lack of evidence establishing a direct link between Al Qaeda's terrorist activities and the drug trade, but also the presupposition that American youth who casually engage in drug use are somewhat responsible for such terrorist acts. The alleged connection between casual drug use among young people and the financing of worldwide terrorist activities is more than a rhetorical stretch: it is a politically irresponsible claim. According to this logic, people who fill up their cars with gasoline or buy diamonds would also be responsible for such acts, since terrorists groups make millions from both oil profits and the diamond trade. But don't expect any ads to appear soon condemning yuppies who buy gas for their SUVs or Hollywood starlets who wear diamonds for sponsoring terrorist campaigns around the globe. Adults would not tolerate such an irresponsible, blanket accusation. But an accusation that appears irresponsible and fallacious when applied to adults seems quite reasonable when applied to young people. Blaming the young for terrorism not only reproduces the worst forms of demonization, it also ignores the complexity of the problems that promote drug use among young people and adults, problems rooted in a culture of commodification and addiction, poverty, unemployment, and deep-seated alienation. One could dismiss this ad campaign as symptomatic of the "war on terrorism" if it were an isolated event. Unfortunately, such representations and the hysteria, fear, and repressive measures used by adults against young people have a long history, but in recent times such attacks seem to be taken up with a methodical zeal unlike anything that has gone before. Moreover, as young people bear the brunt of increasing attacks, children appear unprotected by the state, families, or institutions, such as labor unions and religious organizations, that traditionally have provided support for children's rights.

Similarly, by framing the war against terrorism as a problem of youth, the federal government can keep silent about U.S. foreign policy and how it might explain why we are the object of scorn and derision in so many parts of the world. Moreover, the existence of this ad campaign is indicative of how willing the federal government is to mobilize emergency time and the culture of fear to cover up its own inadequacies by attacking young people, a strategy that reinforces in the public imagination the growing assumption that youth should be treated as a generation of suspects, a potentially dangerous group responsible for many of the social, economic, and political problems that the Bush administration has exacerbated and refuses to address.

The invocation of emergency time profoundly limits the vocabulary and imagery available to us in developing a language of critique, compassion, and possibility for addressing the relationship between the crisis of democracy and the crisis of youth. Limiting civil liberties, cutting back social programs, defining democracy as expendable as part of the discourse of emergency time, and appealing to the culture of fear prevents adults from focusing on young people as a symbol of the future and creating the symbolic and material conditions for increasing the scope of those values and freedoms necessary for the young to become active and critical citizens willing to fight for a vibrant democracy.

CHAPTER 2

Democracy, Patriotism, and Schooling After September 11

Critical Citizens or Unthinking Patriots?

I should like to be able to love my country and still love justice. I don't want just any greatness for it, particularly a greatness born of blood and falsehood. I want to keep it alive by keeping justice alive.

—Albert Camus

This is a difficult time in American history. The tragic and horrific terrorist acts of September 11 suggest a traumatic and decisive turning point in the history of the United States. Some commentators have compared it to the Japanese attack on Pearl Harbor. Others suggest that the history of the twenty-first century will be defined against the cataclysmic political, economic, and legal changes inaugurated by the monstrous events of September 11. Similarly, many people are now aware that, for better or worse, the United States is part of a global system, the effects of which cannot be completely controlled.[1] There is also a newfound sense of unity, organized not only around flag-waving displays of patriotism but also around collective fears and an ongoing militarization of visual culture and public space.

As President Bush declared that the United States was at war, the major television networks capitalized on a militarized notion of patriotism, repeatedly framing their news programs against tag lines such as "America at War," "America Strikes Back," or "America Recovers." Fox News Network delivered a fever-pitch bellicosity in its commentaries and reactions to the terrorist bombings, framed nightly against its widely recognized slogan, "America United." A majority of both the op-ed commentaries in the dominant media and the television commentaries appearing on the major networks proclaimed support for government and military action, including the potential war with Iraq, while giving relatively little exposure to dissenting positions.[2] Many news commentators and journalists in the dominant press have taken up the events of September 11 by invoking daily the symbols of revenge, retaliation, and war. Against an endless onslaught of images amply supplied by the Defense Department of U.S. jets bombing Afghanistan, the dominant media connects the war abroad with the domestic struggle at home by presenting numerous stories about the endless ways in which potential terrorists might use nuclear weapons, poison the food supply, blow up apartment buildings, or unleash biochemical agents on the American population. The increased fear and insecurity created by such stories simultaneously served to legitimatize a host of antidemocratic practices at home, including "the beginnings of a concerted attack on civil liberties, freedom of expression, and freedom of the press."[3] Such anxieties have also produced a growing sentiment on the part of the American public that people who suggest that terrorism should be analyzed, in part, within the context of American foreign policy should not be allowed "to teach in the public schools, work in the government, and even make a speech at a college."[4] Against this censorship of public discourse, Hollywood and television producers provide both Spielberg-type patriotic spectacles such as the HBO dramatic series *Band of Brothers,* and pay uncritical homage to the military in films such as *Behind Enemy Lines, Black Hawk Down, Spy Games, We Were Soldiers,* and *Wind Talkers.* All of these films offer romanticized images of military valor and a hyper-masculine, if not over-the-top, patriotic portrayal of war and violence—while hoping to capitalize on the current infatuation with the military experience.

In this chapter, I illustrate the many ways in which life in post–September 11 America is both a rupture from some of the anti-government politics that dominated before these tragic events and an uncanny continuation of the pre–September 11 worship of global capitalism and the virtual abandonment of any effort to create greater equality, especially for children. In showing both these ruptures and continuities, I hope to help educators contemplate the role that public schools might play in facilitating an alternative discourse grounded in a critique of militarism, consumerism, and racism. Such an alternative discourse would redefine democracy as something separate and distinct from the hyper-individualized market-based relations of capitalism and the retrograde appeal to jingoistic patriotism.

Before the attacks on the World Trade Center and the Pentagon, popular perceptions of politics and government were that they were either corrupt or irrelevant. Recalled from exile, it appears that the government, especially the military and law enforcement, is once again a defining feature of American life, both pressing and despairing at the same time.[5] Still, as significant as September 11 might be as a moment of rupture, it is imperative to look at the crucial continuities that either have remained the same or have escalated since the attacks. For instance, prior to September 11, there was a growing concern with the increasing use of racial profiling, the criminalization of social policies (such as arresting the homeless), the growth of the prison-industrial complex and multilayered systems of social control and surveillance,[6] and the ongoing attacks by the police against people of color.[7] These trends seemed disturbing before the events of September 11, but now they have the cloak of official legitimacy, buttressed and intensified by the sense of insecurity and fear that, in part, mobilizes the call for patriotism and national security. For instance, little has been reported in the dominant media about the violence against people perceived as Middle Eastern. As Mike Davis observes:

> The big city dailies and news networks have shown patriotic concern for the US image abroad by downplaying what otherwise might have been recognized as the good ole boy equivalent of *Kristallnacht*. Yet even the fragmentary statistics are chilling. In the six weeks after 11 September, civil rights groups estimate that there were at least six murders and one thousand serious assaults committed against people

perceived as "Arab" or "Muslim," including several hundred attacks on Sikhs.[8]

While there has been some resistance in both the media and among diverse groups to the accelerated practice of racial profiling, the American public largely supported the indefinite detention by federal authorities of over 1,200 immigrants, only 4 of whom, according to Davis, have direct links to terrorist organizations.[9] Only recently has the opposition been growing to the government's decision to hold alleged terrorists indefinitely, including American citizens such as Yaser Esam Hamdi, as enemy combatants, without charges, bail, and access to lawyers. A successful lawsuit brought against the Bush administration by the American Civil Liberties Union, People for the American Way, and a number of other groups resulted in a federal judge ruling that the U.S. government must reveal the names of the detainees arrested after the September 11 terrorist attacks.

More recently, the immigration and Naturalization Service in Southern California arrested hundreds of Iranians and other Muslim men who complied with an order to register under new residence laws. Many of those arrested had been living, working, and paying taxes in the United States for over a decade. Thousands of people protested in Los Angeles waving signs and banners which read, "What's next? Concentration camps?" and "Detain terrorists, not innocent immigrants." As new anti-terrorist laws have been passed, it has become easier to undermine those basic civil liberties that protect individuals against invasive and potentially repressive government actions. Against a government- and media-induced culture of fear, "Federal law enforcement is being restructured so that the FBI can permanently focus on the War against Terrorism—meaning that it will largely become an elite immigration police—while a mysterious new Pentagon entity, the Homeland Defense Command, will presumably adopt the Mexican border as a principal battlefield."[10] A further threat to democracy can be found in the USA Patriot Act of 2001. This legislation increases law enforcement's power to conduct surveillance, enact wire taps that do not have to be disclosed to the public, engage in secret searches, and detain legal immigrants indefinitely. It also permits the Central Intelligence Agency to resume spying on U.S. citizens. The bill also authorizes secret immigration trials, unreviewable military tribunals, and the monitoring of attorney-client conversations. Not only does the bill introduce a broadly defined crime of "domestic terrorism," it also allows people to be interned and tried on the basis of secret evidence. Many Americans view these laws as both a violation of the Constitution and a threat to some of the most basic freedoms of a democratic state. For instance, David Cole, a progressive lawyer, has argued that the USA Patriot Act "imposes guilt by association on immigrants . . . and resurrects the philosophy of McCarthyism, simply substituting 'terrorist' for 'communist.'" He also argues that "the military tribunals eliminate virtually every procedural check designed to protect the innocent and accurately identify the guilty."[11] There is even more reason for concern about the erosion of civil liberties in light of Attorney General John Ashcroft's willingness to extend the powers of the FBI to monitor and spy on a vast array of citizens and political groups, "even when there is no evidence of criminal activity."[12] The concern over civil liberties is not limited to progressive critics. The widely read conservative op-ed columnist for the *New York Times*, William Safire, has denounced the new unbridled powers given to the FBI without any public debate. He writes that "Attorney General John Ashcroft—working with his hand-picked aide, FBI Director 'J. Edgar' Mueller III—has gutted guidelines put in place a generation ago to prevent the abuse of police power by the federal government. They have done this deed by executive fiat: no public discussion, no Congressional action, no judicial guidance."[13]

The idea of what constitutes a just society is in flux, betrayed in part by the legacy and language of a commercial culture that collapses the imperatives of a market economy and the demands of a democratic society, and a present point in time that makes humanitarian and political goals a footnote to military goals.[14] Under such circumstances, the past simply becomes an advertisement for a market-based society, incapable of offering an ethical and political language that can speak passionately about how to affirm and defend non-commodified public spaces and democratic values. Hence, the most basic principles of citizenship and the freedoms on which it is built get subordinated, if not unduly threatened, amidst the call to war and the language of censorship. Instead of seeing the current crisis as a break from the past, it is crucial for educators and others to begin to understand how the past might be useful in addressing what it means to live in a democracy in the aftermath of September 11. Such an examination suggests that we should establish a vision of freedom, equity, education, and justice, as post-colonialist Homi Bhabha points out, "informed by civil liberties and human rights, which carries with it the shared obligations and responsibilities of common, collaborative citizenship."[15]

Unity, Civil Liberties, and Patriotism

Official calls for unity, burdened with rage and grief for those killed or injured in the terrorist attacks, waver between agitprop displays of patriotism and a genuine attempt to understand and address the problem of balancing civil liberties and national security, fear and reason, compassion and anger. In the political reality that emerges from the crisis, the American people are being asked to make certain choices, for example about ongoing military interventions in Afghanistan, the Philippines, and Iraq, with the possibility of wider military strikes on other Islamic nations, and the sacrifice of some basic civil liberties to strengthen domestic security. Of course, Americans have every right to demand that our children, cities, water supply, public buildings, and most crucial public spaces be safe from terrorists. And we must do something in response to such brutal acts of violence. But the demand for security and safety calls for more than military action, gross violations of international law, and the rescinding of basic civil liberties; it also points to larger political issues that require a diplomatic offensive based on a critical examination of the very nature of our own domestic and foreign policy. Educators have an important role to play in encouraging such an examination of American history and foreign policy among their students and colleagues. Equally important is the need for educators to use their classrooms not only to help students to think critically about the world around them, but also to offer a sanctuary and forum where they can address their fears, anger, and concerns about the events of September 11 and how it has affected their lives. The terrorist attacks provide educators with a crucial opportunity to reclaim schools as democratic public spheres in which students can engage in dialogue and critique about the meaning of democratic values, the relationship between learning and civic engagement, and the connection between schooling, what it means to be a critical citizen, and the responsibilities one has to the larger world.[16]

Nothing justifies the violence committed by terrorists against those innocent people who died or were injured on September 11. Americans should be unified against that type of terror, and rightly so; but we need to define not only what we are against, but also what we stand for as a nation, and how such a posture draws from the principles and values that inform the promise of a more fully developed and inclusive democracy in a global landscape. In a time of crisis, unity is a powerful force, but it is not always innocent, and it must become part of a broader dialogue about how the United States defines itself and its relationship to the rest of the world, particularly to those Western and Middle Eastern societies that reject or are resistant to democratic and egalitarian rule.

If this national crisis has shattered the alleged American sense of complacency and purported self-indulgence, it has also aroused a sense of unity that has sent a chilling message of intolerance towards dissenting opinions about America's role. Early casualties included two journalists, Dan Guthrie, a columnist for the *Daily Courier* of Grants Pass, Oregon, and Tom Gutting of the *Texas City Sun,* both of whom were fired for criticizing President Bush soon after the terrorist bombings.[17] Equally disturbing was a statement issued by both the chancellor and trustees of the City University of New York, condemning professors who criticized United States foreign policy at a teach-in.[18] Neither the trustees nor the chancellor attended the teach-in, basing their response on articles that appeared in the *New York Post.* Similar attacks were made by Lynne Cheney, wife of the vice president and former chairwoman of the National Endowment for the Humanities, and Scott Rubush, an associate editor of *FrontPage* magazine. Cheney denounced Judith Rizzo, deputy chancellor of the New York City schools, because she "said terrorist attacks demonstrated the importance of teaching about Muslim cultures."[19] Rubush, while appearing on National Public Radio in October 2001, argued that four faculty members at the University of North Carolina at Chapel Hill, who had been critical of American foreign policy, should be fired because "They're using state resources to the practical effect of aiding and abetting the Taliban."[20]

Cheney was also involved in what was one of the most disturbing attacks on people who have dissented against American foreign policy. She and Senator Joseph Lieberman founded an organization called the American Council of Trustees and Alumni, which published the recent report, "Defending Civilization: How Our Universities Are Failing America, and What Can Be Done About It."[21] This report includes a list of 117 statements made by faculty and students in the wake of September 11 and points to such comments to argue that American campuses are "short on patriotism and long on self-flagellation."[22] The report not only suggests that dissent is unpatriotic but it also reveals the names of those academics who are allegedly guilty of such crimes.[23] The report was sent to 3,000 trustees, donors, and alumni across the country, urging them to wage a campaign on college campuses to require the teaching of American history and Western civilization and to protest and take actions against those intellectuals who are not loyal to this group's version of patriotism.[24] Commenting on the report, Lewis Lapham, the editor of *Harper's Magazine,* sums up what he considers its contribution to the debate on "preferred forms of free speech." He observes: "I've had occasion to read a good deal of fourth-rate agitprop over the last thirty years, but I don't remember an argument as disgraceful as the one advanced by the American Council of Trustees and Alumni under the rubric of 'academic freedom, quality and accountability.'"[25] Behind the warm glow of American innocence and the brandishing of flag pins, the call to patriotism by Cheney and her ilk undermines the very spirit of liberty and freedom it claims to defend. Patriotism cannot be defended as part of a holy crusade against evildoers, especially when the latter includes anyone who believes that civic mindedness and public conscience demands of any country, particularly a superpower such as the United States, that it pay scrupulous attention to its use of power and the consequences it has on the rest of the world. Dissent is not the enemy of democracy, but an essential element in its ability to make visible the connection between ethics and politics, justice and the exercise of power. As social theorist Jerome Binde observes, "Being able to act also means being able to answer for our actions, to be responsible."[26]

Across the United States, a number of professors have been either fired or suspended for speaking out critically about post–September

11 events.[27] Patriotism in this view becomes a euphemism for shutting down dissent, eliminating critical dialogue, and condemning critical citizenship in the interest of conformity and a dangerous departure from what it means to uphold a viable democracy. Needless to say, teachers in both K-12 and higher education are particularly vulnerable to these forms of censorship, particularly if they attempt to engage their students in discussions that critically explore the historical, ideological, and political contexts of the attacks and the underlying causes of terrorism, not to mention any controversial subject that calls into question the authority and role of the United States in domestic and foreign affairs. Such censorship shuts down critical inquiry in the schools and prevents students from learning how to distinguish an explanation from a justification. Richard Rothstein, a *New York Times* reporter, is right in arguing that "[T]eachers should be encouraged to explore whether there are specific policies that may give rise to terrorism, without being accused of undermining patriotism and national unity. Students who are not taught to question our policies will be ill-prepared as adults to improve on them."[28]

There is a difference between justifying terrorism and trying to historically contextualize and explain it, and this distinction appears to be lost on those who are quick to argue that academic freedom and civil liberties are expendable in a post–September 11 world.[29] Refusing to make a distinction between explaining an event and justifying it not only stifles a full range of public discourse, which would include arguments and perspectives from other parts of the world, it also serves to suppress dissent.[30]

Suppressing a culture of dissent does more than shut down critical voices; it also provides the conditions for intolerance and bigotry. Unfortunately, an unparalleled sense of unity and display of "patriotism" on the part of the American people have also given rise to what some journalists have called "stunning intolerance,"[31] exacerbating an already unrestrained and indiscriminate hatred towards the seven million Americans who are Muslims. In some cases, insults have been replaced by violence and even murder. As the wave of hate speech and incidents escalate, the American people fall prey to the most retrograde and dangerous views. For instance, a Gallup Poll released on

October 4, 2001 "indicated that 49 percent of the American people said yes to the idea that Arabs, including those who are American citizens, should carry special identification," and 58 percent demanded that Arabs, including those who are U.S. citizens, should have "to undergo special, more intensive security checks before boarding airplanes in the United States"[32]

Such views reflect an uncritical notion of "patriotism"[33] and are at odds with the most basic principles of an effective democracy informed by a critical democratic education that encourages dialogue, critique, dissent, and social justice. At its best, patriotism means that a country does everything possible to question itself, and to provide the conditions for its people to actively engage and transform the policies that shape their lives and the lives of others. Patriotism in this sense connects a culture of questioning and dissent with those democratic values that inform public citizenship and legitimate access to decent health care, housing, food, meaningful employment, child care, and childhood education programs for all citizens. At its worst, patriotism detaches itself from public citizenship and turns its back on citizens who are poor, homeless, hungry, and unemployed.[34]

In its most virulent form, patriotism confuses dissent with treason, arrogance with strength, and envisions brute force as the only exemplar of justice. The threat of terrorism will not be eradicated by weakening civil liberties, nourishing bellicose calls for revenge, or drawing lines in the sand between the West and the rest. As journalist George Monblot points out, "[I]t seems that in trying to shout the terrorist out, we have merely imprisoned ourselves. . . . [F]ree speech and dissent have now joined terrorism as the business of 'evil doers.' If this is a victory for civilization, I would hate to see what defeat looks like."[35] Ignorance and arrogance are no substitute for reasoned analyses, critical understanding, and an affirmation of democratic principles of social justice. Any call for further limiting civil liberties and freedom of speech suggests a dangerous silence about the degree to which our constitutional rights are already at risk and how the current call for national security might work to further a different type of terrorism, one not marked by bombs and explosions, but by state-supported repression, the elimination of dissent, and the death of both the reality and promise of democracy.

But unreflective patriotism as home-team boosterism runs the risk of not only bolstering the conditions for what Matthew Rothschild, the editor of *The Progressive,* calls "The New McCarthyism,"[36] but also of feeding a commercial frenzy that turns collective grief into profits—reminding us how easy the market converts noble concepts like public service and civic courage into forms of civic vacuity. Frank Rich, an op-ed writer for the *New York Times,* calls this trend "Patriotism on the Cheap" and captures its paean to commercialism in the following commentary:

> "9/11" is now free to be a brand, ready to do its American duty and move products. Ground zero, at last an official tourist attraction with its own viewing stand, has vendors and lines to rival those at Disneyland. (When Ashleigh Banfield stops by, visitors wave and smile at the TV camera just as they do uptown at the "Today" show.) Barnes & Noble offers competing coffee-table books handsomely packaging the carnage of yesteryear. On Gary Condit's Web site, a snapshot of the congressman's own visit to ground zero sells his re-election campaign. NBC, whose Christmas gift to the nation was its unilateral lifting of a half-century taboo against hard-liquor commercials, deflects criticism by continuing to outfit its corporate peacock logo in stars and stripes.[37]

Red, white, and blue flags adorn a plethora of fashion items, including hats, dresses, coats, T-shirts, robes, and scarves. Many corporations now organize their advertisements around displays of patriotism—signaling their support for the troops abroad, the victims of the brutal terrorist acts, and, of course, American resolve—each ad amply displaying the corporate logo, working hard to gain some cash value by defining commercialism and consumerism as the ultimate demonstration of patriotism.[38] Other companies have seized upon the remarkable flood of giving displayed by many Americans after the tragic bombings to sell their products by suggesting they are working with charities associated with September 11. In many cases, the connection with charities exists, but most of the profits go to the companies rather than to the victims they are supposed to benefit. For instance, Sony Music produced a disc called "God Bless America," which displays boldly on its cover the message, "For the Benefit of the Twin Towers Fund," which refers to "a charity established by former Mayor Rudolph Giuliani for the families of uniformed rescuers killed in the World Trade Center collapse."[39] On the back of the disc in small print is the message that "a substantial portion" of profits from the disc will be donated to the fund. The *New York Times* reported that the company had no formal agreement with the fund and that no money had gone to the Twin Towers Fund, even though the disc had sold over 1.2 million copies.[40] It gets worse. Steve Madden, the shoe designer, produced a sneaker emblazoned with an American flag of imitation gemstones that was part of the "Bravest" shoe line. "The sneakers were promoted across the country as a joint endeavor with a charity run by Denis Leary, star of *The Job* on ABC, to 'raise money for New York City's fallen firefighters.'"[41] According to the *New York Times,* Madden made $515,783 in profits from the sneakers by February 2002, but at that time none of the profits had been distributed to "the families of the firefighters killed September 11." Under pressure to distribute some of the profits, Madden's company agreed to give at least 10 percent to the charity, while retaining "more than $400,000 in profits from the Bravest." When queried about the refusal of the company to hand over the profits made through an appeal to help the families of the firefighters, Jamie Karson, the Madden chief executive, responded without irony that "The most patriotic thing we can do is make money."[42] Of course, making profits is one thing, but making excessive profits through the language of compassion and patriotism at the expense of the bereaved families exploited promotionally to sell products is simply shameful, and makes clear how low corporations can stoop to rake in profits. As I point out in more detail in the following sections, consumerism and the squelching of dissent are mutually reinforcing aspects of a patriotism in which citizenship is more about the freedom to buy than the ability of individuals to engage in "critical public dialogue and broadened civic participation leading (so it is hoped) to far-reaching change."[43]

The general panic following the September 11 attacks not only redefined public space as the "sinister abode of danger, death and infection"[44] and fueled the collective rush to "patriotism on the cheap," but also buttressed the "fear economy." Defined as "the complex of military and security firms rushing to exploit the national nervous breakdown,"[45] the fear economy promises astronomical financial gains for the defense department—already asking for an additional 48 billion-dollar increase from the Bush administration for the 2003 budget. The administration estimates that more than $2 trillion will be spent on the military over the next five years, with annual budgets rising to $451 billion by 2007.[46] In addition to bloated defense budgets, the fear economy also spells big profits for the anti-terrorist security sectors which are primed to terror-proof everything from trash cans and water systems to shopping malls and public restrooms. The war on terrorism cannot justify the profits of a bloated security industry, the imprisonment of American citizens such as Jose Padilla and Yaser Esam Hamdi while not affording them a court hearing and any legal rights,[47] or the war that is being waged against children domestically through the elimination of basic child investments. Security is not limited to military defense, and as the Children's Defense Fund observes, "The war on terrorism is no excuse not to prevent and stop the domestic terrors of child poverty, hunger, homelessness, and abuse and neglect right now."[48]

Democracy and Capitalism Are Not the Same

Based on an appeal to fear and a call to strengthen national security, the space of the social has been both militarized and further com-modified. As a result, there is little public discussion about connecting social life to democratic values and justice, or what the public good might mean in light of this horrible attack as a moral and political ref-erence point to denounce mass acts of violence and to attempt to se-cure freedom and justice for all people. In fact, since the terrorist attacks on September 11, the media has largely treated the notions of freedom and security without any reference to how these terms might be taken up as part of a wider set of political, economic, and social in-terests that were at work before the terrorists wreaked havoc on New York and Washington, D.C. In part, this is due to the willingness of the largely dominant media, politicians, and others to substitute jingoistic drum-beating for a reasoned analysis of what it would mean to "put public affairs back on the American agenda, to revive people's sense that they have a stake in the way our society is run."[49]

Such questions are crucial to any national conversation about the relationship among security, freedom, and democracy, and the future of the United States. But such a task would demand that we remember the social and political discourse and conditions before September 11, and what limited notions of freedom, security, and citizenship were available then to Americans—the legacy and influence of which might prevent them from critically addressing this national crisis. Instead of seeing the current crisis as a break from the past, it is crucial for the American public to begin to understand how the past might be useful in addressing the question of what it means to live in a democracy in the aftermath of the attacks. Public schools should play a decisive role in helping students think about the relationship between history and the present, incorporating a critical understanding of events that are often left out of contemporary interpretations that define the roles students might play as critical citizens. American history should not be presented to students free of the many conflicts and struggles waged by women, workers, people of color, and others who have tried to erase the gap between the reality and the promise of democracy. Of course, this will be difficult because many public schools are overburdened with high-stakes tests and harsh accountability systems designed to get teachers to narrow their curriculum and to focus only on raising test scores. Any struggle to make schools more democratic and socially relevant will have to link the battle for critical citizenship to an ongoing fight against turning schools into testing centers and teachers into technicians.

Notions of freedom and security cannot be separated from a legacy of neoliberalism, in which the space of the social is largely defined by market relations that commodify, privatize, and utterly commercialize the meaning of freedom and security. Construing profit-making as the essence of democracy, neoliberalism provides a rationale for a handful of private interests to control as much of social life as possible to maximize their financial investments. Within this growing marketization and privatization of everyday life, market relations are viewed as a paradigm for democracy itself. Capitalism now defines the meaning of freedom, and to paraphrase Milton Friedman, profit-making is the essence of democracy.[50] Defined almost exclusively through the rhetoric of commercial forces, the economic policies of neoliberalism have undermined the discourses of moral responsibility, democratic values, and political agency by removing from social life considerations of equality, justice, and the value of the public good.

The crucial goal of educating people to be critical agents, capable of making collectively binding choices and to carry them out as part of civic responsibility and the public good, has been eradicated. Even worse, the privatized notion of the social that has dominated American life for the last 20 years makes it increasingly difficult for people to invest in the notion of the public good as a political idea, or to believe they can be agents of change and that political and ethical values matter, or that democracy is worth investing in and struggling over.

The discourse of security and freedom prior to the September 11 attacks pointed to a very different notion of the social, one that had very little to do with democratic social relationships, compassion, and non-commodified values. Freedom was largely defined as the freedom to pursue one's own individual interests, largely free of governmental interference, and seemed at odds with a more democratic notion of freedom—which would include, as Edward Said has argued, the "right to a whole range of choices affording cultural, political, intellectual and economic development—[that] ipso facto will lead to a desire for articulation rather than silence."[51] Decoupled from this higher notion of freedom, security within the last 20 years has become synonymous with big government and a debilitating form of dependency. Security coupled with freedom traditionally also meant providing individuals not only with basic rights, but also making those social provisions that enabled them to develop their capacities as citizens free from the most basic wants and deprivations. This suggested creating a welfare state that provided a modicum of support and services to make sure people had access to decent health care, food, child care, public schooling, employment, basic financial support, and housing.

Under neoliberal social and economic policies, security was no longer valued as a worthy goal or seen as a set of policies designed to protect the most vulnerable in society, such as the poor, elderly, and children. In fact, as the welfare state was hollowed out, governments reduced their investments in public welfare while narrowly redefining the meaning of security. With the election of Ronald Reagan to the presidency in 1980, freedom was defined largely in market terms, removed from questions of equity, and traditional notions of security became a rationale for attacking "big government" and dismantling the welfare state. From the Reagan to the Clinton eras, the idea of the social collapsed under the weight of a market philosophy that could only imagine a privatized notion of agency, and viewed community as an obstacle to market-based values that stressed excessive individualism, privatization, commercialization, and the bottom line. Under such circumstances, the helping functions of society gave way largely to policing functions, and the logic of free market exchange undermined those collective structures that fought for social guarantees, public services, and equality of rights. As the social became individualized, uncertainty and fear worked to depoliticize a population that is educated to believe that social problems can only be addressed through private solutions. Within such a climate, shared responsibilities gave way to shared trepidation.

In light of such views and practices, I want to suggest that while the social is being affirmed and reshaped as a result of the terrible tragedy of September 11, Americans need to critically engage the terms in which public life and citizenship are being invoked if we are to address the responsibilities of critical citizenship and the demands of a democratic society in a time of crisis. For instance, while the roles of big government and public services have made a comeback on behalf of the common good, especially in providing crucial services related to public health and safety, President Bush and his supporters remain "wedded to the same reactionary agenda he pushed before the attack."[52] Instead of addressing the gaps in both public health needs and the safety net for workers, young people, and the poor, President Bush has put into law a stimulus plan based primarily on tax breaks for the wealthy and major corporations, while at the same time "pressing for an energy plan that features subsidies and tax breaks for energy companies and drilling in the arctic wilderness."[53] Investing in children, the environment, and those most in need, as well as in crucial public services, once again gives way to investing in the rich and repaying corporate campaign contributors. This suggests that little has changed with respect to economic policy, regardless of all the talk about the past being irrevocably repudiated in light of the events of September 11.

The collapse of public life over the last 20 years makes it all the more essential that educators rearticulate a notion of the social that is framed not only against the recent terrorist attacks on the United States, but also in light of the emergence of a market-based philosophy. The role of educators, educational researchers, theorists, and policymakers is crucial to an ongoing public conversation with students and others about the current national crisis. At the heart of such a debate is the need to decouple a market economy from the notion of democracy, to refuse the neoliberal notion that market relations and profit-making constitute the meaning and substance of democracy. Political theorist Sheldon Wolin has recently argued that we need to rethink the idea of loss and how it impacts upon the possibility for opening up democratic public life. Wolin points to the need for educators to resurrect and raise questions about "What survives of the defeated, the indigestible, the unassimilated, the 'cross-grained,' the 'not wholly obsolete.'"[54] As I have argued elsewhere, "something is missing" in an age of manufactured politics and pseudo-publics catering almost exclusively to desires and drives produced by the commercial hysteria of the market.[55] What is missing is a language, movement, and vision that refuses to equate democracy with consumerism, market relations, and privatization. In the absence of such a language and the social formations and public spheres that make it operative—grassroots movements, unions, and workers with power, along with schools, a democratically organized media, and an economic system controlled by a popular majority rather than a privileged few—politics becomes narcissistic and caters to the mood of widespread pessimism and the cathartic allure of the spectacle. This issue is especially important for reinvigorating the debate about public education, which in the last few years has been dominated by the discourse of testing, privatization, vouchers, and standards. If schools are not to be defined as either training hubs for the corporations or high stakes testing centers, it is imperative for educators to reassert the discourse of critical citizenship, public participation, and democracy as central to the meaning and purpose of schooling. This means challenging the most basic tenets of neoliberalism, with its central assumption that market relations define schooling, as they do social and public life. Or, as Lewis Lapham puts it, democracy cannot be "understood as a fancy Greek name for the American Express Card."[56]

Education and the Challenge of
Revitalizing Democratic Public Life

Since the beginning of the 1980s, Americans have lived with a heightened sense of insecurity and uncertainty. The tools that were available in the past to deal with the most basic necessities of life such as healthcare, employment, shelter, and education are increasingly disappearing as the welfare state is attacked in the name of market forces that equate profit-making with the core values of democracy and see consumption as the ultimate privilege of citizenship.[57]

As the state is increasingly relieved of its welfare-providing functions, it defaults on its commitment to provide people with basic social provisions such as housing, health care, and public transportation, and simultaneously withdraws from its obligation to create those noncommodified public spheres in which people learn the language of ethics, civic courage, democratic politics, and collective empowerment. Schools are increasingly defined less as a public good than as sites for financial investment and entrepreneurial training—that is, as a private good. As big business comes to play a central role in school reform, public schools are increasingly asked to operate under the imperative to conform to the needs of the market and reflect more completely the interests of corporate culture. Targeted primarily as a source of investments for substantial profits, public schools are under pressure to define themselves as commercial spheres, as part of a broader attempt to restructure civic life in the image of market culture and to educate students as consumers rather than as multifaceted social agents.[58]

Noncommodified public spheres—such as churches, schools, trade unions, and public broadcasting—disappear amid a flurry of commercial activity; shopping malls proliferate, outnumbering both secondary high schools and post offices. Increasingly, the vocabulary of a market-based ideology substitutes the discourse of self-reliance and competition for the language of democratic participation, community, and the public good. One striking example can be seen in the corporate language of schooling, in which the rhetoric of competition, self-reliance, and individual choice dominate the discourse of high-stakes testing, the standards movement, the school choice agenda, and the charter school movement. Another example can be seen in many rural towns, where economic growth is tied to a prison-industry complex that promises jobs by building new prisons. Policing and incarceration emerge as part of a larger pattern of social control, dressed up, in part, as strategic growth to reignite the economies of rural towns.[59] Missing from this unfortunate trend is any mention of the horror "at the spectacle of a society in which local officials are reduced to lobbying for prisons as their best chance for economic growth."[60] Nor is there any mention in the rhetoric of such economic renewal projects that mostly white residents are securing their economic dreams through the incarceration of largely poor African Americans who make up fully half of the two million Americans currently behind bars.[61] Nor is there any room in this discourse for recognizing that increasing militarization abroad will mean more militarization on the domestic front, especially against "vulnerable groups such as immigrants and communities of color bearing the brunt of the intensified assault on civil liberties."[62] Utopia has now become privatized and racialized as social problems are reduced to personal issues. People are now encouraged to overlook public concerns while foregrounding private interests. Instead of being viewed as citizens, workers, union members, or part of a larger social collective, people are encouraged to view themselves in utterly privatized terms—such as property owners, consumers, or simply taxpayers. In the realm of politics, character and individual personality traits replace social problems. For example, rather than focusing on poverty as a systemic problem of manufactured inequality, the media focuses on welfare cheaters who are condemned as lazy and shiftless. Instead of viewing homelessness and inadequate healthcare as a failing of democracy, we are told that the real problem is motivating people to pick themselves up by the bootstraps and gain decent employment and all of its economic rewards. Within this discourse the tools for translating personal considerations into public issues gradually disappear. Instead of complex social analyses, the public is treated by the dominant media to the incessant celebration of those individuals who have made it in the marketplace because of their ability to "go it alone" through the sheer will of their competitive spirit.[63] As the social is envisioned through the privatizing lens of market relations, radical insecurity and uncertainty replace ethical considerations, social justice, and any viable collective hope.

As those public spaces that offer forums for debating norms, critically engaging ideas, making private issues public, and evaluating judgments disappear under the juggernaut of neoliberal policies, it becomes crucial for educators to raise fundamental questions about what it means to revitalize public life, politics, and ethics in ways that take seriously such values as patriotism, "citizen participation, . . . political obligation, social governance, and community,"[64] especially at a time of national crisis when such terms become less an object of analysis than of uncritical veneration. The call for a revitalized politics grounded in an effective and inclusive democracy challenges the dystopian practices of neoliberalism—with its all-consuming emphasis on market relations, commercialization, privatization, and the creation of a worldwide economy of part-time workers. Educators are confronted with the problem as well as the challenge of analyzing, engaging, and developing those public spheres—such as the media, public education, and other cultural institutions—that help create citizens who are equipped to exercise their freedoms, competent to question the basic assumptions that govern political life, and skilled enough to participate in shaping the basic social, political, and economic orders that govern their lives. It is precisely within these public spheres that the events of September 11 and the military action against Afghanistan (and more than likely Iraq), the responsibility of the media, the civic obligation of educators, and America's role in the world as a superpower should be debated, rather than squelched in the name of a jingoistic patriotism.

Two factors work against such a debate. First, there are very few public spheres left that provide the space for such conversations to take place. Second, it is increasingly difficult for young people and adults outside of the market to translate private problems into public concerns or to relate public issues to private considerations. For many young people and adults today, the private sphere has become the only space in which to imagine any sense of hope, pleasure, or possibility. Reduced to the act of consuming, citizenship is "mostly about forgetting, not learning."[65] The decline of democratic values and informed citizenship can be seen in research studies done by The Justice Project in 2001 in which a substantial number of teenagers and young people were asked what they thought democracy meant. The answers testified to a growing depoliticization of American life and were largely along the following lines: "Nothing," "I don't know," or "My rights, just like, pride, I guess, to some extent, and paying taxes," or "I just think, like, what does it really mean? I know it's like our, like, our government, but I don't know what it technically is."[66] Market forces focus on the related issues of consumption and safety, but not on the economic, cultural, and political meaning of a vibrant and substantive democracy. And as social visions of equity and justice recede from public memory, unfettered brutal self-interest combines with retrograde social polices to make security a top domestic priority. One consequence is that all levels of government are being hollowed out, their role reduced to dismantling the gains of the welfare state as they increasingly construct policies that criminalize social problems and prioritize penal methods over social investments. But at the same time, the post–September 11 events have renewed many Americans' belief in the importance of big government as a provider of public services, public infrastructures, and public goods. Hence, it is not surprising that the current concern with security, with its attendant militarizing and policing of ever-more aspects of daily life, is blindly disconnected from the disturbing rise of a prison-industrial complex that also prioritizes punishment over rehabilitation, containment over social investment.[67]

For many commentators, the events of September 11 signaled a turn away from the complacency, cynicism, and political indifference that allegedly attested to civic disengagement and the "weak" character of the American public. A focus on character seemed to replace any sense of either the complexity of the American public or how it has been shaped by dominant political, cultural, and economic forces. Frank Rich argues that the terrorist acts revitalized the patriotic spirit of a "country that during its boom became addicted to instant gratification."[68] Rich seems to forget that the luxury of such "gratification" only applied to the wealthiest 20 percent of the population. He also ignores the fact that while most Americans exhibit a disinclination to vote or put too much faith in their government, they also have been bombarded by a corporate culture that relentlessly commercializes and privatizes non-commodified public spheres, and has almost nothing to say about civic values, civic engagement, or the importance of non-market values in enabling people to identify and fight for those institutions, such as public schools and a non-commercial media, that are essential to any vibrant democracy. When citizenship is reduced to consumerism, it should come as no surprise that people develop an indifference to civic engagement and participation in democratic public life.[69] In fact, I want to stress once again that when notions of freedom and security are decoupled, so that freedom is reduced to the imperatives of market exchange and security is detached from the "helping functions" of the welfare state, then not only does freedom collapse into a brutal form of individualism, but the state is stripped of its duty to make social provisions while its policing functions are inordinately strengthened. Even as the foundations of the security state are being solidified through zero-tolerance policies, anti-terrorist laws, soaring incarceration rates, the criminalization of homelessness, racial profiling, and anti-immigration policies, it is crucial that educators and scholars address the events of September 11 not with a repressive patriotism that stifles dissent and aids the forces of domestic militarization, but as part of a broader effort to expand the United States's democratic possibilities which, in part, suggests being attentive to America's role in the world and the various critiques it engenders both domestically and internationally.

Unlike some theorists who suggest that politics as critical exchange and social engagement is either dead or in a state of terminal arrest, I believe that the current depressing state of politics points to an urgent challenge: reformulating the crisis of democracy as a fundamental crisis of vision, meaning, education, and political agency. If it is possible to "gain" anything from the events of September 11, they must be understood as an opportunity for an international coming together and soul-searching—a time for expanding democratic possibilities rather than limiting them. Politics devoid of vision degenerates into either cynicism, a repressive patriotism, or a concept of power that appears to militarize domestic space as much as foreign policy. Lost from this diminished politics is the recognition that democracy has to be struggled over—even in the face of a most appalling crisis of political agency. Educators, scholars, and policymakers must redress the little attention paid to the fact that the struggle over politics and democracy is inextricably linked to creating public spheres where individuals can be educated as political agents and equipped with the skills, capacities, and knowledge not only to act autonomously but also to believe that such political struggles are worth taking up. Central to my argument is the assumption that politics is not simply about power, but also, as Cornelius Castoriadis points out, "has to do with political judgements and value choices,"[70] meaning that questions of civic education—learning how to become a skilled citizen—are central to democracy itself. Finally, there is the widespread refusal among many educators and others to recognize that the issue of civic education—with its emphasis on critical thinking, bridging the gap between learning and everyday life, understanding the connection between power and knowledge, and using the resources of history to extend democracy—is not only the foundation for expanding and enabling political agency, but also takes place in a wide variety of public spheres through the growing power of mass media.[71]

For many educational reformers, education and schooling are synonymous. In actuality, schooling is only one site where education takes place. As a performative practice, pedagogy is at work in a variety of educational sites—including popular culture, television and cable networks, magazines, the Internet, churches, and the press. As a powerful educational force, culture is now mediated through new informational and electronic technologies that define knowledge as either entertainment or as a largely new and oppositional way of engaging the broader society. As a moral and political practice, the concept of public pedagogy—education produced outside of schools—points to the enormous ways in which popular and media culture construct the meanings, desires, and investments that play such an influential role in how students view themselves, others, and the larger world. Unfortunately, the political, ethical, and social significance of the role that popular culture plays as the primary source of knowledge for young people remains largely unexamined by many educators and seems unaddressed in policy debates about educational reform, particularly as an object of serious analysis. Educators must challenge the assumption that education is limited to schooling and that popular culture texts cannot be as profoundly important as traditional sources of learning in teaching about important issues, for example, poverty, racial conflict, and gender discrimination. At stake here is the responsibility to teach students to engage how popular culture both distorts and seriously addresses these issues. This suggests not only expanding the curricula so as to allow students to become critically literate in those visual, electronic, and digital cultures that have such an important influence on their lives, but it also suggests teaching students the skills to be cultural producers as well. For instance, learning how to read films critically is no less important than learning how to produce films. Critical literacy is not about making kids simply savvy about the media so they can be better consumers, it means offering them the knowledge, skills, and tools to recognize when the new technologies and media serve as either a force for enlarging democracy or when they shut it down. Becoming media literate is largely meaningless unless students take up this form of literacy with a concern for what it means to be a critical citizen and engaged political agent willing to make democracy more just and inclusive. In an expanded pedagogy, examining what constitutes meaningful knowledge, and what the conditions of critical agency are, might point to a wider and more democratic notion of civic education and individual and social agency.

Educators at all levels need to challenge the assumption that politics is dead, or the nature of politics will be determined exclusively by government leaders and experts in the heat of moral frenzy to impose vengeance on those who attacked the Pentagon and the World Trade Center. Educators need to take a more critical position, arguing that knowledge, debate, and dialogue about pressing social problems offers individuals and groups some hope in shaping the conditions that bear down on their lives. Public civic engagement is essential if the concepts of social life and the public sphere are to be used to revitalize the language of civic education and democratization as part of a broader discourse of political agency and critical citizenship in a global world. Linking the social to democratic public values represents an attempt, however incomplete, to link democracy to public action, and to ground such support in defense of militant utopian thinking (as opposed to unadorned militancy) as part of a comprehensive attempt to revitalize individual and social agency, civic activism, and citizen access to decision making while simultaneously addressing basic problems of social justice and global democracy.

Educators within both public schools and higher education need to find ways to engage political issues by making social problems visible and by debating them in the political sphere. We need to build on the important critical, educational theories of the past in order to resurrect the emancipatory elements of democratic thought, while also recognizing and engaging their damaged and burdened historical traditions.[72] We need to reject both neoliberal and orthodox leftist positions (which dismiss the state as merely a tool of repression) in order to find ways to use the state to challenge, block, and regulate the devastating effects of capitalism. Educators need to be at the forefront of the defense of the most progressive historical advances and gains of the state. French sociologist Pierre Bourdieu is right when he calls for collective work by educators to prevent the right and other reactionaries from destroying the most precious democratic conquests in labor legislation, health, social protection, and education.[73] At the very least, this would suggest that educators should defend schools as democratic public spheres, struggle against the de-skilling of teachers and students that has accompanied the emphasis on teaching for the test, and argue for pedagogy grounded in democratic values rather than corporate ideologies and testing schemes that severely limit the creative, ethical, and liberatory potential of education. At the same time, educators must resist the reduction of the state to a policing agency, while linking such a struggle to the fight against neoliberalism and the struggle for expanding and deepening the freedoms, rights, and relations of a vital and contentious democracy. Postcolonial theorist Samir Amin argues that educators should consider addressing the project of a more realized democracy as part of an ongoing process of democratization. According to Amin, democratization "stresses the dynamic aspect of a still-unfinished process" while rejecting notions of democracy that are given a definitive formula.[74] Educators have an important role to play in the struggle to link social justice and economic democracy with human rights, the right to education, health, research, art, and work. On the cultural front, teachers as public intellectuals can work to make the pedagogical more political by engaging in a permanent critique of their own scholasticism and promoting a critical awareness to end oppression and social forms that disfigure contemporary life and threaten democracy. Educators need to provide spaces of resistance within the public schools and the university that take seriously what it means to educate students to question authority, recall what is forgotten or ignored, and make connections that are otherwise hidden, while simultaneously providing the knowledge and skills that enlarge their sense of the social and their own potential as viable political agents capable of expanding and deepening democratic public life. At the very least, educators can challenge the unfortunate correlation between an impoverished society and the increasing impoverishment of intellectuals by offering possibilities other than what we are told is possible. Or as the French philosopher Alain Badiou observes, by "showing how the space of the possible is larger than the one assigned—that something else is possible, but not that everything is possible."[75] In times of increased domination of public K-12 education and higher education it becomes important, as cultural theorist George Lipsitz reminds us, that educators—as well as artists and other cultural workers—not become isolated "in their own abstract desires for social change and actual social movements. Taking a position is not the same as waging a war of position; changing your mind is not the same as changing society."[76] Resistance must become part of a public pedagogy that works to position rigorous theoretical work and public bodies against corporate power and the militarization of visual and public space; connect classrooms to the challenges faced by social movements in the streets; and provide spaces within classrooms and other sites for personal injuries and private terrors to be transformed into public considerations and struggles. Therefore educators should work to form alliances with parents, community organizers, labor organizations, and civil rights groups at the local, national, and international levels to better understand how to translate private troubles into pubic actions, arouse public interest in pressing social problems, and collectively democratize more fully the institutional economic, cultural, and social structures of the United States and the global order.

In the aftermath of September 11, it is time to remind ourselves that collective problems deserve collective solutions, and that what is at risk is not only a generation of minority youth and adults now considered to be a threat to national security, but also the very promise of democracy itself. As militarism works to intensify patriarchal attitudes and anti-democratic assaults on dissent, it is crucial for educators to join with those groups now making a common cause against those forces that would sacrifice basic constitutional freedoms to the imperatives of war abroad and militarism at home.

Toward a Politics of Hope

Rather than define the social through the raw emotions of collective rage and the call for retribution, it is crucial that educators set an example for creating the conditions for reasoned debate and dialogue by drawing upon scholarly and popular sources as a critical resource to engage in a national conversation about the role of the United States in the world, the conditions necessary to invigorate the political arena and shape public policy, and to break what Homi Bhabha has called "the continuity and the consensus of common sense."[77] Against the often uncomplicated and ideologically charged discourses of the dominant national media, educators must use whatever relevant resources and theories they can as tools for critically engaging and mapping the important relations among language, texts, everyday life, and structures of power, as part of a wider effort to understand the conditions, contexts, and strategies of struggle that will enable Americans to be more self-conscious about their role in the world, how they affect other cultures and countries, and what it might mean to assume world leadership without reducing it to the arrogance of power. The tools of theory emerge out of the intersection of the past and present; they respond to and are shaped by the conditions at hand. Americans need new theoretical tools—a new language—for linking hope, democracy, education, and the demands of a more fully realized democracy. While I believe that educators need a new vocabulary for connecting how we read critically to how we engage in movements for social change, I also believe that simply invoking the relationship between theory and practice, critique and social action will not do. Any attempt to give new life to a substantive democratic politics by educators must also address how people learn to be political agents. This suggests taking up the important question of what kind of educational work is necessary to enable people to use their full intellectual resources to both provide a profound critique of existing institutions and to struggle to create, as cultural studies theorist Stuart Hall puts it, "what would be a good life or a better kind of life for the majority of people."[78] As committed educators, we are required to understand more fully why the tools we used in the past often feel awkward in the present, why they fail to respond to problems now facing the United States and other parts of the globe. More specifically, we need to understand the failure of existing critical discourses to bridge the gap between how society represents itself, particularly through the media, and how and why individuals fail to understand and critically engage such representations and to intervene in the oppressive social relationships and distorted truths they often legitimize.

Educators, scholars, and policy-makers can make an important contribution politically and pedagogically by revitalizing a language of resistance and possibility, a language that embraces a militant utopianism while constantly challenging those forces that seek to turn such hope into a new slogan or punish and dismiss those who dare look beyond the horizon of the given. Hope is more than romantic idealism, it is also the condition that highlights images of an alternative politics and pedagogy. It is the basis for prompting modes of resistance, and it offers up glimpses of possibility gleaned from a reading of history. Hope is not simply wishful thinking; it is written into those various struggles waged by brave men and women for civil rights, racial justice, decent working conditions, and a society cleansed of war. It takes its form in both small and large struggles waged by individuals and groups who have not been afraid to step forward and say no to the forces of oppression, greed, and injustice. Hope is the refusal to stand still in the face of human suffering, and it is learned by example, inflamed by the passion for a better life, and undertaken as an example of civic courage. It is embodied in the likes of Howard Zinn participating in anti-war struggles against Vietnam, Mario Savio protesting the corporatization of higher education, Noam Chomsky forever reminding us that a truly democratic society can never be just enough, and Angela Davis putting her mind and body on the line against the military industrial complex. Hope is civic education made concrete in the translation of theory into practice, ethics into action, and compassion into social justice.

Within the prevailing discourse of neoliberalism and militarism, there is little room for a vocabulary of political or social transformation, collective vision, or social agency to challenge the ruthless downsizing of jobs, resist the ongoing liquidation of job security, address the inadequacy of health care and many public schools and public institutions, and oppose the elimination of benefits for people now hired on a strictly part-time basis. Moreover, against the reality of low-wage jobs, the erosion of social provisions for a growing number of people, and the expanding war against young people of color, the market-driven consumer juggernaut continues to mobilize desires in the interest of producing market identities and market relationships that ultimately appear, as Frankfurt School theorist Theodor Adorno once put it, nothing less than "a prohibition on thinking itself."[79]

Against this ongoing assault on the public and the growing preponderance of a free market economy and corporate culture that turns everything it touches into an object of consumption, educators and others must offer a critique of American society and the misfortunes it generates nationally and globally out of its obsessive concern with profits and consumption, and the commercial values of its market ethos. As part of this challenge, educators should help students bridge the gap between private and public discourse, while simultaneously putting into play ideologies and values that resonate with broader public conversations regarding how a society views itself and the world of power, events, and politics. Moreover, as professor Robert Jensen points out, it is crucial for educators and others to recognize free speech as crucial to democratic public life. At issue here is not only a reaffirmation of the formal freedoms that such speech guarantees, but also the economic, political, and social contexts that determine "how effectively citizens can exercise those freedoms in the world in which we live."[80] If we are to avoid the perils of what the *New York Times* writer Paul Krugman calls the existing inequalities and injustices of the New Guilded Age, "democracy must be renewed with politics brought back to life."[81]

Educators cannot completely eliminate crude patriotism, but we can work against a politics of certainty, a pedagogy of conformity, and institutional formations that close down rather than open up democratic relations. This requires, in part, that we work diligently to construct a politics without guarantees—one that perpetually questions itself as well as all those forms of knowledge, values, and practices that the politics of fear places beyond interrogation, debate, and deliberation. Democracy should not become synonymous with the language of the marketplace, oppression, control, surveillance, and privatization. The challenge to redefine the social and imbue it with democratic values that deepen and expand democracy is crucial not only to the forms of citizenship we offer students and the public, but also to how we engage the media, politicians, and others who would argue for less democracy and freedom in the name of domestic security. This is not meant to suggest that national security is not important; no country can allow its population to live in fear, subject to arbitrary and cowardly terrorist acts. But there has to be a balance, and a national conversation must take place among the people of this country about the extent of the terrorist threat, what privileges have to be conceded, and at what point democracy itself becomes compromised. Security means more than safeguarding a country from terrorists. Security also means protecting democratic freedoms and providing every citizen with basic constitutional rights and freedoms—otherwise the United States government begins to develop powers akin to those of a police state, in which people simply "disappear" without due process and legal protections. When an American citizen such as Jose Padilla is accused of plotting to detonate a radioactive "dirty bomb" in Washington, D.C., he should be presumed innocent until proven guilty, and under no circumstances should the Bush administration be allowed to decide arbitrarily to refuse him access to a court hearing while detaining him in secret indefinitely. This breach of due process is all the more insidious in view of the fact that it was later revealed that the Bush administration had no real evidence that Padilla was involved in a terrorist plot or that he was a member of a terrorist organization. The Padilla case is an example of what civil rights lawyer Patricia Williams calls the insidious application of "new martial law," by which American citizens can now be imprisoned without the right to a court hearing.[82] Educators need to raise their voices against such threats to American democracy and its basic constitutional freedoms. Cases such as Padilla's should be discussed as part of a wider analysis of the fundamental tension between the war against terrorism and basic democratic freedoms and rights. Educators have an important role in making their voices heard both in and outside of the classroom and articulating a vibrant and democratic notion of the social in this time of national crisis. Acting as public intellectuals, they can help create the conditions for debate and dialogue over the meaning of September 11 and what it might mean to rethink our nation's role in the world, address the dilemmas posed by the need to balance genuine security with democratic freedoms, and expand and deepen the possibilities of a vitalizing and noisy democracy itself.

CHAPTER 3

Global Capitalism and the Return of the Garrison State

Rethinking Hope in the Age of In-Security

The democratic idea itself is perhaps best thought of as a utopian aspiration. . . .
We need such aspirations if we are to resist the notion, made plausible by the
seeming inevitability of globalization, that democracy, self-determination and the
common good are ideas whose time is past.

—Steven Newman[1]

By the late 1970s, it had become clear to many critical theorists and educators that both the conditions and the social theories that were part of the most basic principles of late modernism had begun to unravel.[2] A new type of social and economic order began to emerge in the advanced industrial countries, marked by a shift away from the old forces and values of industrial production to a new emphasis on "immaterial" production in the information industries, on the one hand, and a much greater ideological emphasis on consumerism on the other.[3] With the move to new types of symbolic production and increasing emphasis on consumption, citizenship, at least in the advanced industrial countries of the West, became defined largely through a narrow notion of choice in which buying and selling constituted the meaning and substance of individual and social agency. The work ethic was now replaced by the aesthetic of consumption as human needs were almost entirely subordinated to the dictates of the market.[4] Under the onslaught of market forces unleashed globally by new information technologies and the mobile power of U.S. capital, the old social contract between labor and capital came under increasing attack as corporations became more global, "continually moving from country to country in search of new markets and untapped low-wage labor."[5] Labor became increasingly temporary and contingent, and the image of labor as long-term, secure, and tied to the traditional work ethic was now viewed more as a burden than an asset. Job security, always fragile at best, came under attack as deregulation, competitiveness, downsizing, and flexibility reduced work everywhere to part-time and minimum-wage jobs, and a future without a vestige of security.[6] Flexibility became the new catchword, signaling that in the new global order, nothing is fixed, permanent, or secure, and that the very nature of identity and agency must be able to change on short notice—willing to change according to the whims of a market economy that appeared largely unchecked by the political power of the nation-state.

But the dismantling and loss of faith in the welfare state did more than inject fear and insecurity into many people's lives, while increasing the hardships and suffering they experienced; it also signaled a redefinition of the notion of agency and the nature of the state itself.[7] Agency no longer was defined as an integral social force in shaping the conditions that constitute the everyday mechanisms and institutional forces that determine the social order. On the contrary, agency became privatized, disconnected from the right of individuals and groups to participate in shaping and transforming society. At the same time, the impoverishment of social agency was being matched by the growing inability of the nation-state to regulate the increasing "globalization of capital, finances and information."[8]

As post-colonial theorist Manuel Castells and others point out, power now flows, escaping from and defying the reach of traditional centers of politics that are nation-based and local.[9] The space of power now appears increasingly beyond the reach of governments and as a result, nations and citizens are steadily losing power as political agents with regard to the multinational corporations that impact their daily lives. As corporate decisions were freed from traditional territorial constraints, capital became more fluid and extended its tentacles far outside the boundaries of the nation-state. As cultural critic Walter LaFeber points out:

> The new transnational [corporation] became so global by the 1980s that a single government had power over only a part of the firm's total operation. The size of many transnationals, moreover, dwarfed the size of many governments. Of the hundred largest economic units in the world of the 1990s, only half were nations. The other half were individual corporations.[10]

Consequently, politics as a matter of state regulation and territorial control—a hallmark of modernism—became substantially weaker in regulating the power of the global multinationals, which had conveniently severed their allegiance to the nation-state. Hence, as sociologist Zygmunt Bauman has written, the unthinkable became thinkable: the state that has emerged relatively recently no longer bears any resemblance to the welfare state; furthermore, the capitalist economy now comes into play, pressuring the state to dismantle any adequate safety nets, and most social provisions for the poor, aged, disabled, and working class.[11] As capital went global, the welfare state, the services it provided, and the workers it served in a neoliberal environment proved to be too expensive.

The obsession with privatization, accompanied by an unadulterated celebration of excessive individualism and "free" market choice, offered a rationale for brutally destroying all those solidarities at odds with market relations, as well as all those non-market based forums and institutions that called into question the commercial culture and the politically impotent forms of democracy and citizenship it legitimated. What emerges is not an impotent state, but a garrison state that increasingly protects corporate interests while stepping up the level of repression and militarization on the domestic front.[12] One consequence in the United States is the growing support among the public for policies, at all levels of government, that abandon young people—especially youth of color—and the poor to the dictates of a society that increasingly address social problems through the police, courts, and prison system. Social problems are now criminalized and can be seen, for instance, in the passing of laws that turn the homeless who panhandle on the street or sleep in public spaces into criminals subject to arrest or oppression. Instead of providing shelters for people reduced to sleeping in doorways and on sidewalks, the state now sends in crews to scrub "down their sidewalk sleeping place with disinfectant, so they have no choice but to move."[13] Poor women who are pregnant and seek medical help in emergency rooms now find themselves subject to blood tests and the possibility of losing their children to the criminal justice system if there is any evidence of their taking drugs. What should be a routine procedure for protecting the life of the mother and fetus now becomes a matter of criminal jurisdiction and punitive action by the state. On a global level, states are either indifferent to or complicit with corporations that refuse to lower the price of drugs to those millions of human beings in sub-Saharan Africa dying in camps from AIDS.

Repression increases and replaces compassion as real issues—such as cities' tight housing markets and massive unemployment, which lead to homelessness, youth loitering, and drug epidemics—are overlooked in favor of policies that favor discipline, containment, and control. The turn towards state repression and social containment is particularly evident in the growth of domestic militarization policies in which practices that are endemic to the penal system are now applied to institutions such as schools—increasingly marked by the growing presence of metal detectors, guards patrolling the corridors, use of surveillance cameras, and harsh zero-tolerance policies.[14] Hence, the distinction between the school and the prison has been blurred. Evidence of a growing culture of control can also be found in the fact that more money is being invested in the growth of prisons in many states in America than in higher education.[15] Rather than being at risk in a society marked by deep racial, economic, and social inequalities, youth and minorities of color and class have been defined as the risk. Such policies signal a growing shift in the public's perception of the state as a source for punishment and containment rather than as a crucial political tool for providing important social provisions and regulating corporate malfeasance.

There is growing support for the neoliberal illusion that "individuals with the same talent and abilities would be equally productive independent of the social resources available to them and thus, owe little to the society that provides the context for their achievements."[16] Even when the social is invoked under neoliberalism, its strongest appeals to community draw people together on the basis of "shared fears rather than shared responsibilities."[17] As Zygmunt Bauman observes, rather than addressing the "deepest causes of anxiety—that is, the experience of individual insecurity and uncertainty,"[18] grounded in concrete social problems, governing elites all over the world exploit the new fears and "terror" as a threat to the body. As such, community is invoked through appeal to military defense, national security, and civil order, and with greater legitimacy after the tragic and horrific terrorist attacks of September 11. As fear is increasingly globalized, anti-terrorist laws are used to target those who fit the "racial profile of white anxiety": Arabs, people of color, Muslims, black youth, "but also anyone with an unusual head-covering."[19] American citizens are now subject to indefinite seizures by the police without even the right of a trial by jury. People can now be held in prison and prosecuted in secret, with the government offering no information regarding who they are or what the nature of their crime might be. The F.B.I. can with impunity and without search warrants search our banking records, telephone bills, computer activity, and travel documents. Libraries and bookstores are now routinely searched by the FBI as civil liberties in general are increasingly under siege—all in the name of protecting national security.

Providing a model for global export, the United States refashions authoritarianism as a form of rabid patriotism, coupled with anti-terrorist legislation that legitimates limiting civil liberties and basic freedoms while sanctioning the surveillance of dissenters and the arrest—if not torture—of those marked as a threat to the collective safety. But as Mike Davis points out, government and corporate elites do more than translate collective fears about uncertainty into privatized concerns about individual safety (legitimating the attack on civil liberties), they also create the conditions for a "fear economy" that fuels corporate profits. In addition to being frisked, searched, monitored, scanned, and interrogated, the populations of the United States and its allies will also be subject to the pressures of venture capital that will make "germ warfare sensors and threat profile software," along with "discrete technologies of surveillance, environmental monitoring and data-processing . . . into a single integrated system. 'Security,' in other words, will become a full-fledged urban utility like water and power."[20]

A critique of globalization called attention to the major transformations taking place in the world and the new dangers that were emerging in full force in the 1990s.[21] As the state increasingly functioned mainly to expand the forces of domestic militarization, surveillance, and control, some critics recognized that the old critical languages that informed the project of modern politics, with its emphasis on equality, freedom, and justice, were incapable of grasping the new conditions of late modernism informed by the forces of economic and cultural globalization. Traditional political discourses such as Marxism, nationalism, and liberalism failed to grasp the complexity and changing nature of the global economy. For example, they undertheorized the growing force of a worldwide media apparatus that is controlled by a handful of corporations and organized through highly complex technologies that redefined the meaning of political education on a global level.[22] These traditional discourses also underemphasized the rise of the prison-industrial complex[23] and the emergence of diverse social movements subjected to forms of domination and oppression that simply could not be captured in the old, narrow language of class exploitation.[24] While the old left provided a class-based critique of capitalism and the intensification of the exploitation of labor, the postmodern left addressed the "cultural disenfranchisement of peoples with nationally marked racial, gender, and sexual identities."[25] While those movements that embraced political economy and identity politics ignored each other, the Green Party in Germany focused on the destruction of the global ecosystem and the issue of sustainability while having too little to say about class and identity politics.

This is not meant to suggest that a viable approach to globalization should dispense with the discourses of Marxism and critical ecology, or consider the identity-based discourse of distinct social movements irrelevant. Actually, I believe that educators need a new political language that links the political economy of labor and political ecology, on the one hand, to a broader concern with the politics of identity and the cultural politics of globalization on the other. A critical Marxism, albeit more nuanced, is probably more relevant to the increasing threat of neoliberal globalization than at any time in the last half century. But central to the emphasis on economic exploitation, class inequalities, the destruction of the environment, and building democratic social movements is the need to focus equally on the pedagogical force of culture as a central aspect of global capitalism. I will return to this theme below.

Critical theories of globalization were born not just out of the crisis of modernism, but also the crisis of democracy, social agency, and politics. Globalization represents both a critical reaction to the "high modernisms which conquered the university, the museum, the art gallery network and the foundations,"[26] and an attempt to provide a language for understanding, critically engaging, and transforming those ideologies, values, social practices, and relations of power that emptied democracy of any substantive meaning while spreading across the globe the inequities and exploitative practices of a consumer society fueled by the worst excesses of neoliberalism.

In opposition to those advocates of globalization, such as Thomas Friedman of the *New York Times,* who believe that if markets and technologies are allowed to do their magical work, the human race will enter into a new golden age,[27] educators and others need to address globalization as a particular form of neoliberal capitalism in which issues regarding democracy, the public good, public participation, or critical citizenship no longer inform mainstream politics. On the contrary, under the auspices of a neoliberal globalization, politics is about privatization, consumerism, deregulation, market-based choice, the spectacle of celebrity, and the revived ethics of Social Darwinism. Abstracted from the ideal of public commitment, neoliberal globalization represents a political, economic, and ideological practice that loosens the connection between substantive democracy, critical agency, and progressive education. It does so, in part, by disconnecting power from politics, "gaining control of the expansion of markets, the looting of the earth's natural resources, [or] the superexploitation of the labor reserves."[28] One of the most important new features of global capitalism is that it constitutes a form of transnational public pedagogy in which the educational force of dominant culture spreads the values, ideologies, and social relations that define global citizenship as a private affair, a solitary act of consumption—rather than as a practice of social and political engagement by people working together to shape the world in which they live.[29] The myth of globalization and the "end of history" narrative proclaiming capitalism's uncontested control over the globe and that only capitalism can resolve future conflicts has gained power from the absence of an ideological challenger. Fortunately, the allegedly unstoppable telos of neoliberal globalization has been opposed in recent times by protests for global justice that have taken place all over the world. Seattle, in particular, has produced a number of counternarratives that challenge neoliberalism's specious global utopianism; as Leerom Medovoi puts it, what must be countered is "globalizations's future-tense narrative of inevitability, demonstrating that the drama of world history remains wide open."[30] Educators and others have an important role to play in undoing the myths and assumptions that give neoliberal globalism the air of historic inevitability. This means reclaiming a language of power, politics, and ethics that is capable of examining the effects of globalization on labor, the environment, culture, and all those spheres and spaces in which democratic identities and relations of power are essential to viable forms of political agency.

In opposition to the forces of globalization, educators must link learning to social change, recognizing that every sphere of social life is open to political action. A politics of globalization linked to democratic struggles and values must also recognize that those pedagogical spheres—such as the media, schools, the advertising industry, and corporations—that convert culture into commercialism and important social and political issues into market spectacles ready for instant consumption constitute a crucial site of political and cultural struggle. Neoliberal capitalism works hard to convince people all over the globe that there is a natural convergence between the market and democracy, in spite of the fact that economic democracy is missing from most capitalist countries and that totalitarian regimes also seem to have a great penchant for embracing market-driven economic systems.

The ideologies and social relations offered by neoliberalism must be challenged by producing democratic spheres that forge the knowledge, identifications, emotional investments, and social practices necessary to produce political subjects and social agents capable of extending and deepening the basis of a global radical democracy.

Unlike many postmodern theorists, I believe that it is foolish simply to dismiss or invalidate completely the legacy of modern Western thought, and to consider all appeals to democracy simply a kind of modernist hangover. On the contrary, it makes more sense critically to engage and appropriate the vital elements of such democratic modernist traditions, while, as cultural critic John Brenkman points out, "assessing their historical burden and criticizing their damaged actuality."[31] As part of the struggle against global capitalism's reduction of critical agency to consumption, educators need to develop a politics and pedagogy that combine the modernist legacy of social justice, equality, freedom, and rights with late modern concerns with difference, plurality, power, discourse, identities, and micropolitics.[32] At the same time, a radical cultural politics must do more than appropriate difference as part of an expanded understanding of how domination, oppression, and struggle are being forged locally within a new global capitalism. Identity politics needs to be stripped of its unquestioned certainties and articulated within a wider set of relations that amplify both its strengths and weaknesses as part of a broader struggle for social transformation, which must be wedded to a notion of general emancipation that refuses to separate culture from history or politics and takes radical democracy as its underlying project. A politics that combines the best of a modernist tradition with elements of a democratic postmodernism is also important because it allows educators and others to recognize that advances in technology (a legacy of modernism) do not have to be used in ways that further the concentration of economic power associated with global capitalism. Technological globalization can be separated from the globalization of concentrated power, and doing so highlights the possibilities of an alternative notion of globalization from what Peter Marcuse has called "really existing globalization."[33]

Educators must also refuse the modernist division between an alleged "real" politics forged in materialist struggles and a cultural politics that is merely a sideshow. Culture is a crucial terrain of politics and struggle, and I believe that the pedagogical force of culture in the age of global capitalism is one of the primary causes for the increasing depoliticization that is the hallmark of monopoly capitalism and that it also affects other elements of society and the global order. Following Stuart Hall, I want to argue that "Cultural change is constitutive of political change and moral awareness of human consciousness."[34] Culture is the terrain where consciousness is shaped, needs are constructed, and the capacity for self-reflection and social change are nurtured and produced. Culture has assumed an unparalleled significance in shaping the language, values, and ideologies that legitimate the structures and organizations that support the imperatives of global capitalism. Rather than being simply a reflection of deeper economic and political forces, culture has become a crucial site for the struggle over those pedagogical and political conditions that determine whether people believe it is possible to be true agents, individually and collectively capable of intervening in the processes that shape the material relations, power, meaning, and practices of their everyday lives. Today, struggles over power have taken on a symbolic and discursive as well as a material and institutional form. The battle over culture, in my view, is about more than the struggle over meaning and identity; it is also about how cultural forms and processes operate within economic and structural relations of power. Culture is not at odds with politics, but rather an important and crucial element in any definition of the political. It offers the theoretical tools for a systemic critique of not only the growing economic but also the pedagogical power of corporations in the age of global capitalism; moreover, a radical cultural politics also offers a language of possibility for creating actual movements for social change. At stake here is combining an interest in symbolic forms and processes with broader social contexts and the institutional basis of power itself. The key point is to understand and engage cultural practices from the point of view of how they are bound up with larger relations of power, signaling not simply a focus on texts and reception but a concern with ownership, political economy, and control.

Educators need to be clearer about how power works through texts, representations, and discourse, while at the same time recognizing that power cannot be reduced to the study of such representations. Changing consciousness is not the same as altering the institutional basis of oppression;[35] similarly, institutional reform cannot take place without a shift in consciousness capable of recognizing the very need for political, economic, and social changes and the need to reinvent the space of collective struggle and the strategies for constructing an inclusive democracy. A critical consciousness, shaped within the contradictory pedagogical registers of lived experience, is precisely what enables individuals, in novelist Arundhati Roy's words, to "push at the frontiers, to worry the edges of the human imagination," and overtly to take a position.[36] In addition, it is crucial for educators and others to raise questions about the relationship between pedagogy and culture and what it takes for individuals and social groups to believe that they have any responsibility whatsoever to *care, have an investment in, or even address* the often unjust consequences of class, race, gender oppression and related material relations of domination. For too long, educators and other activists have ignored the strategic relationship between the sphere of politics and civic education and what it means to make the pedagogical more political and the political more pedagogical. Consequently, critical theorists, especially those outside of education, have paid little attention to the fact that struggles over politics, power, and democracy demand more than creating democratic public spheres where individuals can be equipped with the skills, capacities, and knowledge they need to become critical social agents. In addition, they also must be convinced that such struggles *are worth taking up.* Political agency does not simply follow from having the right analysis. Focusing attention on the deplorable conditions of sweatshops, the ravaging of the global ecosystem, or the commercialization of all cultural spheres and practices does not guarantee that people will pick up the banner of politics or global justice. Analysis has to be coupled with pedagogies that provide people with a sense of meaning and purpose—an emotional investment that connects belief to action, theory to practice.

The cultural politics of capitalist globalization is not only evident in the presence of media conglomerates such as AOL-Time-Warner, Rupert Murdoch's News Corporation, Viacom, Vivendi, Bertelsman, and Disney, but also in the massive advertising campaigns organized internationally by corporations such as Nike, McDonald's, and Reebok.[37] Commercial culture, coupled with popular culture, has become the new transnational force used by global capitalism to both capture and open up markets, as well as to redefine the very nature of identity, needs, desire, and democracy itself. Stripped of its political context, democracy, under the onslaught of global capitalism, is transformed into market relations, and citizenship is reduced to the obligations of consumerism. Moreover, as public space is commercialized on a global scale, the new technologies of communication satellites and fiber-optic cable offer up commodified spaces that not only commercially carpet bomb people with endless images of consumption and a hyper-individualized lifestyle, but also limit those spaces where noncommodified critical discourses, social relations, and policies can be produced that raise questions about the limits of market-based values, interrogate how it might be possible outside the commercial sphere to raise questions about the myriad of anti-democratic forces at work in the world, and what it might mean to create a vision of a global society in which capitalism and democracy do not collapse into each other. The former French minister of culture, Jack Lang, was right when he argued that the United States, as the exemplary model for studying the effects of globalization, has become a "financial and intellectual imperialism which no longer grabs territory, or rarely, but grabs consciousness, ways of thinking, ways of living." [38] Of course, beneath the surface of neoliberal ideology is the ever-present threat of the "U.S. military as the global enforcer of capitalism," the reality of 3 billion people worldwide living on less than $2 per day, and the rampant exploitation of the biosphere, public goods, and communicative space.[39] In addition, there is the intolerable and unforgivable impoverishment of children worldwide. As social critic Thomas Pogge points out, "Worldwide, 34,000 children under age five die daily from hunger and presentable diseases. . . . Two out of five children in the developing world are stunted, one in three is underweight and one in ten is wasted. . . . One quarter of all children between five and fourteen, 250 million in all, are compelled to work, often under harsh conditions, as soldiers, prostitutes, or domestic servants or in agriculture, construction, textile, or carpet production."[40] Such poverty represents more than massive human suffering; it is also evidence of greed and the growing international inequality between rich and poor nations, which can be seen in the fact that "The assets of the top three billionaires are more than the combined GNP of all least developed countries and their 600 million people."[41] In the United States alone, where 33 percent of all children will be poor at sometime in their childhood, Bill Gates in 1998 "amassed more wealth than the combined net worth of the poorest 45 percent of American households."[42] Put in a global context, "Microsoft co-founders Bill Gates and Paul Allen plus Berkshire Hathaway's Warren Buffet have a net worth larger than the combined GNP of the 41 poorest nations."[43]

In what follows, I want to suggest that educators need to develop a critical language for challenging the currently fashionable presupposition that global capitalism represents an "empire" for which there is no outside.[44] This is not to suggest that critics do not offer a language of critique in dealing with global capitalism. Nothing would be further from the truth, but what they often do not provide is a language of possibility, one that engages what it would mean pedagogically and politically to provide the conditions for rethinking a new type of social agent, one that could individually and collectively imagine a global society that combines freedom and social justice modeled after the imperatives of a radical and inclusive democracy.

Against an increasingly oppressive corporate globalism, educators need to resurrect a language of resistance and possibility, a language that embraces a militant utopianism while constantly being on guard against those forces that seek to turn such hope into a new slogan, or that punish and dismiss those who dare look beyond the horizon of the given. Hope is the precondition for individual and social struggle, the ongoing practice of education in a wide variety of sites across the globe, the mark of courage on the part of intellectuals in and out of the academy who use the resources of theory to address pressing social problems. But hope also takes the form of civic courage, with its ability to anticipate a radical democracy against the worldwide experience of injustice as part of a broader attempt to open up new locations of struggle, contest the workings of oppressive power, and undermine various forms of domination. At its best, civic courage as a political practice begins when one's life can no longer be taken for granted. It makes concrete the possibility for transforming hope and politics into an ethical space and public act that confronts the flow of everyday experience and the weight of social suffering with the force of individual and collective resistance as part of the unending project of democratic social transformation. If educators and other cultural workers are to revitalize the language of civic education as part of a broader discourse of political agency and critical citizenship in a global world, they will have to consider grounding such a call in a defense of militant utopian thinking in which any viable notion of the political takes up the primacy of pedagogy as part of a broader attempt to revitalize the conditions for individual and social agency, while simultaneously addressing the most basic problems in the way of social justice and global democracy. Theorists such as Ernst Bloch believed that utopianism could not be removed from the world and was not "something like nonsense or absolute fancy; rather it is not yet in the sense of a possibility; that it could be there if we could only do something for it."[45] Utopian thinking, in this view, is anticipatory not messianic, mobilizing rather than therapeutic. At best, utopian thinking, as Alain Badiou observes, does not defend "the idea that 'everything is possible'":

> In fact, it's an immense task to try to propose a few possibles, in the plural—a few possibilities other than what we are told is possible. It is a matter of showing how the space of the possible is larger than the one we are assigned—that something else is possible, but not that everything is possible.[46]

The longing for a more human society does not collapse into some idyllic or romanticized retreat from the world, but emerges out of critical and practical engagements with present social behaviors, institutional formations, and everyday practices. Hope in this context does not ignore the worst dimensions of human suffering, exploitation, and social relations; on the contrary, it acknowledges the need to sustain the "capacity to see the worst and offer more than that for our consideration."[47] The great challenge to militant utopianism, with its hope of keeping critical thought alive, rests in an emerging consensus among a wide range of political factions that neoliberal democracy is the best we can do. The impoverishment of many intellectuals, with their growing refusal to speak about addressing, if not ending, human suffering, is now matched by the poverty of a social order that recognizes no alternative to itself.[48]

Feeding into the increasingly dominant view that society cannot be fundamentally improved outside of market forces, neoliberalism strips utopianism of its possibilities for social critique and democratic engagement. By doing so it undermines the need to reclaim utopian thinking as both a discourse of human rights and a moral referent for dismantling and transforming dominant structures of wealth and power.[49] Moreover, an anti-utopianism of both the right and left can be found in those views that reduce utopian thinking to state terrorism and progressive visionaries to unrealistic, if not dangerous, ideologues. This alternative is what social critic Russell Jacoby calls a "convenient cynicism,"[50] a belief that human suffering, hardship, and massive inequalities in all areas of life are simply inherent in human nature and an irreversible part of the social condition. Or in its liberal version, the belief that America's best defense against utopianism as a form of terrorism is preserving "democracy as it currently exist[s] in the world"[51]—a view largely shared by the likes of people such as Lynne Cheney, John Ashcroft, and Norman Podhoretz. Within this discourse, hope is foreclosed, politics becomes militarized, and resistance is either privatized or aestheticized, or degenerates into hyper-commercialized escapism. Against a militant and radically democratic utopianism, the equation of terrorism and utopianism appears deeply cynical. Neoliberalism not only appears flat, it also offers up an artificially conditioned optimism—operating at full capacity in the pages of *Fast Company, Wired Magazine, The Wall Street Journal,* and *Forbes,* as well as in the relentless entrepreneurial hype of figures such as George Gilder, Tom Peters, and the Nike and Microsoft revolutionaries—in which it becomes increasingly difficult to imagine a life beyond the existing parameters of market pleasures, mail-order catalogues, shopping malls, and Disneyland. This stills holds true even amid the debris of Enron, Wal-Mart, Xerox, WorldCom and other major companies.[52] The profound cynicism parading as hope that is spurred on by neoliberalism and its myths of the citizen as consumer and markets as sovereign entities, and its substitution of a market economy for a market society, both depoliticizes the realm of the social and commodifies the possibilities of civic agency. There is also the tired lament of some prominent "left" educational theorists who argue that any appeal to utopianism is immediately canceled out because of its refusal to offer critical analyses of the problems that prevent hope from being realized. This view appears more self-serving than insightful, and often confuses romanticism with utopian discourse, while at the same time simply recycling the same old theories of social and economic reproduction. What this view misses is that any viable discourse of hope combines a language of critique and possibility, rather than over-emphasizing or canceling out either side of the equation.

The radical socialist ideal of realizing the potential of the full human being has given way to a debilitating pessimism in which it becomes difficult to imagine a life beyond global capitalism, or for that matter a life beyond the failure of the present. The limits of the utopian imagination are related, in part, to the failure of intellectuals and cultural workers in a variety of public spheres to not only conceive of possibility as a capability for intervention, but also to imagine what pedagogy might help bring into being forms of political agency grounded in the knowledge, skills, and capacities that enable people to govern democratically the major institutions that shape the economy, state, civil society, culture, and everyday life. In opposition to this position, sociologist Ruth Levitas's comment on the need to locate utopian longings in a process of concrete experience and social change points to a notion of hope based on the recognition that it is only through education that human beings can be informed about the limits of the present and the conditions necessary for them to "combine a gritty sense of limits with a lofty vision of possibility."[53] She writes:

> The main reason why it has become so difficult to locate utopia in a future credibly linked to the present by a feasible transformation is that our images of the present do not identify agencies and processes for change. The result is that utopia moves further into the realms of fantasy. Although this has the advantage of liberating the imagination from the constraint of what it is possible to imagine as possible—and encouraging utopia to demand the impossible—it has the disadvantage of severing utopia from the process of social change and severing social change from the stimulus of competing images of utopia.[54]

Educated hope combines the pedagogical and the political in ways that stress the contextual nature of learning, emphasizing that different contexts give rise to diverse questions, problems, and possibilities. Thus, educators and other progressive individuals should be attentive to the ways in which institutional and symbolic power are tangled up with everyday experience. They should also be attentive to how any politics of hope must tap into individual experiences, while at the same time linking individual responsibility with a progressive sense of social destiny and those connections to the world that extend beyond local and national boundaries. Emphasizing politics as a pedagogical and performative act, educated hope accentuates that politics is played out not only on the terrain of imagination and desire, but it is also grounded in relations of power mediated through the struggle to create the conditions for people to become critically engaged political agents. As a form of utopianism, educated hope takes on the pedagogical task of engaging politics through the interconnected modalities of desire, intervention, and struggle. As Houston Baker, Jr., argues in a different context, the imagination does not point simply to the realm of fantasy and escape, but to a form of social practice, a site that is marked by the intersection of politics and pedagogy, on the one hand, and agency and possibility on the other.

> No longer mere fantasy (opium for the masses whose real work is elsewhere), no longer simple escape (from a world defined principally by more concrete purposes and structures), no longer the elite pastime (thus not relevant to the lives of ordinary people) and no longer mere contemplation (irrelevant for new forms of desire and subjectivity), the imagination has become an organized field of social practices, a form of work . . . and a form of negotiation between sites of agency ('individuals') and globally defined fields of possibility.[55]

Educated hope both engages the imagination as social practice and takes seriously the importance of civic education, while recognizing that such education takes place within a vast array of public spheres and pedagogical sites. Part of the challenge of recognizing the diverse spheres engaged in public pedagogy is to construct new locations of struggle, new vocabularies, and a subjectivity that allows people to become more than they are now, to question what it is they have become within existing institutional and social formations and, as political theorist Chantal Mouffe points out, "to give some thought to their experiences so that they can transform their relations of subordination and oppression."[56] As a form of utopian thinking, educated hope provides the foundational connection that must be made among three discourses that often remain separated: democracy, political agency, and pedagogy.

The concept of educated hope rests on an expansive idea of pedagogy, pointing to broader considerations about the role that education now plays in a variety of cultural sites nationally and globally, and how the latter have become integral to producing models of human nature through the pedagogical force of a capitalist "utopia" based almost "exclusively on economic exchange."[57] A democratically engaged cultural politics requires that educators both understand and challenge how neoliberalism and global capitalism undermine inclusive democracy in a relentless attempt to valorize private space over public space, commercial goods over public goods, market fundamentalism over democratic values, and a wholly privatized, personal notion of citizenship over public citizenship. Educators will have to challenge forcefully the portrayal of public space as simply an investment opportunity, as well as the increasing attempt by neoliberals to represent the public good as a metaphor for public disorder. In doing so, they will have to address the profound role that the pedagogical force of the broader culture currently plays on a global level in shutting down democratic relations, identities, and visions. As I have suggested, educators need to make "a timely inventory of democracy's unrealized potential,"[58] but only by bracketing such potential against its unfulfilled promises. Democracy, as Stuart Hall points out, is "haunted by the ghost of its ideal,"[59] and both its burden and urgency lie in recognizing the gap between really existing democracy and its unfulfilled promises—that which is to come. But if educators are to develop an oppositional cultural politics, it will require more than simply spirited criticism.[60] As important as immanent critique might be, it always runs the risk of both representing power as being in the absolute service of domination and failing to capture the always open and ongoing dynamic of resistance at work in alternative modes of representations, oppositional public spheres, and modes of affective investment that refuse the ideological push and institutional drive of dominant social orders.[61]

Combining the discourse of criticism and a hope without illusions is crucial to affirming that critical activity offers the possibility for social transformation. One option that educators might consider is to develop an oppositional cultural politics that engages basic considerations of global social citizenship aimed at expanding democratic rights, while developing collective movements that can challenge the subordination of social needs to the dictates of capital, commodification, and commercialism. Central to such a politics would be a public pedagogy that attempts to make visible alternative models of radical democratic culture that raise fundamental questions about the relationship

between political agency and social responsibility, technology and globalization, and the reinscription of the state as a force for domestic militarization. At the very least, such a pedagogy involves understanding
and critically engaging dominant values within a broader set of historical and institutional contexts. Making the political more pedagogical
suggests producing modes of knowledge and social practices that not
only affirm oppositional cultural work, but offer opportunities to mobilize collective outrage, if not collective action, against glaring material inequities and the growing cynical belief that today's culture of
investment and finance makes it impossible to address many of the
major social problems facing both the United States and the world.
Most important, such work links civic education and modes of oppositional political agency that are pivotal to elucidating a politics that promotes autonomy and social change. Unfortunately, many educators
have failed to take seriously the Italian Marxist Antonio Gramsci's insight that "[e]very relationship of 'hegemony' is necessarily an educational relationship"—with its implication that education as a cultural
pedagogical practice takes place across multiple sites as it signals how,
within diverse contexts, education makes us both subjects of and subject to relations of power.[62]

To confront the deadly politics of capitalist globalization, a
transnational democratic political movement must develop that not
only recognizes the changing nature of globalization under the imperatives of capitalism, but also provides those forms of educated hope
that offer the grounds for creating public intellectuals and social movements capable of linking education to critical agency, and linking
learning to broader global considerations and social issues. As the
French sociologist Pierre Bourdieu points out, intellectuals can play a
key role in filling the empty pedagogical space of transnational struggles. That space can be filled through forms of international mobiliza-
tion that give an important role "to the battle of ideas and in particular
to [the] critique [of those] representations continuously produced
and propagated by the dominant groups and their lackeys in the
media: false statistics, myths about full employment in Britain or the
U.S., and so on."[63] A neoliberal solidarity based on the myth of historical inevitability must be challenged to give way to a solidarity of purpose and social transformation—one in which our lives are viewed as

conditioned but not determined—open to struggle and change. If emancipatory politics is to be equal to neoliberal capitalism, educators need to theorize politics not as a science or set of objective conditions, but as a point of departure in specific and concrete situations. They need to rethink the very meaning of the political so that it can provide a sense of direction, but can no longer be used to provide complete answers. Instead, they should ask why and how particular social formations have a specific shape and come into being, and what it might mean to rethink such formations in terms of opening up new struggles and movements. Politics in this sense offers a notion of the social that is open and contingent, providing a conception of democracy that is never complete and determinate but constantly open to different understandings of the contingency of its decisions, mechanisms of exclusion, and operations of power.[63]

Hopefully, the work done by educators as public intellectuals in an age of global plunder by an unchecked market authoritarianism will manifest itself in a plurality of forms, including: challenging the supposed historical inevitability of global capitalism, defending the historical advances associated with nation-states by pushing for "more education, more health, more guaranteed lifetime income," mobilizing marginalized groups on all fronts to address capitalism's relationship to labor and the environment, and making anti-racist and class struggles paramount to any struggle for democratization.[64] Economic restructuring on a global level makes class a more central category than ever before as a result of the increasing divisions between the rich and the poor, accelerated by the massive transfer of power from nations to transnational corporations, on the one hand, and the equally massive transfer of wealth from the poor and middle class to the upper classes on the other. But any attempt to abolish forms of class, racial, gender, and other types of oppression requires a different kind of politics than what has been traditionally associated with class struggles. A new politics must attempt publicly to confront oppressive relations, explain them, situate them historically, engage how they operate in the intersection between the local and the global, and refuse to accept their inevitability. A pedagogy of persuasion and transformation becomes crucial to any viable politics of democratization. Any feasible movement that challenges neoliberalism and corporate globalization will need to develop pedagogical strategies that debunk the cherished myths of capitalism and offer knowledge, skills, and tools that "will be immediately useful in people's lives" and, at the same time, "point to longer-run, more fundamental changes."[66]

While there have been numerous analyses of globalization, what has been undertheorized is what social critic Imre Szeman has called "the pedagogy of globalization." What Szeman means by this is

> both the conditions of social and cultural learning and reproduction in the context of globalization and the way in which globalization itself constitutes a problem of and for pedagogy. The triumphalist rhetoric of politicians and business leaders, the lessons proffered by newspaper columnists and TV news anchors, as well as the fast-cutting globe-hopping ads of dot.coms, financial services companies, and hardware giants—all of this constitutes a form of public education in the contours and realities of the new global situation.[67]

Szeman argues that any viable understanding of globalization must address the pedagogical conditions for its reproduction. But if educators are to move beyond simply making visible the connection between globalization and new modes of social, cultural, and economic reproduction, they will have to learn both how to engage this newly constituted pedagogical force and how to resist it through new political discourses and pedagogical strategies. Such strategies will have to open up new global spaces of education—employing a vast array of old and new media including digital video, magazines, the Internet, computers, and newspapers. Fortunately, nascent examples already exist in the vast array of student antiglobalization protests that have taken place both on campuses across the United States as well as in Seattle, Washington, D.C., London, Prague, Genoa, and other cities in the last few years. Connecting a wide variety of communicative approaches from street theater to people's summits to inventive uses of the Internet, global justice advocates are rejecting "the official pedagogy of globalization circulated through press releases and the culture industry [by attempting] to construct new modes and sites of learning that might enable a broad, collective response to the powers that be."[68]

I think Szeman is right in claiming that these protests constitute a new space of pedagogy. In addition to picketing, engaging in civil disobedience, and putting their bodies in the way of power, the protestors employ relatively fresh modes of communication such as the Internet and digital video. Such tactics offer the global public new ways of understanding, contextualizing, and engaging issues that are both readily attainable in the dominant media, as well as information that is entirely different and critical—made available to the larger public through new modes such as documentaries, digital photography placed on the Internet, and publicly distributed hand-outs. Citizens, educators, and students need more than rapid-fire sound bytes, disinformation, and outright corporate propaganda. They also need entry to alternative sources of information, new pedagogical sites to access it, and new tools to historicize and critically engage what they confront. The emerging campus student activist and global justice movements offer fresh pedagogical tools and modes of analysis that might prove invaluable in rethinking both the meaning of a pedagogy of globalization and its implications for working with students and adults within and outside of schools.

In addition to the global justice movements such as those that took place in Seattle, youth movements have also taken place on many campuses across the United States and are spreading to other countries as well. Campus activism can be seen in the fight against the growing corporate influence on higher education, attacks on affirmative action, the exploitation of sweatshop workers, the ruin of nature, the prison-industrial complex, low wages for university workers, and university licensing policies, among others. Organizations such as the Student Labor Action Coalition (SLAC) have made great strides in educating students about the importance of unions in preventing corporations from taking over higher education; United Students Against Sweatshops have mobilized thousands of students in support of fair labor policies and economic justice. The Democratic Socialists of American Youth Section tries to bring youth together around a variety of diverse pressing economic, racial, and social issues. Hip-hop mogul Russell Simmons has mobilized a number of artists, executives, politicians, and civil rights leaders to form The Hip-Hop Summit Action Network, which focuses on issues crucial to African American youth such as voter education and encouraging political activism in the hip-hop community. In Boston, Project Hip-Hop consists of students who use the resources of anti-racist struggles to educate youth "to recognize themselves as agents of social change."[69] Through the development of their own curricula, employing the concept of the "rolling classroom," Project Hip-Hop takes students to the South to learn the lessons of civil rights struggles. The group has also taken young people to South Africa to study its ongoing fight against racism and its struggle to create a multiracial democracy.

In all of these instances, students are providing an important political and pedagogical service by connecting corporate power to its social consequences and demonstrating the importance of both collective resistance to the corporations and the need to struggle for global justice through a widely related set of issues. Garment industry abuses are now part of the public lexicon. Sweatshops are no longer removed from public consciousness in the advanced countries of the West. The assault by corporations on public and higher education has become more visible in recent years because of student protests all across the country. Militant, global anti-corporate activism has made debt relief for poor countries a matter of public interest, especially in light of U2 rock star Bono's willingness to take up the issue. The rise in militant student activism not only puts pressure on university administrators, corporate executives, and the leaders of the International Monetary Fund and the World Trade Organization; activists also teach "themselves and their fellow students to question facts of social and economic life that they had long been taught to take for granted."[70] And as such activism gets more media attention, it also offers valuable lessons in global pedagogy, economic injustice, and the politics of globalization to diverse audiences. Moreover, it offers a challenge to the prevailing cynicism that seems to work against any viable notion of a future that does not simply reinvent the present and allow corporations to continue to dominate globally and prevent people from governing themselves. At the same time, student activists on campus as well as the global justice movement face some serious challenges.

The biggest challenge these diverse activists need to confront centers around developing a theoretical language that connects their various struggles to a broader project, such as radical, inclusive democracy, while at the same time being able to develop alliances that provide the collective force of a major international political movement. Inequality and injustice take many forms, and some of the most ruthless include racism, poverty, and class inequities that are not adequately addressed in the anti-corporate rhetoric. If radical ideas and social practices are to become popular, more is needed than creative anarchism, revolutionary theater, and a faith in disparate actions. As Jonathan Rutherford observes, "Politics requires analysis, the connection of disparate issues, and the creation of a coherent argument with which people can understand and sympathize.... The antiglobalization movement has recaptured a sense of idealism and hope in a cynical age. But if it is to consolidate itself as something enduring and politically effective, it needs to be matched by critical analysis and an elaboration of political economy. The politics of spectacle without any accountable forms of leadership or ideology is easily hijacked."[71] While I think Rutherford overstates the shortcomings of the student activists, he is certainly on target with his call for a more careful analysis of how global neoliberalism works and what it would take politically and strategically for these diverse movements to challenge it.

While it is crucial for educators to learn from young people, labor and Green Party activists, and others in order to fight against the effects of neoliberalism and finance capital, academics and other public intellectuals can also offer their own expertise by working collectively with such groups in order to develop global institutions "of effective and political action as could match the size and power of the already global economic forces and bring them under political scrutiny and ethical supervision."[72] Such projects and interventions, while not offering a politics with guarantees, can create a new discourse of politics and hope while simultaneously unleashing the energies necessary to combine a strong hostility to the existence of human suffering and exploitation—especially among children throughout the world—with "a vision of a global society, informed by civil liberties and human rights, that carries with it the shared obligations and responsibilities of common, collaborative citizenship."[73] Instances of such movements, as I have noted throughout this book, can be glimpsed in the antiglobalization protests that have taken place all over the globe. But the move from protest to building astute analyses and international alliances is of particular concern and can be seen in meetings such as the World Social Forum that took place in Porto Alegre, Brazil in 2002.

All of these movements echo David Held and Mary Kaldor's call for a left that is willing to address as part of a broader notion of global justice the ethical issues "posed by the global polarization of wealth, income and power, and with them the huge asymmetries of life chances,"[74] none of which can be left to market solutions. This suggests a non-hierarchical, popular, but organized movement on a global scale that makes pedagogy, economic justice, and cultural recognition central to the goal of creating a world in which democratic principles provide the fertile ground for spreading the values of human rights, the rule of law, and social justice as a way of connecting people of all cultures and places not merely through the abstractions of theory but through the everyday experiences that shape their lives.[75]

CHAPTER 4

Leaving Most Children Behind

Public Education Under Siege

> *The Bush administration's budget choices before and after September 11th leave millions of children behind; favor powerful corporate interests and the wealthiest taxpayers over children's urgent needs; widen the gap between rich and poor—already at its largest recorded point in over 30 years; and repeatedly break promises and fail to seize opportunities to Leave No Child Behind. While thousands of children, parents, and grandparents stand in unemployment and soup kitchen and homeless shelter lines waiting for food and a stable place to live all across America, lobbyists for powerful corporations like Enron and rich individuals and special interests line up inside Congress and the White House to get hundreds of billions of dollars in new tax breaks and government handouts.* —Children's Defense Fund[1]

With the appointment of George W. Bush to the presidency, education initially became an object of intense political, cultural, and social debate, and educational reform a top governmental priority. As one of the few remaining spheres that has withstood the full force of assault against all things public—in spite of the tragic events of September 11 and the anti-terrorist campaign—public education has become a battleground and litmus test for conservatives and business leaders in their attempt to expand the ideology of the market and the control of capital over all aspects of society. But the new assault on education differs from the strategies used by Republicans and the corporate/ religious/radical right, which have dominated the debate since the 1980s. Unlike the Republican party agenda of the past, which called for the abolition of the U.S. Department of Education and a diminished federal presence in shaping educational policy, George W. Bush has called for an expanded federal role in education along with increased funding.[2] And Congress has delivered a huge victory for President Bush by passing one of the most far-reaching bills to overhaul education in the last 40 years. Using the rhetoric of "compassionate conservatism," Bush claims that his educational reform package is aimed at addressing the needs of disadvantaged children, closing the gap between rich and poor kids, improving accountability, and offering schools more financial resources to improve their performance. With what might be viewed as plagiarism of a slogan used by the progressive Children's Defense Fund ("Leave No Child Behind"), Bush has dubbed his education bill the "No Child Left Behind" Act.

Yet, in spite of such promising rhetoric, public schooling currently faces a crisis of unparalleled proportions as at no other time in American history. Bereft of financial support and confronted by myriad problems that include overcrowded classrooms, crumbling school buildings, chronic shortages of classroom materials, demoralized teachers, and budget shortfalls, many of the nation's schools are in dire straits and can no longer provide a decent, quality education, especially to those children who live in poor rural or urban areas. Some major cities such as Philadelphia have even relinquished some of their low-performing schools to for-profit companies such as Edison Schools Inc., in spite of the fact that such companies have not proven that they can run a large urban district and have a track record that belies their claims of improved academic achievement.[3] Within a short time after Bush took office, Harold Levy, who was the chancellor of New York City schools, captured the corporate spirit, animating educational reforms by proposing that advertising be allowed on school grounds as a way of raising funds to help meet educational expenses. Not to be outdone, his successor, Joel Klein, the former Bertelsmann CEO, has promised to give generous bonuses of up to $40,000 annually to school superintendents on the basis of how well they improve standardized test performance in their districts. The overt message here is clear: treat schools like a pseudo-marketplace, bribe superintendents into turning schools into testing factories, and punish them if they do not succeed in raising test scores. The hidden curriculum is that testing is used as a ploy to ensure that teachers are de-skilled as they are reduced to mere technicians, that students be treated as customers in the marketplace rather than as engaged, critical learners, and that public schools fail so that they can eventually privatized. In sharp contrast to the rhetoric coming out of Washington about "no child left behind," the federal government's new educational reform package provides meager assistance to state educational programs whose budgets have been slashed "to accommodate the expense of the war on terror."[4]

As the Bush administration congratulates itself on its new school reform bill, schools are being sold off to corporations and students are quickly being turned into a captive audience for text book publishers and marketeers intent on reducing learning to recognizing brand names and encouraging market identities. Where is the public outrage over a tax stimulus package that gives the wealthiest 1 percent of the population 45 percent of the total tax cut, or a welfare reform bill that leaves millions of children behind because of its refusal to provide adequate child care for welfare recipients and health insurance for poor children, who now number over 41 million?[5] Where is the "compassion," conservative or otherwise, in a 2003 Bush administration budget that "proposes the smallest education increase in the last seven years?"[6] What both the education and economic stimulus packages suggest is that the Bush government, in spite of its claims to improve public schools, has no substantive interest in providing educational support and opportunities for all children in this country. But President Bush is not alone in his willingness to turn his back on the nation's children. Throughout the United States, lawmakers are confronting the challenge and crisis of schooling by supporting either narrow technological fixes, such as standardized testing, or by capitalizing on the hyped-up patriotic post–September 11 fervor by calling for bills that would make the Pledge of Allegiance mandatory in schools. At the same time, few politicians are lending their voices and support to the recommendation proposed by Marian Wright Edelman, president of the Children's Defense Fund, to President Bush and Congress that they rescind the tax cut for the wealthiest 1 percent of Americans and use the funds to "pay for almost all of the provisions of the comprehensive Act to Leave No Child Behind including quality child care, Head Start, after-school programs, health care, nutrition, protections against child abuse . . . and lift millions of children in working families from poverty."[7] The Bush administration's silence suggests that children are not simply being abandoned, they are being ransomed in the interest of profit and greed.

As the obligations of public life are increasingly defined through the narrow imperatives of consumption, privatization, and the dynamics of the marketplace, commercialism encroaches on all non-commodified public spheres. The first casualty is a language of social and political responsibility capable of defending those vital institutions that expand the rights, public goods, and services central to a meaningful democracy. This is especially true with respect to public schooling and the debate over the purpose of education, the role of teachers as critical intellectuals, the politics of the curriculum, and the centrality of pedagogy as a moral and political practice. Certain elements of the religious right, corporate culture, the Democratic party, and the Republican right wing now either argue that free public education represents a massive failure, or they simply hold it in contempt. According to the educational historian, David Labaree, public schools are attacked "not just because they are deemed ineffective but because they are public."[8]

The contradiction between the rhetoric and the reality of investing in the education and general welfare of American children became apparent before the ink was dry on Bush's "compassionate" educational reform proposal. Before the bill even went to the Senate for final approval, President Bush instituted executive orders abolishing aid to international health organizations that supported abortions, reaffirmed his opposition to affirmative action, and proposed cuts in his budget to programs that provide child care, prevent child abuse, and train doctors at children's hospitals. Furthermore, Bush eliminated in his proposed educational budget all federal funds targeted for class size reduction, provided meager funds for school construction (primarily for schools for Native Americans and military personnel), and no tax relief or credits for the millions of families in the nation with the poorest children. In addition, as reported by the Children's Defense Fund, "While the White House and the House of Representatives decided they could not afford to guarantee $1 billion in help for abused and neglected children, they shortly thereafter found they could afford $7.4 billion to relieve 16 powerful corporations from paying a minimum alternative tax."[9] In fact, one of the most misplaced appropriations in Bush's federal funding for schools has been earmarked for increased testing to provide a measure of teacher accountability— as if teachers can be held responsible for crumbling buildings, the disappearance of school lunch programs, overcrowded classrooms, and a chronic shortage of textbooks, computers, and other necessary educational resources. Similarly, Bush has been silent about providing any substantial increases for federal education programs such as Title I, which specifically aid poor and disadvantaged students.[10] In addition, Bush's attempt to move Head Start from Health and Human Services to the U. S. Department of Education has important implications for how the program is assessed and funded. It gets worse. Bush's bill collapses a number of important, targeted, federally funded programs into a general pool of money that states could use at their own discretion, which means that such funds could not only be used largely for promoting testing and accountability mandates, but that school access to such monies would depend primarily on how well they performed in the high-stakes accountability game.

What we are witnessing here is more than the hypocrisy that underlies the contradiction between Bush's humanistic rhetoric and the retrograde policies he is trying to enact. The more telling consequences of Bush's educational reforms are that children in poor rural and urban schools will be systematically deprived of much-needed institutional resources, smaller classes, and a challenging curriculum. In the end, these children will pay in the hard currency of human suffering as money is diverted from public schools to pay for initiatives such as massive testing programs, parental choice schemes, charter schools, scientifically based reading programs, character education, and a lockdown school safety program. Such proposals primarily drain money from underfunded districts; undermine social services, professional development, and drug education programs; and divert attention from reforms that would improve teacher education, reduce class size, and invest in more innovative curricula. It should come as no surprise that Bush's educational reforms have the pivotal support of conservative foundations such as the Lynde and Harry Bradley Foundation as well as many other business leaders and groups.[11] In what follows, I analyze some of the main features of the Bush education agenda, such as parental choice and standardized testing, by examining the broader issues that are at stake, including the implications of such reforms for re-defining the purpose of schooling, the role that teachers might play within such a policy, the nature of learning, the issue of school safety, and the politics of literacy.

The Meaning and Purpose of Schooling

What has become increasingly clear in both Bush's view of education and his educational proposals, with their emphasis on annual testing, parental choice, and drill and skill teaching, is that schools are seen less as a public good than as a private good. Accordingly, they are con-cerned less with demands of equity, justice, and social citizenship than with the imperatives of the marketplace, skill-based learning, and the needs of the individual consumer. It is worth noting that the words "democracy" and "citizenship" are virtually absent from Bush's 28-page educational plan, *No Child Left Behind*. Whatever conception of agency, citizenship, and democracy does exist becomes synonymous with mar-ket-based notions of choice, hyper-competitiveness, and individual stu-dent mobility. Achievement in Bush's proposal means a narrow notion of individual success rather than critical learning linked to improving the collective good. Turning schools into test-prep centers and children into exam fodder becomes the ultimate measure of quality teaching.

Throughout the twentieth century, American public education was viewed by many prominent educational leaders such as Horace Mann, John Dewey, and Lawrence Cremin as a major force for prepar-ing young people to be socially responsible, critically engaged citizens in a democratic society. But after two decades of orchestrated educa-tional reform efforts, conservatives and business leaders have managed to rewrite the meaning and purpose of public education in terms that are both narrowly instrumental and ideologically suspect. As Stephen Metcalf points out,

The new Bush testing regime emphasizes minimal competence along a narrow range of skills, with an eye toward satisfying the low end of the labor market. All this sits well with a business community whose first preoccupation is "global competitiveness": a community most comfortable thinking in terms of inputs (dollars spent on public schools) in relation to outputs (test scores). No one disputes that schools must inculcate the skills necessary for economic survival. But does it follow that the theory behind public schooling should be overwhelmingly economic? One of the reform movements's founding documents is *Reinventing Education: Entrepreneurship in America's Public Schools,* by Lou Gerstner, chairman of IBM. Gerstner describes schoolchildren as human capital, teachers as sellers in a marketplace and the public school system as a monopoly. Predictably, CEOs bring to education reform CEO rhetoric: stringent, intolerant of failure, even punitive—hence the word "sanction," as if some schools had been turning away weapons inspectors.[12]

Bush's reform plan serves up a mixture of assessments, testing, and financial rewards and punishments that allow parents to take their children out of so-called failing schools and, in effect, to abandon such schools. Of course, such a course of action does not promote collective action, debate, and organizational struggles to improve failing schools. In fact, Bush's system of reward and punishment is built on the premise that in the final analysis it is better for parents to seek reform by leaving such schools behind; that is, it is better for them to disengage from broad-based civic participation and struggle rather than fight to improve struggling schools.[13] While the new educational bill does not provide vouchers for public school students to attend private schools, it does allow low-income parents to use federal money to transfer their children to better public schools, including charter schools. Moreover, the bill provides federal money for low-performing students to get outside tutoring, which can be provided by private groups, including for-profit businesses and religious organizations. Within this approach, the crucial problem of how the public might provide a better education for all children is narrowly transformed into the issue of how dissatisfied parents can get a better education for their own children by simply removing them from the schools.[14] Far from abandoning the call for vouchers, the spirit of this highly individualized and privatized approach to schooling has been kept alive through the current reform bill's emphasis on promoting parental choice, private tutoring, and charter schools. In fact, charter schools have a great deal of appeal for entrepreneurial investors such as Chancellor Beacon Academies Inc., which now manages more than 76 charter schools. And conservatives recognize that charter schools not only open the door for the privatization of public education but also offer various for-profit educational companies a market for significant monetary gain. James P. McVety, an analyst with EduVentures Inc., a Boston research company that specializes in the education industry, captures this sentiment with the claim: "There is a big opportunity to serve that market."[15]

Bush's education agenda cannot escape the consequences of schools made dysfunctional because of insufficient funding, decrepit buildings, overworked teachers, and impoverished students by mandating state exams or encouraging parents to withdraw their children from schools that are considered broken. Within this discourse of privatization, test-taking, and choice, it becomes clear that the president's plan for educational reform lacks a vocabulary for discussing the complex issue of schooling and the future in terms that accentuate rather than diminish the importance of equity and collective struggle as a crucial component of democracy. In fact, George W. Bush's educational policies represent an unconscionable withdrawal from what John Dewey called the creation of an articulate public and its attendant concerns with those issues, institutions, and public spheres that are attentive to human suffering, pain, and oppression. And while the ideological issue of vouchers has been removed from the Bush administration educational reform bill, there is little to suggest that conservatives of various party affiliations will refrain in the future from separating educational policy from its legacy of public service while promoting in any way possible the notion of "the public" merely as a source of funding for privatizing the sphere of public education.[16] This educational policy can be understood as part of a wider attempt by conservatives to expand the power of capital, individual competitiveness, and corporate control and regulation. In effect, Bush's plan puts forward a set of initiatives and principles, the aim of which is not simply to restructure schools, but to construct and secure a narrow view of public authority, social morality, and a notion of democratic life that is consistent with corporate culture's view of public education as largely an adjunct of the business community. Educational psychologist and author Gerald Bracey goes even further by suggesting that the "No Child Left Behind Act" is part of a grand scheme on the part of privatizers to set public schools up for failure. He argues that two of the major provisions in the act, those for testing and teacher qualifications, set "up public schools for the final knock down."[17] In the first instance, "The massive testing requirements alone will force almost all states to spend massive amounts of money to develop, administer, analyze and report the test results and other data needed for mandatory 'report cards' for schools. Most states will have to abandon their own programs labored over for the last decade."[18] Similarly, Bush's education bill stipulates that all teachers in schools that receive federal funds must be "highly qualified," which means "those who hold at least a bachelor's degree, have full state certification (or have passed the state's licensing exam), and who have not had any certification requirements waived on 'an emergency, provisional, or temporary basis.'"[19] What Bracey makes clear is that given the existing teacher shortage—which will get especially acute in urban areas—many states will not be able to meet these new teacher qualifications requirements. The consequences for both the public schools and the children who attend them could be catastrophic. Of course, the rationale for these reforms, especially the testing craze, is that they make good business sense and are endorsed by a number of prominent CEOs. The notion that what is good for business is also good for education, or that models of educational leadership should be patterned after corporate leadership, has always been a deeply problematic issue; it has become especially suspect given the scandals surrounding the systematic deceit and imaginative greed that have wracked major corporations such as Enron, KMart, Tyco International, Global Crossing, and WorldCom, "revealing how deeply flawed [corporate management and] US financial markets really are."[20]

At the heart of Bush's vision of schooling is a corporatized model of education that cancels out the democratic ideals and practices of civil society by either devaluing or absorbing them within the logic of the market. No longer a space for relating the self to the obligations of public life, and social responsibility to the demands of critical and engaged citizenship, schools are viewed as an all-encompassing horizon for producing market identities, values, and those privatizing pedagogies that inflate the importance of individual competition. This package of educational reform does more than promote student achievement through scientifically backed research; it also promotes institutionalized class- and race-based forms of tracking and a culture of failure for those who don't have the cultural and academic resources to negotiate successfully a dreary test-based curriculum and the high-stakes sorting mechanisms of a state- and corporate-regulated testing machine.

But the excessive celebration of the sovereign interests of the individual does more than remove the dynamics of student performance from broader social and political considerations, it also feeds a value system in which compassion, solidarity, cooperation, and social responsibility—attributes of education as a social good—get displaced by a definition of education exclusively as a private asset. If education is about, in part, the creation of particular identities, what is privileged in Bush's model of education is a notion of the student as an individual consumer and teachers as either de-skilled technicians or multinational operatives.[21] Education reformer David Labaree rightly argues that such a model undermines the traditional idea that education should be viewed as a public good that should benefit all children and should be embraced as central to the health of a democratic society. But when viewed as a private good, whose organizing principle is simply to mimic the market, education is transformed into a discourse and ideology of privilege driven by narrow instrumental and individual interests at odds with real democracy. Labaree is quite clear on this issue:

> In an educational system where the consumer is king. . . . Education . . . is a private good that only benefits the owner, an investment in my future, not yours, in my children, not other people's children. For such an educational system to work effectively, it needs to focus a lot of attention on grading, sorting, and selecting students. It needs to provide a variety of ways for individuals to distinguish themselves from others—such as by placing themselves in a more prestigious college, a higher curriculum track, the top reading group, or the gifted program.[22]

Education in this framework becomes a vehicle for social mobility for those privileged to have the resources and power to make their choices matter—and a form of social constraint for those who lack such resources and for whom choice and accountability reflect a legacy of broken promises and bad faith.

Bush's educational policy represents an attempt on the part of right-wing conservatives, corporate interests, and the religious right to privatize social services formerly provided by the state, to consolidate wealth among affluent groups, and to construct a market-based value system which enshrines individualism, self-help, bureaucratic management, and consumerism at the expense of those values that reflect the primacy of the ethical, social, and civic in public life.[23] Couched in the language of educational reform, corporate values and test-driven competition become the sources of individual initiative and cancel out those collective values and experiences that provide the foundation for democratic civic life. This privatizing morality is reinforced as corporate culture becomes increasingly the only legitimate model of educational leadership and moral authority.[24] Such a model of leadership, with its inability to make a distinction between market relations and a market society, lacks the vocabulary for addressing broader conceptions of democratic citizenship and encourages schools to sell their curriculum, students, and space to the highest corporate bidder. Many of the proposals in Bush's reform bill are, in fact, designed to both liquidate the gains of the welfare state, disempower working-class children, and actively pursue the ongoing quest to privatize health, education, and other public goods—extending an agenda that has dominated American political life since the beginning of the Reagan era in 1980. The notion of parental choice, at the heart of Bush's initial educational proposal, was simply a thinly veiled attempt to cater to the religious right by undermining the separation between church and state by allowing public funds to be used to support religious interests. It was also designed to further the ongoing privatization of education, removing religious schools from viable forms of public accountability, including the need for open meetings, public oversight, implementation of civil rights legislation, and adherence to the widely acclaimed Americans with Disability Act. None of these would have any bearing on the functioning of private schools. At issue here, as educator Jeffrey Henig points out, is not simply that public money would support private schools or that some students would be given the option to attend privately run schools at the public's expense, but that Bush's initial market-based proposals would serve to "erode the public forums in which decisions with societal consequences can be democratically resolved."[25] This is the key issue that drives the conservative educational agenda, and while it did not attain its full ideological expression as a result of the defeat of school vouchers in the current educational legislation, its presence in the new bill is evident in its endorsement for punishing failing school districts by turning them over to the state, which in turn can invite for-profit institutions such as Edison Schools, Inc., to manage them—precisely what is currently happening in Philadelphia, the seventh-largest school system in the United States.

The most fundamental goal of school reform is to improve the educational opportunities for all children who attend public schools. But this would demand more than simply tougher accountability schemes, expanded choice programs, privatization, more testing, and increased security. It would mean embarking on what Amy Gutman calls systemic reforms, which include: "decreasing class size, expanding pre-school programs, setting high standards for all students, engaging students in cooperative learning exercises, empowering principals and teachers to innovate, increasing social services offered to students and their families, and providing incentives to the ablest college students to enter the teaching profession and, in particular, to teach in inner city schools."[26] Such a task would not be exclusionary or punitive, as in the Bush model, but would demand a democratic vision made concrete through political, economic, and social reforms that would hold society accountable to the very meaning and promise of an inclusive democracy, especially those promises aimed at creating a decent future for the next generation of young people. School reform in this context would include addressing those underlying causes of educational inequality such as family poverty, massive discrepancies in school funding, racism, and other subtler injuries of class and racial discrimination.

Accountability and the De-Skilling of Teachers

According to the Bush educational plan, the unfairness of the present system of public schooling resides in the absence of accountability, tough standards, and rigorous modes of testing. Bush's emphasis on high standards (as if anyone is for low standards) translates into a heavy emphasis on standardized tests as the most important way to measure how students learn and "to determine if high standards [are] being met."[27] While Bush wants to spend more money on education, much of that funding would be used to support an accountability scheme largely developed around the push for improved standards measured by the results of new state-developed reading and math tests. According to the new bill, beginning in the 2005–06 school year, annual testing of all third through eighth graders in math and reading will be required. In addition, mandated annual science tests, beginning in 2007, would be required once each between grades 3–4, 6–9, and 10–12. Schools that failed to close the achievement gap between the races and different socio-economic levels would face a number of sanctions. Educator Stan Karp observes that the sanctions are not necessarily new, but they do signal a "rightward turn in education policy." He writes that the Bush administration's new elementary and secondary education act mandates:

> Sanctions for the schools receiving federal Title I funds that don't reach their "adequate yearly progress" goals, which most likely will be impossible to meet. The sanctions include now-familiar "corrective measures" like outside intervention by consultants, replacement of staff, or state takeover. Additional sanctions reflect the administration's privatization agenda that lurks just below the surface of the legislation. This includes use of federal funds to provide "supplemental services" to students from outside agencies, imposing school choice or charter plans, or transferring management of schools to private contractors. Tenure reform, merit pay, and teacher testing are also potentially in the mix, though they are not mandated by the new law.[28]

Bush's primary emphasis on standardized testing is based on the alleged success of the use of state-wide achievement tests to narrow the gap between the scores of minorities and whites in Texas while he was governor. But a number of educators, such as Walter Haney and Linda McNeil, have argued that the "Texas miracle in education" is a myth. They argue that the standardized tests used in Texas are too easy, promote a curriculum primarily concerned with aggressive test-drilling, and that the system of accountability has not only failed to close the achievement gap, as measured by the NAEP—a test used across the country—but has also undermined educational quality.[29] For example, Texas schools have some of the nation's highest dropout rates, particularly among minorities. Funds are often spent on commercial test- preparation materials rather than on more important resources, and "many schools, especially in working class areas with low pass rates, are virtually handed over to 'test-prep' from New Year's through April, when the tests are given."[30] In order to secure money for their schools, many principals hold pep rallies and bribe kids with financial incentives, movie tickets, pizza, and other consumer items in order to raise test scores. Beyond using the schools to motivate students around crass market appeals and turning teachers into commercial hawkers, such "incentives" not only take up valuable class time, they put excessive pressure on students and teachers alike. In one of the largest studies done on standardized testing, researchers found that students are being educated so narrowly that they are performing less well in other independent measures of academic achievement such as the SAT, ACT, and reading tests. The research also demonstrated that states that use high-stakes testing have the highest drop-out rates and that fewer students get diplomas.[31]

Under Bush's educational reform policy, statistical accountability replaces real accountability, and the consequences do not bode well for schools. Not only will the huge emphasis on testing result in the squandering of valuable school resources on testing programs at the expense of developing enriched curricula, providing valuable support services for students, and hiring qualified teachers, but, as educational theorists Wayne Ross and Sandra Mathison point out, it will also reinforce a number of unjust and unsound educational practices, including: "increased drop out rates, teacher and administrator deprofessionalization, loss of curricular integrity, [and] increased cultural insensitivity."[32]

Legitimating self-interest as the only readily acceptable standard of human behavior, framed within the logic of consumer sovereignty and abstracted from the material relations of power that give it meaning, Bush's emphasis on accountability and testing has nothing to say about poor urban and rural students who are taught by inexperienced teachers, attend overcrowded classrooms, lack adequate school supplies, inhabit decrepit buildings, and live, in some cases, in districts that receive $39,000 less per pupil than children in the richest suburbs.[32] Rigid accountability schemes and high-stakes testing models offer no guidance on matters of justice, equality, and freedom, and condemn both poor students and public schools to failure. Moreover, Bush's emphasis on standardized testing appears utterly unaware of the extensive body of research that problematizes some of the most basic assumptions behind the use of high-stakes testing, and demonstrates how such testing has actually exacerbated the problems it sought to alleviate.[34] In addition, there is the added cost of subjecting 10-year-olds to test drills 4 months out of a 9-month school year as a solution to drop-out rates and failing schools.

To promote testing as a centerpiece of educational reform while saying nothing about how student achievement and learning are linked to the distribution of resources, power, and politics represents more than the rhetoric of insincerity; it also translates the alleged virtues of the marketplace into an object lesson of punitive hypocrisy. But Bush's emphasis on accountability does more than separate academic performance from issues of equity. It also has devastating consequences for undermining the autonomy of teachers, lowering the quality of the curriculum, and reproducing those tracking and stratification policies that bear down so heavily on minorities of class and color. Patricia Williams has noted that at a time when state and federal budgets are being slashed to accommodate the war on terror, those schools that need the most help are penalized while the emphasis on testing and achievement makes these into thinly coded terms for legitimizing the narrowing of access to the most privileged students. According to Williams,

> A parsimony of spirit haunts education policy, exacerbated by fear of the extremes. Under the stress of threatened budget cuts, people worry much more about providing lifeboats for the very top and containment for the "ineducable" rock bottom than they do about properly training the great masses of children, the vibrant, perfectly able middle who are capable of much more than most school systems offer.[35]

Williams is right, but she underestimates what groups are being contained and how the culture of schooling is changing under the umbrella of such approaches. In light of the emergence of high-stakes testing and zero-tolerance policies, the vast majority of those being either contained in low track classes, expelled from schools, or pushed into the criminal justice system are primarily students of color and poor students. High-stakes testing does nothing to address this racial and class divide in the schools and, in fact, actually reproduces forms of tracking that perpetuate it. I take this issue up in more detail later in this chapter.[36]

It is no secret that the test-based reforms called for by President Bush are imposed on administrators and teachers by state legislatures and overly powerful school boards. The high stakes mean that schools can either receive extra money or be shut down, and such tests put enormous pressure on teachers to teach to the test, abandon their sense of creativity and autonomy in the classroom, ignore the specificities of children's lives and problems, and, in general, be less attentive to the vast differences that often exist among students. As conception is divorced from implementation, teachers are often stripped of their authority, skills, and creative possibilities, and reduced to technicians—drill sergeants working under the imperatives of a handful of corporate test makers, who rake in millions in profits and also play a major role in shaping both the nature of teaching and the shape of the curriculum. These were precisely the effects of such testing found by Linda McNeil in her study of the Texas Accountability System: As she puts it,

> a very narrow set of numerical indicators (student scores on statewide tests) has become the only language of currency in education policy in the state. Principals report that there can be little discussion of children's development, of cultural relevance, of children's contributions to classroom knowledge and interactions or of those engaging sidebar experiences at the margins of curriculum where children often do their best learning. According to urban principals, many have supervisors who tell them quite pointedly, "Don't talk to me about anything else until the TAAS (Texas Assessment of Academic Skills) scores start to go up."[37]

Under such conditions, teachers are prevented from taking risks and designing their own lessons as the pressure to achieve passing tests scores produces highly scripted and regimented forms of teaching. In this context, worksheets become a substitute for critical teaching and rote memorization takes the place of in-depth thinking. Behaviorism becomes the preferred model of pedagogy and substitutes a mind-numbing emphasis on methods and techniques over pedagogical practices that are critical, moral, and political in substance. Learning facts and skills in reading and math becomes more important than genuine understanding. Academic success therefore becomes largely a measurement of one's speed in taking high-stakes standardized tests, rather than the ability to engage knowledge with thoughtfulness and critical analytical skills. Testing is not simply an alleged measure of "achievement," as the conservatives put it, but also constitutes a pedagogy of testing in which students are often taught to believe "there is only one right answer, that the objective is to find the right answer, that the right answer is in the mind of the text drafter."[38] This type of pedagogy is at odds with learning that stresses creativity, critical thinking, leadership skills, autonomy, and self and social development.

Pedagogy as a critical practice in which students learn to be attentive and responsible to the memories and narratives of others disappears within corporate and test-driven learning. Unfortunately, the reductive transmission, or banking, approach to pedagogy underscored in Bush's reforms cancels out some of the most important aspects of critical teaching: making knowledge relevant to students' lives; providing supportive environments in which students can learn; and developing a range of teaching approaches and forms of assessment based on the recognition that not every student learns the same way. But focusing on test scores does more than de-skill teachers and squeeze any critical, moral, and intellectual life out of the process of learning. Drill-and-skill teaching also removes pedagogy from the selective operations of power and ideology, even as it results in schools "cutting back or even eliminating programs in the arts, recess for young children, electives for high schoolers, class meetings, discussions about current events, the use of literature in the early grades, and entire subject areas" that are not easy to test.[39] Clearly, such cuts have the most devastating affects on those schools that barely can afford such programs in the first place, schools already suffering because they are underfunded. Moreover, researchers have found standardized tests to be racially biased, condemning students of color to bottom slots within the educational hierarchy where there is bad teaching, emphasis on worksheet knowledge, and alienating social relations.[40] Standardized tests have always favored the rich and the powerful,[41] and their origins in the eugenics movement in the earlier century, as well as the recent rantings of Charles Murray in *The Bell Curve,* should serve as a forceful reminder of the legitimating connection between such testing and the prevailing racist discourse on IQ as a valid way to identify "superior" from inferior students. Put simply, such tests often discriminate against those children who are not from the upper- and middle-classes—who can afford private lessons in test-taking—just as they discriminate against students who do not grow up in what can be termed acceptable race- and class-specific modes of cultural capital—dressing, speaking, experiencing, and being in the world. Moreover, such tests are often used to promote the dreadful practice of sorting students of color in ways that make it difficult for them to take high-powered classes that address serious issues, link learning to empowerment, and gain access to forms of political and social agency in which they learn how to intervene in and challenge those forms of economic and political power that are closing down all possibility of a multicultural, transnational, and radical democracy.

Testing has become the code word for training educational leaders in the language of management, measurement, and efficiency. It has also become the new ideological weapon in developing standardized curricula that ignore cultural diversity by defining knowledge narrowly in terms of discrete skills and decontextualized bodies of information, ruthlessly expunging the language of ethics from the broader purpose of teaching and schooling. What knowledge is taught, under what conditions, for what purpose, and by whom has become less important than developing precise measuring instruments for tracking students and, increasingly, for disempowering and de-skilling teachers.

In terms of accountability, this discourse offers few insights into how schools should prepare students to push against the oppressive boundaries of gender, class, and racial domination, and help those dealing with sexual preference. Nor does this approach provide the conditions for students to explore how questions of knowledge that inform curricula are, in fact, closely linked to struggles over identity, culture, power, and history. Similarly, the crisis of schooling is grounded in a refusal to address how particular forms of authority are secured and legitimized. Refusing to analyze the values that frame how authority is constructed and to define leadership as a critical political and democratic pedagogical practice, Bush's educational reforms end up celebrating the bureaucratic rules of management, regulation, and control at the expense of substantive democracy, critical citizenship, and basic human rights.

Market values under neoliberalism encourage a competitive individualism in which teachers must out-perform their peers in order to receive requisite rewards, while at the same time students are encouraged to separate themselves from others, often through the discriminatory terms of race, class, and gender. Kenneth Wesson, a founding member of the Association of Black Psychologists, has raised a question worth pondering regarding the reduction of assessment in public schools to the use of standardized tests: "Let's be honest. If poor, inner-city children consistently outscored children from wealthy suburban homes on standardized tests, is anyone naive enough to believe that we would still insist on using these tests as indicators of success?"[42]

I am not arguing against forms of assessment that enhance the possibility for self and social empowerment among children, forms of assessment that promote critical modes of inquiry and creativity as opposed to those that shut down self-respect and motivation by instilling a sense of failure or humiliation. On the contrary, assessments are important to get students to reflect on their work and the work of others—not as a test of speed or a function of what I have called corporate time—but as a measure of deliberation, critical analysis, and dialogue. But if such assessments are to be useful, they need to be part of a broader agenda for equity, and must be understood within a notion of schooling that rejects learning simply as the mastery of discrete skills and precise bodies of information. Moreover, any viable notion of assessment needs to be removed from the politics of mandated curricula, a culture of punishment, and those modes of discrimination that currently drive much of the testing craze. Assessment strategies cannot be used to dictate top-down teaching practices—not only because such practices define teaching less as an intellectual activity and more as a standardized, mechanical, and utterly passive mode of training, but also because "teachers and communities shorn of the capacity to use their own ideas, judgments, and initiative in matters of importance can't teach kids to do so."[43] Such practices have little to do with teaching students to develop critical skills, sociocultural "maps," and an awareness of the operations of power that would enable them to both locate themselves in the world and to effectively intervene in and shape it.[44] The use of punitive, standardized, high-stakes testing undermines teacher autonomy, imposes harsh restrictions on academic labor, disables critical approaches to teaching, and promotes pedagogical practices that supposedly "measure" student progress while reproducing a tracking system that parallels the deep racial and economic inequalities of society as a whole. The first responsibility of public schools is not to test students as if they were empty containers to be measured, stamped, and processed, but to address what it means to provide them with the critical reading, writing, language, technological skills, knowledge, social experiences, and resources they need—in order to enhance their capacity to understand, comprehend, engage, and, when necessary, to transform the world in which they live. Of course, President Bush has plenty of ardent supporters for his testing proposals, and most influential are the testing and textbook companies, such as McGraw-Hill, whose owners are long-standing friends of the Bush family. One executive from the publishing giant NCS Pearson, cited in *Education Week,* could barely hide his enthusiasm for Bush's educational policy and claimed that Bush's call for state testing "reads like our business plan." Indeed, Fair Test, a Boston nonprofit company puts it more bluntly: "This promises to be a bonanza for the testing companies."[45]

Schooling and the Culture of Fear

Schools in Bush's proposal function primarily as agencies of social and cultural reproduction. For instance, Bush has allocated a substantial amount of money to the education budget to develop programs that would instill "character" in students; that is, teaching students right from wrong. Bush's support of character education, or "character"-building lessons, coupled with his endorsement of reading programs based on phonics or correct sounding of letters—rather than meaningful communication, or the struggle with ideas, or even writing—turns teaching and learning, at best, into a crushing bore, and at worst, into a form of ruthless disempowerment for students. Such traditional and rote approaches to teaching are passionately ideological in the most retrograde sense and utterly instrumentalist. As one critical educator observes, "Phonics is a way of thinking about illiteracy [especially for adolescents and young adults] that doesn't involve thinking about larger social injustices. To cure illiteracy, presumably all children need is a new set of textbooks."[46] Character education as a basis for promoting a highly restricted notion of literacy and moral reasoning has long been supported by conservatives such as William Bennett, Diane Ravitch, Dinesh D'-Sousa, Chester Finn, Jr., and others who see it as a way of imposing rigid restrictions on what can be taught in schools, particularly in regard to subjects considered dangerous—such as sex education, evolution, and bilingual education—or subjects viewed as irrelevant to the Western canon—anything to do with multicultural education.

The ideological nature of character education can be seen in the new education bill's program for strengthening American history instruction by offering grants for training teachers who teach "traditional" American history. Clearly, this program is another example of how the appeal to "character" education is used to deter educators from including the voices of minorities, women, labor activists, and others, as well as those struggles waged from the bottom up that are often left out of traditional history. As Richard Rothstein, an education reporter for the *New York Times* observes, it is difficult to believe that any "respected teacher wants a return to the traditional teaching of only facts about leaders. Yet this approach is a matter of law for schools that accept this federal money."[47] In this perspective, character is allegedly developed by memorizing dates and facts, on the one hand, while on the other the history of great men overrides any understanding of those struggles waged by labor, feminists, and civil rights movements that have shaped the history of the United States. Critical historical narratives are viewed as dangerous by the Bush administration, as are any pedagogical approaches that encourage teachers and students to become responsible agents actively questioning and negotiating the relationships between theory and practice, critical analysis and common sense, and learning and social change. To the conservatives, teaching history is not concerned with providing students with the skills and knowledge to expand their critical capacities and enter into dialogue with the multiple narratives of history. Nor is it concerned with going beyond treating history as an assemblage of facts to be memorized in the spirit of promoting a form of jingoistic "patriotism." This perspective lacks any notion of what it means to teach history through a culture of questioning, in which students become the subjects of learning and in doing so also become responsible for their own ideas, while learning how to take risks, negotiate differences, be respectful of others, and think critically in order to function within a wider democratic culture. This is not a matter of separating pedagogical processes from content, as many conservatives suggest, but making historical content meaningful so it can become critical and transformative. This critical approach to teaching history, and to pedagogy in general, is based on the idea that there is more hope in the world when teachers and students can question what is often taken for granted in their textbooks, classrooms, and the larger social order. The purpose of learning history is not to promote some self-serving notion that views progressive initiatives and dissent as unpatriotic and critical learning as undermining social agency; on the contrary, history should be taught in order to provide students with the knowledge and skills they need to come to terms with their own power as individual agents and critical citizens. The study of history should enable students to learn about the relationship between knowledge and the power of self-definition, and what it means to use knowledge to understand the world—as well as to be able to influence those who are in power and help to mobilize those who are not. Learning history in this sense is not simply a matter of competency as the testmakers suggest, but a matter of the possibility of intervention into the ideas, values, and institutional structures that reproduce existing hierarchies of power and privilege that undermine the most basic premises of a democratic society. At the same time, history as a critical narrative can be used to help students explore patriotism, as cultural historians Peter Dreier and Dick Flacks suggest, through the writings and struggles of Americans who "expressed a patriotism rooted in democratic values and consciously aimed at challenging jingoism and 'my country, right or wrong' thinking . . . [associated with] blind nationalism, militaristic drumbeating and sheeplike conformism."[48]

Given the blatant ideological nature of the traditional history provision in "No Child Left Behind," it seems impossible not to recognize the sheer hypocrisy and partisanship of an educational bill that uses the phrase "scientifically-based research" 111 times to justify funding particular policies that are in line with traditional approaches to teaching subjects such as reading, math, and science. Ironically, the Bush administration's appeal to "scientifically-based research" seems to have little bearing on either teaching evolution or sex education that does not rely primarily on abstinence. There is more at work here than turning scientific research into an instrumental ideology that can be used by any politician to justify particular proposals and policies to "shape" student character. There is also the sheer hypocrisy of using a different standard of legitimation for judging forms of knowledge that actually *are steeped* in scientific rules of evidence and stringent modes of evaluation. As Richard Rothstein argues:

> Congressional enthusiasm for science, however, does not seem to apply to evolution and sex education. In the case of evolution, the law says that teachers must "help students understand the full range of views on controversial topics," science notwithstanding. And sex education programs must emphasize abstinence, despite the lack of scientific data showing [the teaching of abstinence] to be an effective way to reduce AIDS, venereal disease or teenage pregnancy. The law actually does its best to discourage scientific data on this topic, prohibiting Department of Education surveys from asking students, even anonymously, about their sex behavior or attitudes. Effective programs cannot be developed without such information.[49]

Character education is not aimed at schools for the rich and privileged, who would hardly tolerate the strictures of such obedience training and modes of authoritarianism. Educating the managerial and cultural elite cannot be grounded in the imperatives of character education, which promotes passivity rather than leadership. Learning to follow the rules, adapting rather than critically engaging the values that reproduce existing structures of power, and developing a curriculum around "patriotic" and traditional views of history are meant largely for those students who are either a threat to or are completely dispensable to Bush's version of America. Character education, as it has been defined among conservative cultural warriors such as Lynne Cheney, is a euphemism for promoting pedagogical practices in which students learn core values that reproduce "good" habits of conduct such as being polite, learning how to compete with others, providing the "right" answers, keeping classrooms tidy, and returning library books on time. Character education shifts attention to the moral values that guide student behavior, but has nothing to say about how institutions assume, and should be held accountable ethically and politically for, the ways in which they exercise power and how it affects others. Character education focuses on controlling individual behavior but totally neglects the relationship between individual behavior and the responsibilities of social life, or ethics as a social discourse grounded in public struggles. Moreover, character education is part of the discourse of right-wing conservative and religious groups who exercise an enormous influence over Bush's policies. In this context, character education is used to impose a highly charged conservative set of values upon schools, and its consequences will strengthen the spirit of reverence, authoritarianism, and control that is central to Bush's view of schooling and educational reform. The effects will be devastating for those teachers and educators who believe that a spirit of diversity, critique, and public discussion are central to a democratic education.

Public schools don't need character education, which is just a euphemism for conservative modes of moral and social regulation. Instead, schools should provide forms of critical education in which ethics and values are used to teach students to keep the spirit of justice alive in themselves, embrace the need to be compassionate, respect the rights of others, and be self- conscious about the consequences of their actions. Public schools need to do more than teach students to "just say no" to drugs and sex. Moral education, in the best sense, means taking a hard look at what we as adults and educators impart to kids in schools and the larger society on a daily basis—and understanding how they tend to mutually inform each other. Seeing schools as a site of moral and political education means developing curricula and classroom social relations that teach students the basic values of tolerance, acceptance, decency, civic courage, gender equity, fairness, and racial justice. Moral education also means giving students the knowledge and skills to enable them to interrogate and defend the values and norms that are crucial to recognizing anti-democratic forms of power and expanding the operations of freedom and democracy.

Closely linked to Bush's call for character education is his emphasis on providing funds for schools to "remove violent or persistently disruptive students from the classroom." Moreover, "to receive funds from this program, states must adopt a zero-tolerance policy for violent or persistently disruptive students."[50] Bush's proposal also provides funds for children to transfer from dangerous schools to safe ones. Again, choice and flight, rather than engagement and struggle, becomes the antidote for dealing with failing public schools. It is difficult to understand the rationale behind this policy, except as a way of linking character education to the culture of fear and punishment. As many educators have indicated, schools are among the safest places for kids to be.[51] Pushing the moral panic button in "No Child Left Behind," Bush paints public schools as dangerous, and in doing so grossly exaggerates the statistics on crime and violence in schools. As Richard Rothstein has pointed out in a *New York Times* article, "In fact, of the 2,000 killings of children a year, only about 10 occur in or near schools. . . . Even gun violence is not a significant school problem, despite some highly publicized, horrifying instances. For every teenager killed by a gun in school, more than 300 are killed by guns elsewhere. . . . To enhance child safety, we would do better to control drunken driving on weekends than to turn schools into lock-down facilities with metal detectors."[52] Exaggerations aside, Bush and Attorney General John Ashcroft believe that guns, poverty, racism, the hyper-commercialism of corporate culture, and the brutal machismo at the heart of American society have nothing to do with the problems and violence that students sometimes face in and out of schools.

Under Bush's plan, those students who don't fit in, resist the new testing orthodoxy, or organize opposition to lock-down schools can now be removed from schools, and, under the imperatives of zero-tolerance policies, be handed over to the police or other elements of the criminal justice system.[53] Moreover, Bush wants to standardize such policies so as to further undermine the possibilities for administrators, teachers, and others in schools across the country to make judgments and deliberations about student behavior that take account of a wide range of considerations and factors and guarantee a genuinely fair appeals process. But Bush's policies do more than turn administrators into unwitting supporters of a rigid and harsh criminal justice system: they also further abet the discriminatory policies against minorities that are already deeply entrenched in school practices, such as tracking, inordinate rates of expulsion and suspension for students of color, the warehousing of black and brown kids in dead-end schools and classrooms, and the underfunding characteristic of schools inhabited by poor and minority kids.[54] Every parent wants their child in a safe school, not only because such environments provide a basic condition for learning, but because schools are one of the few places left where adults do make a commitment to invest in the quality of children's lives. When schools become unsafe, punitive measures should not be enacted against children, but against those adults and institutional forces that allow such negligence to take place. Discipline policies should educate kids and not merely punish them. School safety policies should offer kids a second chance, not simply dump them into the criminal justice system, and students should be given the power to play a governing role in shaping such policies.

Conclusion

Bush's educational agenda represents one of the most conservative and powerful assaults ever faced by advocates of public education. It exemplifies a willingness to deny an entire generation of youth the possibility of a quality public education and is an attack on both education as a social force and all those institutions of public life that "encourage disempowered citizens to imagine a future beyond the status quo."[55] Against the current onslaught to privatize and undermine public education, educators, parents, community leaders, and others must offer a staunch defense of public education as a resource vital to the democratic and civic life of the nation. They also need to engage in the hard work of making the pedagogical more political by providing analysis of the crisis of education on multiple fronts, particularly in relation to those wider economic, political, and social forces that exacerbate tensions between those who value education as a public good and those advocates of neoliberalism who see market culture as a master design for all human affairs. Any attempt to rally to the defense of public schools must make clear that Bush's education agenda is closely connected to the ongoing attempts on the part of conservatives, religious right-wingers, and neoliberals to undermine substantive democracy by reducing it to the imperatives of hyper-capitalism and the glorification of financial markets. In opposition to this multi-faceted attack on democratic public life, educators must address the political and pedagogical importance of struggling over the meaning and definition of education, authority, and social responsibility as part of a broader debate over human rights, social provisions, civil liberties, equity, and economic justice.

Activists and educators must make clear that the struggle over education is part of this wider struggle over class, community control, and public resources. As oppositional public intellectuals, educators need to create a broad-based movement for the defense of public goods and democratic public spheres, one that links the struggle for autonomy within the public schools to universities, workplaces, and other social settings. Similarly, supporters of public education must ally themselves with groups opposing privatization in spheres such as housing, transportation, the prison system, child care, and health services. Such a movement suggests that educators take seriously the symbolic and pedagogical dimensions of these diverse struggles and be able to mobilize resources in a variety of public spaces to fight for equality, freedom, public services, and rights, especially the right of children to decent health care, education, housing, and work. Moreover, educators and others interested in the well-being of children must make clear that the priorities shaping Bush's policies have little to do with protecting and educating children and a lot to do with leaving most children behind. For instance, the Bush administration claims that Head Start, one of the most successful educational programs, is a top priority, and yet "Its 2002 budget would have cut children from Head Start and its 2003 budget will not give even one more child a Head Start." Equally disturbing is the fact that Bush's 2002 welfare bill not only "provides a $1.6 trillion tax cut that disproportionately benefit[s] the wealthy" while limiting gains in the child tax credit to upper- and middle-class families, "leaving 17 million children behind, including a majority of Black and Latino children."[56]

Educators both within and outside of the public schools must find ways to connect their work to social policy, especially by addressing the role that public policy currently plays in undermining the basic foundations of democratic public life. The link between education and social policy is important and complex, and—as social activists and engaged citizens—educators, parents, and others need to address and support such connections. Though far from widespread, groups such as Fair Test, *Teachers College Record* online, and the Media Education

Foundation do precisely this kind of work around questions of assessment, testing, critical pedagogy, and media education, and they have offered a welcome opposition to many of Bush's testing schemes and other important aspects of education.[57] I also want to stress that while it is important for educators to link their work to policy, this call remains too abstract unless it engages the critical role of pedagogy in developing and enabling forms of political agency among both professionals and the broader public in order to make such a connection both attractive and viable. Without a viable notion of political agency, such calls for linking theory and practice become empty and miss the crucial importance of making the pedagogical more political. To do so, educators need to find a way under present conditions to redefine public schooling as a public good and teachers as critical intellectuals whose pedagogical role, in part, is to link learning to social change, but also to join with community and other activists to change social policy and to struggle against the Bush agenda. This will entail exposing the ideological and political interests at work in such a proposal, while creating new forms of communication and solidarity capable of addressing and challenging the dangerous threats that the Bush plan represents to public schools, minorities of class and color, and democracy itself.

Challenging the Bush agenda at the level of daily school experience means, in part, reaffirming the importance of the classroom as a site of critique, critical exchange, and social transformation. The struggle over curricula, both hidden and overt, provides educators with the opportunity to challenge those approaches to pedagogy in the Bush agenda in which knowledge becomes capital—a form of investment in the economy—that appears to have little value in terms of self-definition or the ability of youth to expand the scope of individual and social freedom. By viewing the curriculum as a site of critical inquiry, contestation, and resistance, pedagogy is defined as a normative and political practice rather than as a neutral methodology or a fixed, a priori discourse. Engaging the relationship between knowledge and power highlights the socio-historical formations and ideologically laden assumptions that determine how teaching and learning are framed in the curriculum. Rather than viewing teaching and learning as a sacred ritual buttressed by modes of authority that are held to be unproblematic and beyond debate, educators have an ethical obligation to provide students with the tools to challenge all types of authority "that would fail to render an account and provide reasons . . . for the validity of its pronouncements."[58] A vibrant democracy demands citizens who can examine how language is tangled up with the operations of power, the value-based interests underlying knowledge claims, and the consequences of diverse modes of authority. Central to this task is the need for educators to provide students with the critical knowledge, personal experiences, and critical skills to challenge those moral and political regulations that define public education as both a training ground for corporate berths and as an unquestioned guardian of dominant cultural values designed to benefit a privileged minority of students. The model for some of these practices can be see in the work of *Rethinking Schools, Radical Teacher,* and Youth United For Change. But, again, these groups occupy marginal positions in the struggle against dominant neoliberal and conservative forces driving the education agenda.

Under the Bush educational agenda, the concept of the social is being refigured and displaced as a constitutive category for making democracy operational and making political agency the condition for social transformation. The ideas of the social and the public are not being erased as much as reconstructed, under circumstances in which public forums for serious debate, including public education, are being eroded. Within the logic of neoliberalism and the culture of fear, teaching and learning are removed from the discourse of democracy and civic freedom—now defined as a purely private affair. Divorced from the imperatives of a democracy, pedagogy is reduced to a matter of technique, individual choice, and job training. Pedagogy as a mode of witnessing—a public engagement in which students learn to be attentive and responsible to the experiences of others—disappears within a corporate-driven agenda in which the logic of the market devalues the opportunity for students to make connections with others through social relations that foster compassion, ethics, and hope. The crisis of the social is further amplified by the withdrawal of the state as a guardian of the public trust and its growing lack of investment in those sectors of social life that promote the public good.

I think it is fair to say that educational theories that pose fundamental questions about the democratic possibilities of schools as genuine sites of learning and democratic values have largely disappeared from the national debate about the meaning and purpose of public schooling. Schools are in crisis, and critical theories of teaching and learning seem to have either fallen on deaf ears or have been consigned to the dustbin of history. In 2001, one of the major debates over public schools concerned putting the Ten Commandments on public display. In 2002, the Bush administration proposed that one viable form of educational reform is to reinterpret Title IX legislation passed in 1970 so as to encourage the creation of single-sex classrooms and schools. Against the new "common sense" of educational reform, teaching is not about processing received knowledge but actually transforming it. In opposition to the profound anti-intellectualism and corporate ideology that currently drive mainstream school reform, educators, parents, students, and others need to promote a more democratic vision for improving both the quality of schooling and the pedagogical practices in which teachers and students engage.

The greatest threat to our children does not come from lowered standards, the absence of privatized choice schemes, or the lack of rigid testing measures. On the contrary, it comes from a society that refuses to view children as a social investment, that consigns 12 million children to live in poverty, replaces critical learning with massive testing programs, promotes policies that eliminate most crucial health and public services, and defines masculinity through the degrading celebration of a gun culture, extreme sports, and the spectacles of violence that permeate corporate-controlled media. Students are not at risk because of the absence of market incentives in the schools. Young people are under siege in American schools because far too many schools have become institutional breeding grounds for racism, right-wing paramilitary cultures, social intolerance, sexism, and homophobia.[59] We live in a society in which a culture of punishment, fear, and intolerance has replaced a culture of social responsibility and compassion. Within such a climate of harsh discipline and disdain, it is easier to put young people in jail than to provide the education, services, and care they need to face the problems of a complex and demanding society.[60] As intolerance replaces critical judgment, right-wing religious, corporate, and conservative advocates refuse to address what it would mean for a viable educational policy to provide reasonable support services for all students and viable alternatives for troubled ones. As the criminalization of young people finds its way into the classroom and every other aspect of social life, it becomes ever-easier for school administrators, educators, and legislators to punish students rather than listen to them, work with parents, community justice programs, religious organizations, and social service agencies. The idea that children are a crucial social resource for any healthy society, presenting important ethical and political considerations about the quality of public life, the allocation of social provisions, and the role of the state as a guardian of the public interest, appears to be lost in a society that refuses to invest in its youth as part of a broader commitment to a fully realized democracy. As the social order becomes more privatized and militarized, we are in danger of losing a generation of young people to a system of increasing intolerance, repression, and moral indifference. Bush's agenda for education embodies and exacerbates these problems, and as such it leaves a lot more kids behind than it helps.

President Bush's 2002 budget is designed to benefit the wealthy rather than the nation's children. Moreover, Bush's 2003 education budget cut and froze far more children's programs than the few it increased, allocating $2.8 billion in net increased spending while cutting $3.2 billion from the education budget. But the real scandal is not simply the government's refusal to invest in public education; it is its refusal to invest in a wide range of crucial programs that would offer children a decent life. As is well documented, 1 in 5 children is poor during the first 3 years of life, and child poverty rates for blacks and Hispanics are 30 and 28 percent, respectively. Nine million children lack health insurance; 12 million children are poor and many millions more are either at risk of hunger or homelessness; the U.S. child poverty rate of 14.8 percent is the highest among the 19 richest countries, and making matters worse is the unconscionable fact that the United States has a greater gap between the rich and the poor than in any other rich nation; infant mortality rates are only slightly better than in Cuba, and because of such high rates rank 33rd in the world; 18 percent of American women have minimal or no prenatal care, higher than in any other advanced industrial nation; and "only 60 percent of 3- and 4-year-olds go to child care, well below the European rate, and many of those go to centers that are inadequate."[61] Less we descend into cynicism, the Children's Defense Fund reminds us that:

> These facts are not acts of God. They are our moral and political choices as Americans. We can change them. We have the money. We have the power. We have the know-how. We have the experience. We have the vision. And we have the moral and social responsibility. What we lack is the civic and spiritual engagement of enough citizens, and political faith, and media leaders to pierce the profound lack of awareness about the indifference to preventable and solvable child suffering; the poisonous politics of self-interest and greed; narrow ideological agendas which reflect the belief that government should help the rich and powerful most and the poor and powerless least; and the political hypocrisy of leaders at all levels of government and in all parties who leave millions of children behind while pretending to do otherwise.[62]

CHAPTER 5

Teen Girls' Resistance and the Disappearing Social in *Ghost World*

Children are the future of any society. If you want to know the future of a society look at the eyes of the children. If you want to maim the future of any society, you simply maim the children. Thus the struggle for the survival of our children is the struggle for the survival of our future. The quantity and quality of that survival is the measurement of the development of our society.

—Ngugi Wa Thiong'O[1]

Murdering the Social

Every society creates images and visions of those forces that threaten its identity.[2] In the aftermath of September 11, 2001,the most pressing danger facing the United States appears to come from Muslims and Arab Americans, and other alleged "terrorists." But the foremost danger facing the United States predates the terrorist attacks on the Pentagon and the World Trade Center and, in fact, provides a crucial continuity bridging the past and the present. That danger is nothing less than the devaluing of the social and the growing foreclosing of a democratic future that such a devaluing implies. Underlying a refusal of the future is a notion of the social world bereft of ethics, social justice, and any viable notion of democratic public culture.[3] But our thinking about the future can harbor impulses and a horizon of expectations that challenge the narrow conceptions of a society dominated by market relations and the transformation of the citizen into a consumer, and also embody those social bonds that entail a responsibility to others, and especially to young people.

Prior to the events of September 11, democracy was defined largely through the relations and values of the market. Labor was increasingly seen as an obstacle to productivity, and citizenship was being rewritten so as to strip it of any critical substance. Emptied of any social content, the public sphere was reduced to a phantom largely dominated by the vocabulary of the private. Politics for the most part turned inward as the language of community, public action, and citizen participation were redefined as matters of private choice and individual desire. Such changes can be traced to two major events that have recast both the nature of politics and the relevance of the social.

First, power has become increasingly detached from politics. As power travels beyond national boundaries, it is largely disconnected from any moral obligations and accountability to employees, the young, the aged, the local community, and the larger social order. In the age of neoliberal globalization, as Manuel Castells and others have observed, power extends across, around, and over territorial boundaries, disrupting the neat correspondence between the sovereignty of the nation-state and the space of the political. Power is now more extraterritorial, increasingly placed beyond the reach of political institutions. As such, power moves freely, escaping the reach of the average citizen as it casts its net beyond the borders of the town, city, state, and nation.[4] As Zygmunt Bauman points out, one consequence of globalization is that politics is more place-based while at the same time power defies the traditional regulations and governance imposed by nation-states:

> Our dependencies are now truly global, our actions however are, as before, local. The powers which shape the conditions under which we confront our problems are beyond the reach of all the agencies invented by modern democracy in the two centuries of its history. . . . Real power, the extraterritorial global power, flows, but politics, con-

fined now as in the past to the framework of nation-states, stays as before attached to the ground.[5]

As power distances itself from traditional modes of politics, nation-states have lost much of their capacity to control and regulate the powerful—except to become the security service and watchdogs for major corporations and the wealthy. The state under such circumstances does not disappear as much as it gets reconstructed, largely as a repressive force for providing a modicum of safety for the rich and privileged classes while increasing its focus on disciplining those populations and groups that pose a threat to the dominant social order.[6]

Under neoliberal policies, identities based on stable work disappear as the success of new technologies and productive forces is judged by "the replacement and elimination of labor."[7] In the current neoliberal economy, labor has become a constraint on profits not only because of the emergence of new labor-saving technologies, but also because much less labor is needed to produce huge volumes of goods—and even if it is needed, corporations can simply relocate in order to capitalize on the availability of cheap labor.

Secondly, as globalization saps the power of the state and individuals to influence the modalities of power, politics, and ideology, collective action seems improbable and politics turns inward. Individuals now assume the burden of their own fate, even though the forces that shape their destiny are beyond the scope of individual behavior. Under such circumstances, all problems are defined as self-made, reduced to matters of character and individual initiative (or its lack). The result is that personal worries and private troubles are disconnected from public issues and social problems. For millions, the political economy of insecurity now becomes endemic to everyday life and is understood in relation to a depoliticized notion of citizenship, largely defined as the right to consume rather than as the ability of individuals to shape the basic economic and political structures of their society. As the vast majority of citizens becomes detached from public forums that nourish social critique, personal agency not only becomes a mockery of itself, it is replaced by market-based choices in which private satisfactions replace social responsibilities and, as Ulrich Beck suggests, biographical solutions become a substitute for systemic change.[8] In a world marked by deregulated markets, downsizing, and growing unemployment, the uncertainty and insecurity that individuals experience appears to be matched by a retreat from, if not indifference to, a politics of collective struggle and social transformation.[9]

As the state is hollowed out and public services are either cut or privatized, security is decoupled from freedom, and freedom is reduced to a matter of individual resources and choices. Moreover, as many centralized forces are ceded to the market (with the exception of those state forces that provide policing or military functions), the public treasury is emptied and nearly all of the "public infrastructure—roads, water systems, schools, powerplants, bridges, hospitals, broadcast frequencies—that provide the country with a foundation for its common enterprise" falls into disrepair.[10] Lacking a critical vocabulary as well as those non-commodified public spaces necessary for young people and adults to defend those institutions crucial to a democracy, the American public finds it more difficult to acknowledge and understand how the growth of individual freedom under consumerism coincides with the growth of collective impotence.[11] Put differently, the language of market-driven individualism is used to unleash and legitimate what Herbert Marcuse once called all those "forces of brutal self-interest which the democratic countries have tried to curb and tried to combine with the interest of freedom."[12]

The call for self-reliance in the place of collective struggles, and the prioritizing of private considerations over social needs and collective safety now assume the form of unquestionable "common sense." This hyper-individualism has done more than dissolve the bonds of sociality that underscore the very meaning of social citizenship and civic obligation; it has also proved to be a powerful ideological force in transforming the individual from a political citizen into a spectator. This development has undermined the very possibility of viable and critical forms of political agency that enable individuals to influence the conditions that shape their lives. The citizen's right to interfere in shaping the forces that govern his or her life is replaced by the individual's liberty from interference. All references to the social or public sphere and its attendant concerns with ethics and justice as a common good, especially as defined through the role of government in providing a collective safety net for those who are relatively powerless (such as the poor, disabled, young people, and the aged), are now disparaged as a form of debilitating dependency. Within this discourse of neoliberalism, big government appears wasteful and incompetent, capitalism becomes synonymous with democracy, and history allegedly reaches its apogee with the celebration of market forces, identities, and relations.[13]

As the social was depoliticized and the safety net provided by the welfare state dismantled, the poor and young people, especially during the 1980s and 1990s, were removed from the universe of moral obligation.[14] As the ideal of public commitment was undermined, issues of human suffering, the growing inequalities between the rich and the poor, persistent racism, violence against women, the collapse of social housing, the breakdown of public health, and the crisis of public education were erased from the inventory of public concerns. The connection between education and democracy was broken, and the importance of the education of young people for the future of society was downplayed. The welfare society's most vulnerable citizens—the young and the poor—were no longer a focus of social investment but a matter of social containment. Youth, indeed, became a target of disciplinary control, surveillance, and punishment, especially on the streets and in the public schools. Monitored, regulated, and disciplined, youth were increasingly viewed as depraved rather than deprived, troubling rather than troubled. In the last decade, schools passed harsh zero-tolerance policies, set up dress codes, regulated hair color, imposed drug testing, banned certain forms of music, and monitored much of the movements and behavior of students.[15] Young people were viewed as either a threat to society or too infantile to protect themselves from being corrupted. Adult society refused to view young people as responsible citizens with a sense of independence and agency—yet they were treated as adults when they committed allegedly irresponsible acts. The contradiction speaks to more than generational conflict or even hypocrisy, it points to an all-out assault on youth that has emerged since the 1980s. Cultural studies theorist, Lawrence Grossberg writes in the following terms about the chilling contradictions that mark what he calls the "war" on youth:

> In most states in the United States, at 16 today, you cannot get your ears pierced without the permission of your parents. You cannot get

a tattoo, and you cannot buy cigarettes. In fact, people under 16 cannot go to the Mall of America in Minnesota (the largest shopping mall in the country) after 6 P.M. on Friday or Saturday without a parent. But you can be tried and jailed as an adult, and more and more kids are. And in a growing number of states, you can be put to death as a penalty. Think of that—you can't get your ears pierced, but you can be put to death.[16]

Social guarantees are now provided for only the most privileged youth, and those less fortunate, such as poor inner city kids, are offered inspirational tales (if not by Hollywood then by conservative luminaries such as William Bennett) about the virtues of self-reliance, competition, picking oneself up by the bootstraps, and reaching deep down into one's character to find the virtues needed to survive in a world increasingly wedded to the ruthless tenets of social Darwinism. When self-reliance doesn't work in a world of endemic uncertainty and universal struggle, a ballooning prison industrial complex offers a different alternative to the current youth "problem." As their behavior is increasingly criminalized, youth are suspended or expelled from schools and incarcerated in record numbers, even though crimes by youth have been declining sharply in the last decade. It is not surprising that in a society that largely constructs other subordinate groups as failures, youth marginalized by class and color either vanish from the agenda of public concerns, or evoke the wrath of an increasingly repressive state that sees them as a threat to the social order.

As a symbol of our collective future, youth remind us of the presence of the social, our responsibility to others, a concern for wider public interests, and social relations that cannot be judged exclusively within the parameters of profit, consumerism, and commercialism. Grossberg rightly argues that "The war against youth is a war against youth's ability to embody the very necessity of commitment to a future and to a particular future insofar as it entails certain kinds of political and economic visions of the [democratic] American dream."[17] Young people evoke a utopian principle that challenges the privatized dreams of neoliberal capitalism, and as such symbolize one of the most important tensions in American life—the contradiction between those values that are central to a democracy and those competitive, individualistic values at the heart of market fundamentalism.[18] But, as Grossberg suggests, young people do more than evoke a tension in American life, they also symbolize one of society's greatest threats.

Resisting Youth in the Age of Cynicism

The terrible events of September 11 opened up a new possibility for engaging the relationship between the concepts of the social, the future, and youth. In many ways, the terrorist attacks pointed to the importance of the social in providing crucial public services in order to save lives, put out fires, provide funds for decimated families, and offer some modicum of protection against further terrorist actions. But this reliance upon and celebration of public services and public life itself seemed short-lived, as the Bush administration seized upon the insecurities and fears of the populace in order to expand the policing and military powers of the state through a series of anti-terrorist acts that compromised some of the basic freedoms provided by the Bill of Rights. At the same time, as I have mentioned previously, Bush and his supporters pushed through legislation that once again drained projected public surpluses by offering tax breaks—approximately 1.6 trillion dollars—for the wealthy and major corporations. Tax cuts that mostly benefit the top 1 percent of the population at a time when "the financial wealth of the top one percent of households now exceeds the combined wealth of the bottom 95 percent"[19] do more than undermine any pretense to democratic values. Such welfare schemes for the rich also blatantly exhibit the ruthlessness of a society that, on the one hand, allows one American, Bill Gates, to amass "more wealth than the combined net worth of the poorest 45 percent of American households"[20] and, on the other hand, refuses to provide adequate health care to 14 million children. It is difficult to understand how democratic values are deepened and expanded in a society in which, according to the Bureau of Labor statistics, the typical American now works 350 hours more per year than a typical European—almost 9 full weeks. Under such conditions, parents are not only working longer, they are also spending 40 percent less time with their children than they did 40 years ago.[21] While it is too early to see how this tension between democratic values and market interests will be played out in society, it is crucial to recognize that young people more than any other group will bear the burden and the consequences of this struggle in their everyday lives. Clearly, these are poor conditions under which to learn to assume the mantle of leadership necessary to shape the future that they will inherit.

The continuity that bridges a pre– and post–September 11 social reality resides in the relationship between a depoliticized public sphere and the current attack on youth. These related crises are best exemplified in various representations of youth that shape the contemporary political landscape of American culture. How a society understands its youth is partly determined by how it represents them. Popular representations, in particular, constitute a cultural politics that shapes, mediates, and legitimates how adult society views youth and what it expects from them. Such representations, produced and distributed through the mass media in television, video, music, film, publishing, and theater, function as a form of public pedagogy actively attempting to define youth through the ideological filters of a society that is increasingly hostile to young people. All of these sites make competing claims on youth and their relation to the social order. At worst, they construct youth in terms that largely serve to demonize, sexualize, or commodify them, to reduce their sense of agency to the consumerist requirements of supply and demand. Such images not only resonate with larger public discourses that contribute to a panic about youth, they also help to legitimize policies aimed at both containing and punishing young people, especially those who are marginalized by virtue of class, gender, race, and sexual orientation. At best, such representations define youth in complex ways that not only capture the problems, issues, and values that bear down on them, but also illustrate how varied youth in diverse circumstances attempt to negotiate the contradictions of a larger social order.

In what follows, I examine an exemplary independent film, *Ghost World*, as part of a broader attempt to address how popular representations of youth signal a particular crisis—but do so through a discourse of privatization that fails to locate youth and the problems they face within the related geographies of the social and political. *Ghost World* is a particularly interesting film because it is sympathetic to the plight of alienated, downwardly mobile teenage girls and goes to great lengths to let the principal characters speak in a way that gives meaning and affect to their sense of despair, their ennui, and their resistance to the adult world. This attempt at "authenticity" has won praise from critics and viewers alike, and makes the film all the more important to analyze as a form of public pedagogy that provides a unique opportunity to take up the troubled dynamic between teenage resistance and the privatization of the social.

Loosely adapted from an underground comic book by Daniel Clowes and directed by Terry Zwigoff, who also directed the 1995 documentary *Crumb*, *Ghost World* presents a portrait of two teenage malcontents, Enid (Thora Birch) and Rebecca (Scarlett Johansson), whose adolescent angst and resentment inform both their resistance to a phony middle-class world and their attempts to adjust to it without losing their self-ascribed marginal status. Best friends since elementary school, the lonely, sardonic Enid and Rebecca, her slightly more conventional companion, negotiate the complex territory between high school graduation and the plunge into adulthood. *Ghost World* also chronicles the story of their increasingly strained friendship.

In the opening scene of the film, which takes place during the high school graduation ceremony, Enid and Rebecca are clearly out of sync with the boorish world of dominant school culture and the deadness of American suburbia—a world embodied by testosterone-driven surfer-like athletic drones, obsequious academic climbers, and pompom-waving cheerleaders just waiting to become soccer moms. They snarl through a graduation speech by a classmate in a head brace and wheelchair that begins with the cliche: "High School is like the training wheels for the bicycle that is life." While listening to the speech, Enid whispers, "I liked her so much better when she was an alcoholic and drug addict. She gets in one stupid car crash and suddenly she's Little Miss Perfect." When their classmates throw their caps in the air and cheer, Enid and Rebecca respond accordingly by giving their fellow students a middle finger, and to bring the point home, Enid throws her cap on the ground, stomps on it, and shouts, "What a bunch of retards." Rebecca nods in approval, making clear their shared and active refusal to buy into a world filled with what Enid calls "creeps, losers, and weirdos."

When we meet the adults who touch Enid's life, they seem to give legitimacy to her presumption that most adults are either phonies or losers. Her timid dad (Bob Balaban) fits into the latter category. Living with him in a small but comfortable apartment in Los Angeles, Enid seems to be in pain every time he approaches. Not only does he call her "pumpkin" and mutter imperceptibly practically every time he opens his mouth, he is also about to ask his corny girlfriend, Maxine (Teri Garr), who tries to befriend Enid by involving her in the exciting world of computer retailing, to move in with them. Needless to say, Enid despises her.

The other adult Enid has to put up with is a gushy, purple-clad performance artist–teacher named Roberta (Illeana Douglas), who is a comically drawn mix between a hippie leftover from the sixties and a recruit from the take-no-prisoners and I-am-always-right-and-righteous strand of feminism. Enid is forced to take Roberta's lame art class during the summer in order to graduate officially, and she sits in class rolling her eyes every time Roberta speaks. Roberta operates on the pedagogical assumption that the only way to reach her students is to relate to their lives, speak in terms they understand, and help them to "find themselves." The problem is Roberta confuses her own ideological interests with her students', and rather than listen to them, she simply rewards those students who feed back to her what she wants to hear. From day one, this art teacher rubs Enid the wrong way, so she passes time by adding to her repertoire of violent comic book drawings, which she eventually shows Roberta. Roberta soon displays some interest in Enid and even helps her to get a scholarship to an art school. But her convictions go out the window when she receives a lot of flack from the school and community for showing a piece of Enid's work—one of her friend Seymour's racist ads called "Coon Chicken"—at an art exhibition ironically titled, "Neighborhood and Community: Art and Dialogue." As a result of school and community indignation over Enid's artwork, which was, after all, an attempt to foster real dialogue about the community's racist history, Roberta withdraws the art school scholarship and joins the rest of the adult creeps and hypocrites who seem to inhabit Enid's life.

These adults seem to fuel Enid's desire to inflict ridicule and pain on every adult she and Rebecca come across. With high school behind them, Enid and Rebecca hang out in retro 1950s diners and record stores. At first, their friendship is fueled by their mutual disdain for everyone around them. "Like totally losers," Enid scoffs, and Rebecca fully agrees. Biting sarcasm is interlaced with Enid's comic-like portraits of the various adults they encounter along the way. Nobody appears to escape their sardonic looks, commentaries, and visual escapades. When not ridiculing people and indulging their unlimited capacity for scorn, Enid and Rebecca embark on their shared dream of renting an apartment together and putting their lives in order. Somewhat bored, they set up a meeting with a hapless schmuck—Seymour (Steve Buscemi)—who they discovered in the personal ad section of the local newspaper. Seymour used the ad to solicit a woman he briefly met and became entranced with while in an airport. Enid and Rebecca respond to the ad and set up a meeting in a diner, wait for him to show up, then watch him drink milkshakes as he waits for a woman who they know will never appear.

As the summer unfolds, a strain develops between the two girls as Rebecca moves into high gear by getting a job working in a local Starbucks-like emporium, earnestly starts looking for an apartment, and uses her free time to spend money in typical consumer fashion on cheap wares for her new place. Nonetheless, Enid resists what appears to be her only option, disinclined to adapt to an adult world she loathes. She is put off by the colorless neighborhood in which Rebecca tries to find an apartment, has no interest in shopping for mall goods to clutter the apartment, and just can't seem to bring herself to look for a job in the corporate world that sickens her. The one job she does get is a short-lived stint at a local multiplex theater. But she is soon fired because she cannot bring herself to prod customers into buying oversized drinks or to suggest that the movies they are watching are worth the effort. Rebecca disapproves of Enid's inability to move forward, and Enid is confused by Rebecca's easy adaptation to a world they both despised while in high school.

The relationship is further strained as Enid's life takes an unexpected turn when she meets Seymour, the victim of her personal ad prank. While hunting for an apartment together, Enid and Rebecca come across him at a garage sale, where he is selling some of his vintage 78 rpm collection of blues records out of milk crates. Rebecca finds the 40-something Seymour gross, and admits to Enid that she has "a total boner" for some wholesome-looking young blond guy who likes to listen to reggae. But Enid is intrigued by Seymour's sad-sack looks, his commitment to old blues music and various collections of Americana, his intelligence, and his utterly alienated life. Before long, Enid begins to see him less as a pathetic, middle-aged geek than as a poster boy for permanent rebellion. Things soon begin to click between them, especially after Seymour gives Enid a copy of his 1931 recording of Skip James's "Devil Got My Woman." Enid decides she is going to be a matchmaker for Seymour, with each attempt instituting a series of inevitable disasters. Seymour sees himself as a bad candidate for a relationship with a woman, telling Enid "I don't want someone who shares my interests. I hate my interests." This makes Seymour all the more odd—a mixture of unapologetic loneliness and refreshing honesty, and hence all the more attractive to Enid, who tells Rebecca, "He's the exact opposite of all the things I hate." Each "date" disaster seems to feed their own relationship as they end up spending more time with each other. Enid tells Seymour, "Only stupid people have healthy relationships." And Seymour, sharing her own sense of alienation and cynicism counters, "That's the spirit." Unfortunately for Enid, Seymour does meet up with the personal ad girl, Dana (Stacy Travis), and the relationship between Seymour and Enid begins to sour. Seymour's new girlfriend represents everything Enid despises. Dana and Seymour go shopping together and she buys him stone-washed jeans in an attempt to transform him into a prototype for an Eddie Bauer ad. She works as a real estate agent, and seems utterly attached to a world that is far too normal and far too removed from the self-deprecation, misery, and disdain that keeps Enid alert to everything that is phony and empty in middle-class suburban life. Moreover, Seymour seems attracted to his new girlfriend's utterly bourgeois lifestyle, though she sees his music and art collection as so much junk—compromising Enid's view of him as an oddball resister. Enid wages a desperate campaign to win Seymour back and rekindle her friendship with Rebecca, but to no avail. In the end she boards a bus during the middle of the night and leaves both Los Angeles and her adolescence behind her.

Ghost World is an important film about youth, friendship, alienation, and survival. Many commentators have named it as one of the top ten films of 2001, if not the best film yet produced about youth. And one critic for *USA Today* actually named it as the best film of the year.[22] Some critics labeled it the film equivalent of *Catcher in the Rye*. Most have celebrated the film for its dead-end irony, its hilarious dialogue, and its honest portrayal of the posturing and superiority befitting youth who drape themselves in the cloak of rebellion. Unlike many other youth films of the past decade—for example, *kids* (1995), *American Beauty* (1999), *American Pie* (1999), or *Murder by Numbers* (2002)—*Ghost World* refuses to trade in either caricatures, stereotypes, or degrading representations of youth. Moreover, *Ghost World* rejects the traditional Hollywood narrative that chronicles teenage rebellion as part of a rite of passage towards a deeper understanding of what it means to join adult society. Instead, the film focuses on the dark side of teenage alienation, exploring the fractures, cracks, and chasms that locate teenagers in a space that is fraught with resentment, scorn, and critical insight. *Ghost World* gently and movingly attempts to explore in uncondescending terms the pain of broken relationships, the justifiable teenage fear of being trapped in an adult world that offers little rewards and even less fulfillment, and the difficulty of choosing an identity that is critical of such a world yet not so removed as to become marginalized or irrelevant. Moreover, this film rightly appealed to critics who celebrated its refusal to offer a predictable Disney-like solution to the problems teenagers face and its ability to capture, with depth and empathy, the tensions and ambiguities that shape the lives of many teenagers on the margins of a throwaway culture. Underlying almost all of the reviews I have read of this film is an affirmation, if not a romanticizing, of an alleged kind of "authenticity" as the ultimate arbiter of the film's worth.

Ghost World arguably may be, as many critics suggest, one of the most important youth films of the decade—its importance stemming, in part, from its attempt to address how marginalized youth attempt to negotiate, if not resist, a political and social system that offers them few hopes and even fewer opportunities to see beyond its ideological boundaries. At the same time, *Ghost World* is notable for its complicity with a dominant discourse that, in spite of its emphasis on youth resistance among teenage girls, too easily depoliticizes rebellion by displacing the social as a crucial political concept that could provide a sense of what it might mean to struggle individually and collectively for a more just and democratic future. The most important pedagogical issues that hold this film together appear to resonate with a much broader set of discourses and values that increasingly celebrate and romanticize individual youth rebellion while denying young people "any significant place within the collective geography of life in the United States."[23] Irony, pathos, rebellion, and gritty dialogue may help to capture the spirit of teenage girls who "talk back," but depictions in terms of these elements remain utterly privatized and ineffectual unless they are situated in relation to broader social, economic, and political forces—the crisis of labor, political agency, democracy, and the meaning of the future itself.

While *Ghost World* is certainly not a comforting depiction of youth for the middle class, it also does nothing to link the current war being waged against youth with any of the political, economic, and cultural realities that for the last 20 years fueled yuppie greed and spectacle. Nor does it address the poverty of public discourse about youth and the breakdown of civic culture in American life during the same period. Unwilling to do justice to the urgency of the crisis that youth face in the United States, or to the complexity of violence, meanings, and practices that shape children's lives, *Ghost World* ignores the possibility of a pedagogy of resistance that disrupts and challenges conventional narratives of marginalized youth. Enid may live in a world of existential angst, but her anger seems to be so diffuse as to be meaningless. Why is it she displays so little understanding of an economic order in which the future for young people like herself seems to offer up nothing more than the promise of fast food jobs and low-skilled labor? Why is it that few commentators on the film in the national media point out that both Enid and Rebecca seem to define their sense of agency exclusively around consuming, whether it be housewares or bohemian artifacts? Cynthia Peters begins to answer this question with her comment:

> Somehow, when young adulthood should be an ample universe of growth and discovery—one that gives kids the chance to learn, contribute, experiment, envision, and carve out a meaningful role in the world—it is instead shrunk into the pinpoint activity of buying and selling. We treat kids contemptuously by herding them into deskilled, meaningless, low-wage jobs and by taking them seriously only insofar as they might divulge to marketers how they plan on spending their on-average $84 per week.[24]

Why is it that audiences watching this film are never given a clue that Enid and Rebecca live in a society that bears down particularly hard on the lives of young people? Why do so few critics note that Enid and

Rebecca's society is the wealthiest nation on earth, but allows one third of its children to live in poverty, and invests more in building prisons for young people than in institutions of higher learning? Consider the statistics: 1 in 6 children in the United States—12.1 million—still live in poverty. Nearly 9 million children are without health insurance, 90 percent of whom have working parents. One in 8 children never graduate from high school and "children under 18 are the fastest growing and largest portion of the population of homeless in America, with an average age of 9 years."[25] By contrast, the "crisis" experienced by Enid and Rebecca is shown over and over as a personal, individualized affair.

Ghost World hammers home the lesson that in a world of high youth unemployment, poverty, incarceration rates, and a disintegrating urban education system, youth have only themselves to rely on and only themselves to blame if they fail. Against the constant reminders of a society that tells youth it neither particularly needs them nor wants them, youth in the film are offered only right-wing homilies about relying on their own resources and cunning. In the context of this rhetoric of nomadic subjectivity and privatized resistance, the pessimistic notion that there are no alternatives to the present order reinforces the message that young people should avoid at all costs the prospect of organizing collectively in order to address the social, political, and economic basis of individually suffered problems. Resistance in this film rarely touches upon the possibility for recovering the ideals of a democratic social order or a robust form of collective intervention. So *Ghost World* is defined less by what it says than by what it leaves out. This absence is precisely what is necessary for engaging *Ghost World* within a broader set of historical and political contexts. And though *Ghost World* lampoons the middle-class mores of a market-driven society, it ends up replicating rather than challenging the privatized utopias and excessively individualistic values it sets out to critique—a position that both undercuts its progressive implications and begs for more analysis. Resistance as presented in *Ghost World* points approvingly to how insightful and nuanced young people can be about the phoniness and emptiness of adult society, but the film refuses to expand and deepen this notion of resistance in order to see it in terms of the obligations of critical citizenship, the power of collective struggle, or the necessary translation of private troubles into larger public considerations. There is a historical, political, and social void in this film that not only isolates and privatizes teenage resistance within the narrow confines of an art-film sensibility, but also fails to address the role that adults play in creating many of the problems that young girls like Enid and Rebecca face on a daily basis. Adults are not simply boors or phonies, for example; they also pass legislation that deny children the most fundamental and basic services. Adults commit 75 percent of the murders of youth in America; they also sexually abuse somewhere between 400,000 and 500,000 young people every year. Talking back to adults through clever irony and sarcasm points to neither an understanding nor a way of challenging the attacks often waged on young people by adult society.

Enid may strike a blow for a hip teenage aesthetic with her black fingernail polish, excessive makeup, and *de rigeur* combat boots, but these are only the trappings of resistance without any political substance and can be easily bought at any Hot Topic store along with a $20.00 Che Guevara shirt. Enid and her companion display few if any insights into a society marked by massive youth unemployment, the commercialization and sexualization of kids, the increasing incarceration of young people—especially those marginalized by virtue of their class and color—and the collapse of health care, decent public education, drug programs, and job training for teenagers. These are the problems that real youth face, and it is hard to believe that Enid and Rebecca can be oblivious to them as they get caught in the very dynamics such issues produce. But when it comes to regarding the relevance of the future for Enid, and by implication for marginalized youth in general, the film and many of its critics seem to waver badly. At various points throughout the story, Enid comes across an older man, sitting on a bench at a bus stop that has been closed down for quite some time. He seems to be there at all hours of the day. One day Enid tells him the bus route has been cancelled and that he is wasting his time, but he simply snarls at her and tells her to leave him alone. But near the end of the film, while Enid is approaching the bus stop, a bus mysteriously arrives and the man boards it and is never seen again. In part, this symbolizes in rather dramatic form the idea that there is a possibility within the realm of the impossible; that as bleak as the future might seem, there is hope. This scene is all the more poignant since in the last scene in the film, Enid is seen boarding that same mysterious, cancelled bus, uncertain of where she is going or what she is going to face in the future. Making the possible out of the impossible surely opens up the issue of how the future is being shaped for children as we enter the twenty-first century. But with no analysis grounded in the brutal social realities she must live with, *Ghost World* romanticizes Enid's contempt for the world yet offers no sense of how she might find her way without being subject to oppression. By privatizing and romanticizing Enid's resistance, *Ghost World* ignores the more serious reality of a society that wages a war against children precisely because they embody a notion of the future that calls into question the nature of adult obligations and responsibilities.

It is hard to imagine that Enid will hold on to her critical intelligence and biting wit without eventually succumbing to cynicism, and this is where the film reveals its most egregious shortcoming. It resonates too intimately with a major aim of neoliberalism, which is to "make politics disappear by, in part, producing cynicism in the population."[26] Cynicism does more than confirm irony as the last resort of the defeated; it also substitutes resignation and angst for any viable notion of resistance, politics, and social transformation. It is precisely on these terms that *Ghost World* both indicts and reflects the very society it attempts to portray through the eyes of alienated teenage girls.

A society that views children as a threat has no way of talking about the social or the future as central to a vibrant democracy. Moreover, such a society often finds it increasingly difficult to address the importance of those non-commodified values and public spaces that keep alive issues of justice, ethics, public opportunities, civic courage, and critical citizenship. Youth make visible the ethical consequences and social costs of losing a language of political and social responsibility, not to mention real spaces informed by the discourse and practices of civic engagement, critical dialogue, and social activism. Youth is troubling because as a social category it demands a politics of responsibility that rejects the notion of market freedoms that absorb every other freedom and accentuate, as Lani Guinier observes, the collective gaze of "atomized individuals operating in their own spheres" with "no sense of citizenry, no sense of community that is committed to a set of common values that they have to hold each other accountable to."[27] As I mentioned in the beginning of this chapter, if youth in the past were "the privileged sign and embodiment of the future,"[28] that has all changed under the regime of neoliberalism. Youth now symbolize a threat to the social order, a population under siege by a dominant class eager to erase its responsibility to a democratic future.

As a symbol of contemporary culture, *Ghost World* points to crucial problems without fully engaging them, and by never adequately attending to "questions of politics, power, and public consciousness"[29] it displaces political issues to the realm of aesthetics and depoliticized forms of transgression. This is not to suggest that the film does not offer any real pleasures in its depiction of teenage rebellion. On the contrary, its richly textured script of sensory experience and comic pleasure is woven into the girls' speech, punkish style, and offhand body language. If pleasure and knowledge intersect in this film in a way that allows students to make a real affective investment in Enid and Rebecca's lives, all the more reason to connect the pleasures of entertainment that the film provides with the "learned pleasure of [critical] analysis."[30] *Ghost World* both shapes and bears witness to the ethical and political dilemmas that structure teenage life. If youth are viewed as a threat to the larger social order, it becomes necessary to raise pedagogical questions about how *Ghost World* works in diverse ways to challenge, but also reinforce, this perception. Making the pedagogical more political in this instance serves not only to locate *Ghost World* within a representational politics that bridges the gap between private and public discourses, but also to offer students the space "to break the continuity and consensus of common sense"[31] and to resist forms of authority that deny the value of political agency, the importance of the social, and the possibility of social change. By examining *Ghost World* in conjunction with a broader assemblage of dominant texts, discourses, and institutional forces, it becomes less difficult to recognize that the struggle over meaning is, in part, defined as the struggle over identity, agency, power relations, and the future. Maybe the value of this film resides not only in what it says, but also in the discussions it might provoke about what it ignores. When read against itself, *Ghost World* offers a rich pedagogical terrain for critically engaging the limits of an utterly privatized notion of resistance and for reclaiming utopian possibilities by reasserting the inseparable connection between private troubles and public discontents, between social transformation and democratic struggles, between political agency and public life.

CHAPTER 6

From "Manchild" to *Baby Boy*

Race and the Politics of Self-Help

If Reno was in a bad mood—if he didn't have any money and he wasn't high—he'd say, "Man, Sonny, they ain't got no kids in Harlem. I ain't never seen any. I've seen some real small people actin' like kids, but they don't have any kids in Harlem, because nobody has time for a childhood. Man, do you ever remember bein' a kid? Not me. Shit, kids are happy, kids laugh, kids are secure. They ain't scared-a nothin'. You ever been a kid, Sonny? Damn, you lucky. I ain't never been a kid, man. I don't ever remember bein' happy and not scared. I don't know what happened, man, but I think I missed out on that childhood thing, because I don't ever recall bein' a kid."

—Claude Brown[1]

When Claude Brown published *Manchild in the Promised Land* in 1965, he wrote about the doomed lives of his friends, families, and neighborhood acquaintances. The book is mostly remembered as a brilliantly devastating portrait of Harlem under siege, ravaged and broken from drugs, poverty, unemployment, crime, and police brutality. But what Brown really made visible was the raw violence and dead-end existence that plagued so many young people in Harlem, stealing not only their future but their childhood as well. In the midst of the social collapse and psychological violence wrought by the systemic marriage of racism and class exploitation, children in Harlem were held hostage to forces that robbed them of the innocence that comes with childhood, forcing them to take on the burdens of daily survival that an older generation seemed unable to protect them from in the face of a hostile environment and social system. At the heart of Brown's narrative, written in the midst of the civil rights struggle in the 1960s, is a "manchild," a metaphor that indicts a society that is waging war on those children who are black and poor and have been forced to grow up too quickly. The hybridized concept of manchild marked a space in which innocence was lost and childhood stolen. Harlem was a colony and its street life provided the condition and the very necessity for insurrection. But rebellion for young people came with a price, which Brown reveals near the end of the book: "It seemed as though most of the cats that we'd come up with just hadn't made it. Almost everybody was dead or in jail."[2]

Childhood stolen became less a plea for self-help than a clarion call for condemning a social order that denied children a future. While Brown approached everyday life in Harlem more as a poet than as a political revolutionary, politics was embedded in every sentence in the book—not a politics marked by demagoguery, hatred, and orthodoxy, but one that made visible the damage done by a social system characterized by massive inequalities and a rigid racial divide. *Manchild* created the image of a society without children in order to raise questions about the future of a country that turned its back on its most vulnerable population. Claude Brown's lasting contribution was to reconfigure the boundaries between public issues and private sufferings. For Brown, racism was about power and oppression and could not be separated from broader social, economic, and political considerations. Rather than erasing the social within a discourse of individual pathology or self-help, Brown insisted that social forces had to be factored into any understanding of group suffering and individual despair. Brown explored the suffering of the young in Harlem, but he did so by refusing utterly to privatize it, to elevate the private over the public, or to separate individual hopes, desires, and agency from the realm of politics and public life.

Since the 1980s, various conservatives and liberals have attempted to rework the language of racism and social responsibility in ways that eliminate those larger systemic and structural inequalities that give racism such persistence and provide only moderate change. Theorists such as Shelby Steele, Thomas Sowell, Ward Connerly, Richard J. Herrnstein, Charles Murray, and Dinesh D'Souza, among others, have become prominent in spearheading a counter-movement in which problems of race have been psychologized either as issues of character, individual pathology, or genetic inferiority. In these perspectives, the language of social analysis has given way to the discourse of self-help; the call for social provisions has been transformed into punitive assaults on the character of the poor; and the struggle for enlarging social entitlements for those suffering under the weight of unemployment, hunger, homelessness, and inadequate health care has given way to policies of containment, control, and criminalization. Racism and poverty in the new millennium are now defined largely through the language of privatization and punishment, and can be seen in two interrelated discourses. First, there is the discourse of self-help, which displaces responsibility for social welfare from government to individuals. Self-help is reinforced by representations that portray black men as utterly infantile, lacking moral values, and in need of character development so that they can pick themselves up and allegedly take responsibility for their lives. The doctrine of self-help is invariably bolstered by allusions to a few African Americans—Tiger Woods and Michael Jordan, for example—and is aimed at youth who supposedly can achieve the American dream if they quit whining and "just do it." This highly individualized and privatized discourse has been very important as a rationale for dismantling the welfare state while simultaneously ignoring corporate policies that create downsizing, unemployment, toxic waste dumps in poor neighborhoods, and a lowering of urban tax revenues. The ideology of privatized agency has been promoted by prominent white conservatives and black public intellectuals from various conservative think-tanks, neoliberals, and the Christian right. Historically, the rhetoric of self-help has been intertwined with racist representations of colonized subjects as children. Frantz Fanon, among others, makes this clear in his claim that for many white Europeans "The Negro is just a child."[3] Second, and closely related to the discourse of self-help, is a much more entrenched politics of demonization, which portrays black men as dangerous—"the prototype of violent hyper-masculinity."[4] In their depiction of gangsta rap artists such as Tupac Shakur and Snoop Doggy Dog, as well as sports figures such as Mike Tyson, the popular media has seized upon this representation of black men as dangerous, misogynist, and threatening. Such representations are also pervasive in the culture industry and can be seen in numerous Hollywood films about African American youth, such as *187*, *Belly*, and *Black and White*, as well as in an endless array of reality-based television shows such as *Cops* and *Wildest Police Videos*. This discourse plays a crucial role in criminalizing social policy and justifying repressive measures, especially those aimed at African American youth. Like the language of self-help, the representational politics of pathology is purely psychological—devoid of any social context within which to situate behavior—and further mobilizes mainstream contempt for victims while securing the indifference of government.

The discourses of self-help and demonization, while appearing to serve different purposes, end up complimenting each other. The discourse of self-help ignores those larger structural determinants that promote racism and poverty while simultaneously blaming African American youth for their plight. With the global proliferation of singular American black male "success" stories; the absence of any viable form of social analysis; and the dismantling of state provisions to eliminate racism and poverty, the problem of racism is presented as solved, while its ongoing effects are addressed as a matter of criminal policy. The language of self-help makes it possible to ignore the deeper causes of racial inequality while both justifying and expanding the prison-industrial complex. If the discourse of demonization inspires moral panics among whites and blacks alike, the punitive policies of social containment ameliorate that fear. The consequences are as undemocratic as they are appalling, and have resulted in the incarceration of over a million African American males, as well as rising crime rates in poor areas. These policies have also left thousands of children without fathers and a significant proportion of the African American community without jobs, voting rights, and decent health care. In addition, the connection of black masculinity and criminality, on the one hand, and reform policies that rely exclusively upon the ethos of self-help, on the other, does more than mobilize racist contempt and fear in whites; it also "has resulted in the deaths of many innocent boys and men of darker hue."[5]

Although there can be little doubt that racial progress has been achieved in many areas in the last 50 years,[6] it is also true that such progress has not been sustained. This is particularly evident in the dramatic increase in black prisoners and the growth of the prison-industrial complex, spiraling health crises such as AIDS, crumbling city infrastructures, segregated housing, soaring unemployment among youth of color, exorbitant school drop-out rates among black and Latino youth (coupled with the realities of failing schools more generally), and deepening inequalities of incomes and wealth between blacks and whites.[7] The legacy of racism and its persistence in everyday life, especially for poor youth of color, is still, as Supreme Court Justice Ruth Bader Ginsburg observes, "evident in our workplaces, markets and neighborhoods."[8] It is also evident in child poverty rates for "blacks and Hispanics, which is an unconscionable 30 percent and 28 percent, respectively."[9]

David Shipler argues powerfully that race and class are the two most powerful determinants shaping American society. After interviewing hundreds of people over a five-year period, Shipler wrote in *A Country of Strangers* that he bore witness to a racism that "is a bit subtler in expression, more cleverly coded in public, but essentially unchanged as one of the 'deep abiding currents' in everyday life, in both the simplest and the most complex interactions of whites and blacks."[10] Pushing against the grain of civil rights reform and racial justice are reactionary and moderate positions, ranging from the extremism of right-wing skinheads and Jesse Helms–like conservatism, to the moderate "color-blind" positions of liberals such as Randall Kennedy, to tepid forms of multiculturalism that vacuously celebrate diversity while undermining any critical discourse of difference.[11] But beneath its changing veneers and expressions, racism, however ignored, embodies the relationship between politics and power—a historical past and a living present where racist exclusions appear "calculated, brutally rational, and profitable."[12]

Crucial to the re-emergence of this "new" racism is a cultural politics that plays a determining role in how race shapes the popular unconscious. This is evident in the widespread articles, reviews, and commentaries in the dominant media that give inordinate amounts of time and space to mainstream conservative authors, filmmakers, and critics who rail against affirmative action, black welfare mothers, and the alleged threats black youth and rap artists pose to middle-class existence. Rather than dismiss such rampant conservatism as either indifferent to the realities of racism or deconstruct its racialized codes, concerned citizens, educators, and others can engage these commentaries more constructively by analyzing how they function as public discourses, how their privileged meanings resonate with ideologies produced in other contexts, and how they serve to construct and legitimate racially exclusive practices, policies, and social relations. Central to such a project is the need to produce a representational politics of popular culture that offers educators and the wider public opportunities to critically engage how certain racialized meanings expressed in culture are construed as common sense in light of how racialized discourses and images are articulated in other public spheres and institutionalized sites.

In order to deepen the cultural politics of democratic transformation, educators and others can address questions of culture, power, identity, and representation as part of a broader discourse about public pedagogy and social policy. Power thereby becomes central to the study of cultural texts and practices, and socially relevant problems can be explored through theoretical engagements with wider institutional contexts and public spaces in which racialized discourses gain their political and economic force. If interrogating, challenging, and transforming those cultural practices that sustain racism is a central objective of any critical politics and pedagogy, such a task must be addressed in ways that link cultural texts to broader social problems. Texts in this instance would be analyzed as part of a "social vocabulary of culture" that points to how power names, shapes, defines, and constrains relationships between individuals and their society, constructs and disseminates what counts as knowledge, and produces representations that provide the context for identity formation.[13] Educators and other public intellectuals must find ways to acknowledge the political character of culture through strategies of understanding and engagement that link an antiracist and radically democratic rhetoric with strategies to transform racist institutions within and beyond the university.

At its best, a democratic cultural politics and public pedagogy should forge a connection between reading texts and reading public discourses in order to link the struggle for equality and social justice with relations of power in the broader society. It is precisely within cultural politics that educators and engaged citizens can develop pedagogical practices that close the gap between intellectual debate and public life not simply as a matter of academic relevance, but as a process through which students can acquire the skills and knowledge to develop informed opinions, make critical choices, and function as citizen activists. Historian Robin D. G. Kelley indicates one direction such a project might take. He insightfully argues:

> [A democratic cultural politics cannot ignore] how segregation strips communities of resources and reproduces inequality. The decline of decent-paying jobs and city services, erosion of public space, deterioration of housing stock and property values, and stark inequalities in education and health care are manifestations of investment strategies under de facto segregation. . . . [Educators must address] dismantling racism, bringing oppressed populations into power and moving beyond a black/white binary that renders invisible the struggles of Latinos, Asian-Americans, Native Americans and other survivors of racist exclusion and exploitation.[14]

Implicit in Kelley's call for action is the recognition that any viable pedagogy and politics of representation needs to address the realities of historical processes, the actuality of economic power, and the range of public spaces and institutions that constitute the embattled terrain of racial difference and struggle. This suggests developing a critical vocabulary for viewing diverse cultural texts not only in relation to other modes of discourse "but also in relationship to contemporaneous social institutions and non-discursive practices."[15] Within this approach, cultural texts cannot be isolated from the social and political conditions of their production, nor can the final explanation of such texts be found within the texts themselves. On the contrary, such texts become meaningful when viewed both in relation to other discursive practices and in terms of "the objective social field from which [they] derive."[16] Pedagogically, this demands addressing how cultural texts in the classroom and other spheres are constructed in response to institutions, power, and the social relations that they both legitimate and help to sustain. Needless to say, while I will focus on how such texts can be taken up in the classroom, such analyses can go on in a variety of public spheres outside of public and higher education and can include influences as diverse as media and popular culture, peer groups, and parents.

In what follows, I demonstrate the theoretical relevance for developing critical pedagogical practices in which issues of representation and democratic social transformation mutually inform each other. In doing so, I want to focus on that regime of representation that seeks to both individualize and privatize the experiences of African Americans as it places them in a state of arrested development and renders them criminally pathological. I will use a popular Hollywood film, *Baby Boy* (2001), to demonstrate how such texts can be used as both a social transcript and a form of public pedagogy that produces images, ideas, and ideologies that powerfully shape both individual and collective identities. The growing popularity of film as a compelling mode of communication and form of public pedagogy suggests how important it has become as a site of cultural politics, particularly as it contributes to a public discourse and policy about racial injustice. While films play an important role in promoting particular ideologies and values, they also provide an educational space that opens up the "possibility of interpretation as intervention."[17] As public pedagogies, they make clear the need for new vocabularies and modes of analysis that address the profoundly political and pedagogical ways in which knowledge is constructed and enters our lives, in what Susan Bordo calls "an image saturated culture."[18] For educators and others, this suggests critically analyzing how films function as social practices that influence everyday life and positioning them within existing social, cultural, and institutional machineries of power, as well as examining how the historical and contemporary meanings that film's produce align, reproduce, and interrupt broader ideas, discourses, and social configurations at work in society.[19] Films both shape and bear witness to the ethical and political dilemmas that animate the broader social landscape, and they often raise fundamental questions about how we can think about politics and political agency. I want to explore how *Baby Boy* embodies a particular view of racial politics in American society; how it connects the discourses of infantilization and black pathology with broader considerations about public life; and how it simultaneously offers opportunities to read against its ideology of self-help in order to fight anti-black racism in contemporary American society.

Racial Coding in the Hollywood Text

During the last ten years, Hollywood has cashed in on a number of young, talented black directors such as Spike Lee, Allen and Albert Hughes, Ernest Dickerson, and John Singleton. Films such as *New Jack City* (1991), *Boyz 'N the Hood* (1992), *New Jersey Drive* (1995), *Clockers* (1995), *Belly* (1999), and *Baby Boy* (2001) have not only appealed to a lucrative black audience but have crossed over and become successful with white audiences as well. Many of these films in varying degrees have offered up homogeneous images of the inner-city ghetto as largely inhabited by illiterate, unmotivated, and violent urban youth who are economically and racially marginalized. The increasingly familiar script suggests a correlation between urban public space and rampant drug use, daily assaults, welfare fraud, teenage mothers, and young black men caught in the ritual behavior of thug life, prison, and moral irresponsibility. Missing from these highly sensationalized and exoticized celluloid ghetto neighborhoods is any sense of the complexity of life there. As Robin D. G. Kelley says in another context, what a film like *Baby Boy* avoids are representations of:

> men and women who [go] to work every day in foundries, hospitals, nursing homes, private homes, police stations, sanitation departments, banks, garment factories, assembly plants, pawn shops, construction sites, loading docks, storefront churches, telephone companies, grocery and department stores, public transit, restaurants, welfare offices, recreation centers; or the street venders, the cab drivers, the bus drivers, the ice cream truck drivers, the seamstresses, the numerologists and fortune tellers, the folks who protect . . . or clean . . . downtown buildings all night long.[20]

Baby Boy is yet another controversial addition to this genre, because it makes an attempt both to represent and critically engage the arrested development of black male youth in the South-Central section of Los Angeles. Rather than address the economic, political, and social forces at work in the dehumanization, exploitation, and pathologizing of poor urban youth of color, *Baby Boy* focuses on the refusal of such youth to grow up and assume the responsibility of getting jobs, taking care of their families, and becoming productive members of the community. *Baby Boy* is less interested in the broader forces that produce racism than it is in the way in which the effects of racism are experienced by those who bear the burden of its consequences. This is not an unimportant project, but it is taken up within an ideological register that is all too characteristic of the 1990s and the new millennium. Social problems in this film become personal problems, and systemic issues are reduced to private considerations. Matters of personal commitment and character push aside broader questions of how individual incapacities and misfortunes intersect with larger systemic forces. Private struggles replace social struggles, and collective solutions give way to individual responsibility. *Baby Boy* echoes the conservative call for black males to stop complaining, pick themselves up, take personal responsibility for their behavior, and do themselves and the larger society a favor by exercising some self-criticism aimed at the infantile and irresponsible lives they lead.[21] Needless to say, black conservatives such as Stanley Crouch and white liberals such as Roger Ebert closed ranks in praising *Baby Boy* as both an honest and deeply serious film. Crouch claims it is one of the few black films ever made that has the courage to "look at those strutting young Los Angeles black men who father children by various women and make little or no effort to support them."[22] Roger Ebert, the film critic for the *Chicago Sun-Times,* exalts in *Baby Boy*'s "message to men like its hero: yes, racism has contributed to your situation, but do you have to give it so much help with your own attitude?"[23]

Written and directed by John Singleton, *Baby Boy* is the follow-up to his 1991 hit *Boyz 'N the Hood.* Both films deal with the rite of passage young black men face in South Central Los Angeles. Whereas *Boyz 'N the Hood* explores the connection between racism, violence, and the militarized masculinity associated with gang warfare, *Baby Boy* narrows its focus and addresses the theory that racism and macho fantasy infantalize African American males who cannot assume the responsibilities that come with being a mature adult. To prove his point, Singleton explains his theme in the first few minutes of the film through a mix of spectacle and scientific rhetoric. The film opens with a surreal, dreamlike image of a fully grown, naked black man, the 20-year-old protagonist Jody (Tyrese Gibson), floating in his mother's womb. Jody is curled up in a fetal position and imagines that he is about to be aborted. Jody's imagined, infantile fears become the backdrop for a voiceover quoting a "lady psychiatrist," Dr. Frances Cress Welding, author of the 1991 book *Isis Papers: The Keys to the Colors,* who asserts that African American men both baby themselves and believe that they deserve to be treated with the indulgence accorded an infant. To support the claim that racism has made black men think of themselves as babies, Welding offers the following: "What does a black man call his girlfriends? momma; his acquaintances? boyz; and his place of residence? crib." Far from rupturing this absurd reductionism, Jody's character seems to embody it to its fullest. Early on we're told that Jody has two young children, a boy and a girl, each of whom has a different mother. Yet he lives at home with his own mother, who is constantly telling him to grow up, while he watches cartoons on television and builds and plays with model cars. When he is not sponging off his mother, he is taking advantage of his girlfriend, Yvette (Taraji P. Henson), constantly borrowing her car and fooling around with other women. When Yvette "steals" back her car, he ends up riding around the neighborhood on a ridiculously garish child's bicycle.

Next, we find him outside an abortion clinic waiting for Yvette, one of the two women with whom he has fathered children. Jody drives Yvette home and puts her to bed, but because she is in pain, distraught, and slightly drugged from the painkillers, she doesn't want to talk to Jody, whose present irresponsibility appears as an uncomfortable reminder of why she got the abortion in the first place. Lacking the compassion or sensitivity to stick around and offer some comfort, Jody borrows Yvette's car and takes off to visit his other girlfriend, Peanut (Tamara LaSeon Bass), the mother of his other baby.

His self-absorption wavers as Jody begins his journey from an unremitting display of narcissism, selfishness, and grossly infantile behavior to some semblance of adult responsibility. Jody's rite of passage is marked by four significant events. First, Jody's domestic life is shattered when his mother brings home a boyfriend, Melvin (Ving Rhames), whose presence Jody bitterly resents. Melvin is an old-style gangsta whose history of violence and 10 years' imprisonment is boldly displayed in the words "Thug" and "187" tattooed on his huge, muscular arms. Melvin is a painful reminder that Jody's mother, Juanita (A. J. Johnson), a youthful 36-year-old, has her own desires and needs a life of her own. But more is at stake than his mother's independence and pleasure; there is also the possibility that Jody will be forced to leave the house and go out on his own once Melvin settles in. In fact, Melvin becomes a grim reminder of when Juanita allowed a former boyfriend to join the household and as a result Jody's brother was asked to leave the house—eventually to be killed in the streets. In a scene combining stereotypes of rapacious sexuality and criminality, Melvin's increasing presence around the house becomes more threatening to Jody (and presumably the audience) when he wakes up one morning and finds his mother's suitor stark naked in the kitchen, scrambling eggs for Juanita. Melvin now owns a landscaping business and has given up the thug life, but when dealing with Jody, whom he resents, he quickly resorts to both the reasoning and violence of his past. Melvin may no longer kill people, but his sense of agency is still firmly rooted in a macho ebullience that appears removed from any kind of critical understanding that might question the allure of violence for men and how it functions to numb them to the plight of others. Jody, on the other hand, fears that Melvin might eventually abuse his mother, a pattern he has seen in her relationships with other men. But while such a fear is legitimate, it becomes a self-serving rhetorical tool for Jody to try to convince his mother to get rid of Melvin. Jody's insincerity is echoed in his lack of self-consciousness regarding his own treatment of women as objects, which not only reproduces a particularly repugnant form of moral insensitivity, but makes it all the more predictable that he will engage in the very abuse that he believes Melvin is capable of producing.

The second turning point in Jody's life occurs while hanging out with Sweetpea (Omar Gooding), his unemployed childhood friend, in a liquor store parking lot. Observing various individuals engage in small-time boosting, he realizes that he will never make it out of South Central until he can become, as he puts it to Sweetpea, the master of his destiny. According to Jody, "Everybody moving is making money." As far as Jody is concerned, the world is divided into "buyers" and "sellers." Jody wants to be a seller. But Jody doesn't want to sell drugs, the trade of so-called choice in his neighborhood. To become a seller, Jody begins boosting women's clothes from the fashion district and peddles them in neighborhood beauty parlors. Jody has a vague feeling that his own sense of manhood depends on getting a job and becoming more independent, but he has no sense of the political and economic forces in his neighborhood that construct the problem as a social issue and not merely as a problem of individual initiative or character. Manhood for Jody is about making money—hardly an oppositional stance toward the system that punishes young black men like himself. In other words, Jody's newfound sense of agency is entirely entrepreneurial and privatized; it offers little understanding of how the racialized stratification of power and opportunity limits his own sense of possibility, not to mention the possibilities of the young men and women who populate his impoverished neighborhood. Jody lives in an ideological universe in which the "deeply etched historical inequities and inequalities" of state-sponsored racism disappear from historical memory purged of ethical responsibility into the "relative invisibility of private spheres, seemingly out of reach of public policy intervention."[24] Jody recognizes that to be a consumer you have to be a producer, but he has little sense of the economic, historical, and political dynamics and inequities at work in shaping the relations of the marketplace.

While making some extra cash, Jody's life takes a third critical turn for the worse when he angrily confronts his mother and demands that she throw Melvin out of the house. At first Melvin lays back and says nothing, but finally he explodes and tells Jody to grow up and be a man, adding that he needs to stop blaming everyone else for his problems. But to add insult to injury, Melvin suggests that Jody has an oedipal complex and that the root of his problem is a repressed desire for his own mother. Melvin then decks Jody, and Jody leaves the house for good. Jody has no place to go, and to make matters worse he no longer has a car, because Yvette has taken hers back. Reduced to riding around the neighborhood on his childhood bike, Jody suffers another indignity when he is attacked by a group of neighborhood teens. Jody finds Sweetpea and they cruise the streets until they find the group of

14-year-old punks in a park. Sweetpea and Jody give all of them a beating that redeems Jody's manhood, but the violence makes him uncomfortable and serves as a marker for him to rethink his own relationship to violence. Jody's crisis of masculinity faces another challenge when Rodney (Snoop Dogg), a dope-smoking gangbanger and former lover of Yvette's, comes to town after being released from jail and wants to resume his place in her life. Rodney offers the flip-side of Singleton's altogether simplistic and reductive understanding of young black masculinity.

Rodney ends up in Yvette's house and tries to pick up the relationship again. Rodney is a menacing figure who settles in against Yvette's desire to get him out of the apartment. Resentment soon turns to violence as Rodney tries to rape Yvette, but gives up the attempt when her baby boy, JoJo, enters the room and pleads for Rodney to leave her alone. Rodney's rage then turns on Jody as he gets some of his "boyz" together and drives over to Jody's house in order to shoot him. Jody and Sweetpea get caught in the line of fire but manage to escape unhurt. Jody and Sweetpea now have to face the challenge to their manhood of both the failed rape attempt against Yvette and the assault by Rodney and his "boyz" against their own lives. Their identities, if not masculinity, are now on trial, and though they hesitate about committing a violent act, they hunt Rodney down and murder him.

Jody is completely shaken and learns about male responsibility through a street code that offers few rewards, except survival. He goes back to his mother's house, sinks into a corner, trembling while holding the gun he used to shoot Rodney. Melvin finds him in the room, takes the gun, wipes off the prints, and leaves the room. No words are exchanged between them. Melvin and Jody have now bonded through the ritual of masculine violence, removed from either the sphere of moral responsibility or the necessity for argument. Violence is not renounced in this instance, but harnessed for the greater good of the family. Macho fantasy still feeds adult reality, but in the service of helping Jody overcome his immaturity and selfishness. The film ends with Jody leaving his mother and moving in with Yvette, the implication being that he is finally willing to try to live up to his responsibilities as a father and husband.

Film as Public Pedagogy

Films such as *Baby Boy* can be interrogated initially by analyzing both the common sense assumptions that inform them, the affective investments they evoke, and the absences and exclusions that limit the range of meanings and information available to audiences. Analyzing such films as public discourses also affords pedagogical opportunities to engage those complex institutional frameworks that are brought to bear in producing, circulating, and legitimating the range of meanings associated with such cultural texts. As public discourses, these cultural texts can be seen as objects that gain their relevance through their relationship to other social institutions, resources, and non-discursive practices. *Baby Boy*'s racialized representations gain legitimacy because they resonate so powerfully with the "war on crime" and the generalized culture of fear it produces to legitimize punitive policies against black and brown youth since the 1980s, but especially so under the Clinton and both Bush administrations.[25] For example, when viewed within the dominant racial ideology of mainstream popular culture, *Baby Boy* registers the rightward shift in race relations, especially among social conservatives and mainstream media, in which black youth are both demonized and subjected to mounting surveillance by the police and increased control under the criminal justice system. As cultural critic S. Craig Watkins observes, "Black youth seemingly have been in the eye of a public storm against crime, drugs, and the alleged erosion of traditional values. As a result, new punitive technologies and legislation have been initiated in order to exercise great control over black youth."[26] But Watkins understates the case. The vast majority of youth who are incarcerated are black or Hispanic kids of color, and as journalist Paul Street points out, "a young black man age sixteen . . . faces a 29 percent chance of spending time in prison during his life. The corresponding statistic for white men in the same age group is 4 percent."[27] Youth culture has always incurred the wrath of adults, but young people have never been persecuted with such methodical zeal as they are at present. Catherine Campbell, a civil rights attorney in Fresno, California, argues that:

> The point is not that youth is criminalized, but that only certain kids are criminalized, and these are kids from bad neighborhoods. . . .

They get them, and then if they're the right kind, if they're poor, of color, angry, and unsuccessful in school, they keep them. Through all means available, they keep them in the system. They search them, harass them, follow them, watch who they talk with, what they wear. The most minor infraction, they are back in jail, they are sent away, or placed on probation, and they are watched more.[28]

It is against this social and political backdrop that *Baby Boy* needs to be engaged as part of a broader politics of racial representation.

According to filmmaker John Singleton, Jody, the main character in *Baby Boy,* is one of the most dangerous young men around "because he is hypersensitive," a young man who is trying to negotiate what it means to be a man, while laboring under a social code that says "you're not a man unless you are a killer."[29] Singleton rightly views this behavior as utterly dysfunctional, and crafted the film to explore the relationship between the crisis of masculinity and violence on the one hand, and the politics of agency and responsibility on the other. But the landscape used to frame these issues operates within a political register that almost completely ignores broader historical, economic, racial, and political contexts. Nor does it comment on the centrality of violence to either white masculinity or American culture generally. As popular culture critic Michael Eric Dyson points out,

> It does no good to reprimand black youth for their addiction to violence. Our nation suffers the addiction in spades, as even a cursory read of pop culture suggests. But it is not just pop culture that is implicated. American society was built on violence, from the wholesale destruction of Native American culture to the enslavement of Africans.[30]

Moreover, the crisis of identity and masculinity that Singleton constructs finds its resolution in integration into the existing social order rather than a challenge that calls for its transformation. Singleton wants to capture what it means for some young black men to grow up in poverty without fathers, how they are raised by mothers who do their best, and how both get by without the benefit of older role models. But against this seemingly severe deprivation is not only the presumption that women do not do enough to help these young men reach a state of maturity and independence, but also the sense that the traditional nuclear family is the normalizing space where these problems can be resolved. This is a deeply flawed and conservative position because it never confronts the misogyny and inequalities that structure such families, especially amid a disturbing legacy of machismo and severe social problems. Moreover, this position affords no way of understanding how the family is connected to larger social forces that it cannot shape or control. All of these issues offer an opportunity for educators and students to take up this film as part of a broader understanding of the racial, economic, and political forces that both frame its major assumptions and connect it to those ideologies and public spheres that exist outside of the often isolated space of higher education.

Singleton's conservative ideology is most evident in his refusal to raise questions about the larger forces that bear down on Jody's sense of agency and possibility. What does it mean to be a man in a neighborhood marked by deep racial and economic inequalities? To what degree does self-responsibility become the only referent of possibility when neighborhoods such as the one Jody lives in are burdened by poverty; segregated housing; a lack of decent schools, healthcare, and neighborhood organizations; high unemployment; and, usually, a hostile police force? How does one talk about individual initiative in a system when the poverty rate for blacks is 28.3 percent, more than double what it is for whites (11.2 percent)? What role do individual solutions play in dealing with systemic problems such as the ongoing discrimination against African American youth in the workplace and schools? How does one theorize the concept of individual responsibility or character within a social order in which the national jobless rate is about 6 percent, but unemployment rates for young men of color in places such as South Central Los Angeles have topped 30 percent? How does one ignore the fact that while it is widely recognized that a high school diploma is essential to getting a job, it is increasingly difficult for large numbers of African American youth to even stay in school, especially with the advent of zero-tolerance policies now driving school policy? As a result of such policies, the rate of expulsion and suspension for such students is increasing at an alarming rate. For instance, journalist Marilyn Elias reported in *USA Today* that "In 1998, the first year national expulsion figures were gathered, 31% of kids expelled were black, but blacks made up only 17% of the students in public schools."[31] Moreover, as many states invest more in prisons than in schools, more African Americans are dropping out of school and ending up under the control of some aspect of the criminal justice system. The figures on this are extraordinary. Of the two million people behind bars, 70 percent of the inmates are people of color, with 50 percent being African Americans and 17 percent Latinos.[32] Law professor David Cole, in his book, *No Equal Justice,* points out that while "76 percent of illicit drug users were white, 14 percent black, and 8 percent Hispanic—figures which roughly match each group's share of the general population," African Americans constitute "35 percent of all drug arrests, 55 percent of all drug convictions, and 74 percent of all sentences for drug offences."[33] A Justice department report points out that on any given day in this country "more than a third of the young African American men aged 18–34 in some of our major cities are either in prison or under some form of criminal justice supervision."[34] The same department reported in April of 2000 that "black youth are forty-eight times more likely than whites to be sentenced to juvenile prison for drug offenses."[35] Within such a context, the possibilities for treating young people of color with respect, dignity, and support vanishes, and with it the hope of overcoming a racial abyss that makes a mockery out of justice and a travesty of democracy.

Rather than point to the weakness of Jody's character in addressing what it would mean for him to be a man, students might ask how Singleton might have addressed prevailing social conditions and what resources Jody had to expand his capacities, knowledge, and skills to make informed choices. Singleton might have acknowledged the need for eliminating racism in the workplace, addressed the ongoing discrimination in the schools, or the growing violence and militarization waged against black youth by what David Theo Goldberg has called "the racial state." Yet it appears that Singleton has no sense of how the historical burdens of racism work through the "technologies employed by the [modern racial state] to fashion, modify, and reify the terms of racial expression, as well as racist exclusions and subjugation."[36] Singleton could have acknowledged not only the practices, social conditions, and institutional structures that make up the racial state, he could have also brought attention to the need for the federal government to provide funds for a range of proven programs that improve the life of impoverished communities with limited jobs and institutional infrastructures. For example, he might have pointed to the need for Head Start and drug prevention programs, youth centers, urban school reform, and subsidizing of low-income housing as well as child care and health care programs. Clearly, these are far more important than moralistic appeals to self-responsibility in establishing the conditions for giving young men and women in the urban cities an opportunity to lead their lives as responsible adults and critical citizens. Moreover, Singleton could have pointed to the myriad forms of inventive resistance that black youth have produced, particularly within the realm of media and popular culture, to redefine "alternative notions of their racial, gender and generational identities in the face of an ascending conservative hegemony that was making its own set of distinctive claims about black youth."[37] But apparently this is not the stuff of Hollywood entertainment. It doesn't titillate. It doesn't shock. It can't offer the same mechanisms for exotic escape that mainstream white audiences crave in their consumption of blackness.

Black youth are neither irresponsible nor passive victims of the racial apartheid so rampant in urban centers in this country. Black youth display a remarkable degree of agency and resistance, and in doing so "they provide a valuable set of diverse resources within black popular culture to challenge the conservative claim that blacks are responsible for urban poverty, violence, and a drain on our national resources."[38] This is not meant to suggest that such resistance should be over-valorized in the face of massive inequalities, power, and modes of discrimination. But it should be mined as a way to rethink and repoliticize agency, collective movements, and "the central constituting factor of power in social relations."[39]

Any attempt to address *Baby Boy* as a form of public pedagogy would have to analyze the largely privatized and individualized analysis that shapes this film and how it resonates with the ongoing privatization and depoliticization of the public sphere. As neoliberalism has gained momentum since the 1980s, one of its distinguishing features has been an assault on all those public spheres that are not regulated by the language of the market. Civil freedoms degenerate into market freedoms, and the very idea of the sanctity of the public good and public service are increasingly viewed as either an unacceptable extravagance or as useless luxury, if not pathological "dependency." The onslaught of neoliberal ideology and its turn toward the free market as the basis for human interaction attempt to alter radically the very vocabulary we use to describe and appraise human interest, action, and behavior. Individuals are now defined largely as consumers, and self-interest appears to be the only factor capable of motivating people. Public spaces are increasingly displaced by commercial interests, and constructing private utopias becomes the only model for the good life. As public life is emptied of its own separate concerns—importance of the public good, civic virtue, public debate, collective agency, and social provisions for the marginalized—it becomes increasingly more difficult to translate private concerns into public ones. The Darwinian vision of universal struggle pits individuals against each other, while the misfortunes and problems of others are represented as both a weakness of character and a social liability. Moreover, it holds the needs of racialized minorities as an impossible drain on already scarce resources. Within such a system, the state gives up its obligations to provide collective safety nets for people while the ideology of "going it alone" furthers the myth that all social problems are the result of individual choices.[40] As all levels of government move from social investment to racial containment, the state makes more visible its militarizing functions, and as David Theo Goldberg brilliantly argues, begins to function more visibly as a racial state through its control over modes of rule and representation. He contends that the state uses:

> physical force, violence, coercion, manipulation, deceit, cajoling, incentives, law(s), taxes, penalties, surveillance, military force, repressive apparatuses, ideological mechanisms and media—in short, all the means at a state's disposal—ultimately to the ends of racial rule. Which is to say, to the ends of reproducing the racial order and so representing for the most part the interests of the racial ruling class.[41]

Unfortunately, *Baby Boy* acknowledges neither the state's implication in racial violence and social disintegration, nor its refusal to assume any responsibility for preventing it. One consequence is that

Baby Boy leaves intact the myth of individual motivation and pathology as the source of unemployment, violence, welfare dependency, bad housing, inadequate schools, and crumbling infrastructures. It reproduces this conservative myth by suggesting that collective problems can only be addressed as tales of individual survival, coming of age stories that chronicle either selfishness, laziness, and lack of maturity or individual perseverance. Under such circumstances, conservatives such as Thomas Sowell and Shelby Steele invoke the language of personal responsibility to blame African Americans for the poverty and discrimination they endure on a daily basis. But the language of personal responsibility does much more. It also makes invisible and literally unaccountable those state-supported economic, political, and educational policies that reproduce racially predicated forms of exclusion and discrimination.[42]

Dependency in this film and the broader society is a dirty word; charges of "dependency" resonate with right-wing attacks on the welfare state and the alleged perils of big government. Granted, *Baby Boy* is supposedly about the refusal of immature African American youth to grow up, but the film's attack on dependency is so one-sided that it reinforces the comfortable illusion (to some) that social safety nets simply weaken character. The film supports this ideology in part by refusing to acknowledge how so-called dependency on the welfare state *has worked* for those millions for whom it has "made all the difference between wretched poverty and a decent life."[43] Similarly, if Jody's dreams are limited to the demands of the traditional family structure and the successes associated with the market ideology, there is no room in *Baby Boy* to recognize that democracy, not the market, can be drawn upon as a force of dissent and a relentless critique of institutions. Democracy rather than the market provides a vocabulary for civic engagement as well as a discourse for expanding and deepening the possibilities of critical citizenship and social transformation. In the end, *Baby Boy* fails to offer a space for translating how the private and public mutually inform each other; consequently, it reinforces rather than ruptures those racially oppressive trends in American society that disfigure the possibility of racial justice, democratic politics, and responsible citizenship. More importantly, the characterizations of black men and women offered up by Singleton, to quote film critic Armond

White, "are reactionary throwbacks . . . a sign of that national epidemic that deforms discourse on race: denial."[44]

Agency and Masculinity as the Politics of Pathology

Questions of identity are central to *Baby Boy* and to Jody's development as a character. Identities are neither fixed nor unified but are about an ongoing process of becoming. Identities are constructed through the differences and exclusions, mediated within disparate and often unequal relations of power, that largely determine the range of available resources—history, values, language, and experiences—through which individuals and groups experience their relationships to themselves and others. While the link between agency and identity is a complex one, agency is at the center of the connection between the private and the social, the individual and the public sphere both as a matter of politics and power. Agency, as Lawrence Grossberg observes,

> involves the possibilities of action as interventions into the processes by which reality is continually being transformed and power enacted. . . . [I]n Marx's terms, the problem of agency is the problem of understanding how people make history in conditions not of their own making. Who gets to make history? That is, agency involves relations of participation and access, the possibilities of moving into particular sites of activity and power, and of belonging to them in such a way as to be able to enact their powers.[45]

Identity in *Baby Boy* is shaped outside of the discourse of political power, and as a result enacts a notion of agency for Jody that is defined primarily through the discourse of immaturity and self-inflicted injury. Identity does not become a site of social contestation, but collapses into a static notion of masculinity in which the body occupies a limited sense of agency defined primarily through violence, crime, dependency, pleasure, and social pathology.[46] Within this commonplace Hollywood stereotype, black male power is removed from the realm of critical thought and plays out in a display of excessive machismo, lurid sexuality, exoticized athleticism, and patriarchal masculinity. Trapped within a discourse of identity and agency mediated through a form of masculinity reduced to affirming and negotiating the dynamics of violence, Jody has no tools for understanding how power actually works in society or what it would mean to favor "negotiation over violence and the will to justice over the will to dominate."[47] *Baby Boy* presents its viewers with a "flattened moral landscape bereft of difficult choices," one in which limited visions are matched by a cynical politics that parades as part of a naturalized morality.[48] Missing from this analysis of power and its collapse into a traditionally racist notion of black masculinity is the use of state violence and how it not only disciplines bodies of color through a range of practices extending from racial profiling to incarceration, but also, as David Theo Goldberg argues, how it is used to "systematically close off institutional access on the part of individuals in virtue of group membership (while hiding) the very instrumentalities that reproduce that inaccessibility."[49]

Violence in this film operates as both a constant threat and a medium for men to express their masculinity. Jody is haunted by the death of his brother and harbors fears of being murdered in the streets in his dreams. At one point, he tells Yvette that he wanted their child so something of him would be left behind once he is killed. Jody is also ambivalent about his relationship to street violence, and this is evident when he participates in beating up the young punks who robbed him and when he hunts Rodney down and murders him. There is also the sense that Melvin, while still a tough guy, no longer resorts to the kind of brutalizing violence that defined his life in the past. But in all of these cases, violence is still the only terrain on which these men move, define themselves, and work out their problems. This is violence packaged as a critique of masculine crisis, but it is a decontextualized violence, more intent on an aesthetics of posturing than on disrupting conventional stereotypes that portray black youth and men in the image of Richard Wright's character Bigger Thomas. In the end, *Baby Boy* falls prey, regardless of how it attempts to complicate masculinity, to constructing black men homogeneously through the performance of violence, and in doing so it both infantilizes them and portrays them as numb to the plight of others. Similarly, by decontextualizing the violence in their lives, it mystifies the sources and real nature of violence that assaults the minds and bodies of black men throughout the United States in the form of poverty-ridden schools, low teacher expectations, racist profiling, housing discrimination, joblessness, shrinking public services, and police repression. Robbed of all concreteness and stripped of any historical context, representations of violence in films such as *Baby Boy* are "flattened to caricatures of villains and victims [and] the radical demand for equality in personal life is displaced onto a profoundly conservative appeal for law and order."[50]

Masculinity in *Baby Boy* is not only defined through the posture of menacing toughness, promiscuity, and the infantilization of the black male psyche; it also works to preserve male power while legitimizing iniquitous power relations between men and women. Freedom in this film is about redeeming black masculinity, but the notion of manhood that is redeemed "makes masculinity synonymous with the ability to assert power over [individuals] through acts of violence and terrorism,"[51] particularly against women. What is left unproblematized in this notion of masculinity is its intimate connection to a notion of patriarchy in which the power to act is equated with the power to control or abuse women. For example, all of the major women characters in this film are defined largely as props for men's pleasures and as integral to maintaining some semblance of family values, and all their actions are devoid of contextualization. The framing of black women's sexuality in this way says nothing about the dominant culture all women endure. As Michael Eric Dyson astutely observes,

> perhaps there's no excuse for poor young black women believing that their bodies are their tickets to pleasure—besides, that is all the cues they get from pimps, playas, teachers, preachers, daddies, hustlers, and mentors. Apparently, there are no cultural influences—no magazines or television shows—that lead them to believe that their sexuality might suspend their misery, if even for a few gilded moments at the end of the night in the backseat of a car on the edge of town—and perhaps their sanity.[52]

Jody's lovers and his mother, even when they display some insight about the difficult nature of their lives, never rise to the occasion of challenging the wider misogynist structures in which they live out their daily existence. All of these women are caught within a violence that carries an erotic charge, and all of them experience the pain and suffering that comes with the submission to male power, but none of them can imagine themselves outside of its dominating influence. At most, they try to do the best they can to control its worst excesses. Singleton not only defines women as the binary opposite of masculinity in this film; he goes a step further and suggests that "African American men are systematically prevented from assuming adult responsibilities by their mothers, who insist on smothering them with affection."[53] For all of Singleton's emphasis on critiquing black masculinity, it is ironic that his only attempts to contextualize its most abrasive forms are at the expense of black women. As Dyson argues, representations of black women, it appears, engender or are ascribed even less complexity.

> If social empathy for young black males is largely absent in public opinion and public policies, the lack of understanding and compassion for the difficulties faced by poor young black females is even more deplorable. There exists within quarters of black life a range of justifications for black male behavior. Even if they are not wholly accepted by other blacks or by the larger culture, such justifications have a history and possess social resonance. Young black males hustle because they are poor. They become pimps and playas because the only role models they had are pimps and playas. Black males rob because they are hungry. . . . Yet there are few comparable justifications for the black female's beleaguered status. The lack of accepted social justifications for black women's plight would lead one to assume that black women do not confront incest, father depravation, economic misery, social dislocation, domestic abuse, maternal abandonment, and a host of other ills.[54]

Given the film's view of the relationship between masculinity and women, this seems to be a predictable response to a dreadful form of misogynist logic. Through its representations of masculinity, violence, and women, *Baby Boy* dissolves politics into pathology and agency into narcissistic modes of self-absorption. By relying on a cheap moralism as a substitute for any viable analysis, *Baby Boy* reduces the struggle to overcome racism and inequality to the lack of individual discipline, and in doing so "discourage[s] rebellion in favor of guilty, resigned acquiescence."[55] Public politics becomes difficult to imagine when issues of agency, vision, and transformation are collapsed into the realm of the personal and the psychological, as opposed to the collective and social. Commenting on representations of black masculinity, bell hooks provides an important insight into the ideological and political shortcomings at work in *Baby Boy:*

> The portrait of black masculinity that emerges in this work perpetu-
> ally constructs black men as "failures" who are psychologically'
> "fucked up," dangerous, violent, sex maniacs whose insanity is in-
> formed by their inability to fulfill their phallocentric masculine des-
> tiny in a racist context. . . . It does not interrogate the conventional
> construction of patriarchal masculinity or question the extent to
> which black men have historically internalized this norm. It never as-
> sumes the existence of black men whose creative agency has enabled
> them to subvert norms and develop ways of thinking abut masculin-
> ity that challenge patriarchy.[56]

Conclusion

Baby Boy is an important film that can be used to address the stereotypes and the conservative ideology that currently construct specific notions of race, agency, masculinity, violence, and politics. But *Baby Boy* represents more than a text that portrays a particularly offensive image of black men and women. The film, like the advertising and culture industries, also teaches and legitimates those images and values that undermine a democratic language for defending vital social institutions that oppose racist values and practices. As a public text, *Baby Boy* resonates powerfully with those forces in American society that condemn minorities of color and class to the most debilitating and exploitative aspects of racism. Ad-dressing *Baby Boy* as representative of reactionary racialized texts is par-ticularly important at a time in American history when racism is once again on the rise, as the war on terrorism—which reinforces policies of racial profiling, anti-immigrant legislation, and the suspension of basic civil liberties—combines with neoliberal policies that reinforce a rabid individualism and free-market ideology that, in addition to turning citi-zenship into the act of consuming or patriotic jingoism, also leave no room for understanding the effects of racist practices and policies as public concerns deeply threatening to democracy.

Framed against a culture of commercialism and fear, *Baby Boy* be-comes not simply another text to be consumed but also a pedagogical device for legitimating a market-based notion of self-help and individualism, while reinforcing the idea that racism is a problem best understood as a lack of character or individual motivation—a problem that can only be understood and resolved within the privatized discourse of self-help or, if need be, through the disciplinary practices of punishment and containment. Zygmunt Bauman observes that as collective interests are reforged as private pursuits, "The new across-the-board consensus . . . is not about making the plight of the poor easier, but about getting rid of the poor; deleting them or making them vanish from the agenda of public concern."[57] What is crucial to recognize here is how different groups and individuals respond to a film such as *Baby Boy* is, in part, conditioned by the dominant ideologies that shape the public sphere, and what John Brenkman calls "the material, institutionalized space of expression and criticism,"[58] which is currently under assault by Bush, Ashcroft, and others waging a war against terrorism (and civil liberties). Given the current assault on public life and dissent, it becomes all the more necessary to make the politics of films such as *Baby Boy* both visible and problematic.

There are no "manchildren" in *Baby Boy*, because the film mirrors the increasing attempt in American society to remove the plight of poor black and Hispanic children from the inventory of public concerns. Hence there is little consideration of what it might mean to address individual problems as public issues, or connect individual choices to the realms of power and politics. In this sense, *Baby Boy* reinforces both the rise of "blame the victim" ideology and those political forces that claim that persistent racism is not a white problem, that the welfare state must be dismantled in favor of market freedoms, and that the increasing criminalization of social problems is a legitimate response by the racial state to the racial intolerance, economic inequalities, and class antagonisms shaping American life. Clearly such policies threaten dire consequences for those youth who are poor, black, and Hispanic.

If the dominant codes at work in such a film are to be questioned, it is imperative for students to address how the absences in such a film become meaningful when understood within a broader struggle over issues of racial identity, power, and representation.

Depictions of urban youth as dangerous, pathological, and violent must be part of a larger examination of how such representations shape the contexts of everyday life, and how they could be used as sites of struggle for racial justice in spaces other than the university. For example, the depictions of youth in *Baby Boy* resonate powerfully with the growth of social policies and an ever-expanding, highly visible criminal justice system whose get-tough policies fall disproportionately on poor black and brown youth. Students might be asked to weigh what the potential effect of a film such as *Baby Boy* might be in addressing the political, racial, and economic conditions that threaten to wipe out a whole generation of young black and Hispanic males who are increasingly incarcerated in prisons and jails whose populations are growing at the rate of about 7 percent a year and cost more than 30 billion annually to operate.[59] What might it mean to expand the concern for racial justice from the analysis of a film to forms of intervention that not only challenge assumptions about color blindness and the alleged "end of racism" but also address actual struggles being waged against racism in a variety of public spheres such as education, the prison-industrial complex, the dominant media, and the state? How might *Baby Boy* be used educationally to address the contradiction between the attempts on the part of conservatives and liberals to insist on the irrelevance of a vocabulary of race with the reality of racist imagery that has real political effects? How might a cultural text such as *Baby Boy* be used to address the apparently persistent stereotype of black men as lazy; the ongoing attack on the welfare state; the dismantling of affirmative action policies in higher education; and the plight caused by industrial downsizing and rising unemployment among young black men across America's inner cities? What might it mean for students to address their own responses to the panics concerning crime and race that have swept across the middle classes in the last decade, made manifest in strong electoral support for harsh crime laws and massive increases in prison growth?[60] At the very least, educators can address *Baby Boy* not merely in terms of what such a text might mean but how it functions within a set of complex social reactions that create the conditions of which it is a part and from which it stems. Lawrence Grossberg insightfully argues that such a pedagogy would:

involve the broader exploration of the way in which discursive practices construct and participate in the machinery by which the ways
people live their lives are themselves produced and controlled.
Rather than looking for the "said" or trying to derive the saying from
the said, rather than asking what texts mean or what people do with
texts, [a critical pedagogy] would be concerned with what discursive
practices do in the world.[61]

Films such as *Baby Boy* become important as part of a politics and
pedagogy of difference because they play a powerful role in mobilizing
racial ideologies, investments, and identifications. They produce and
reflect how race functions as a structuring principle in diverse relations
in a wide variety of social spheres. Put differently, Hollywood films represent an important form of public pedagogy and play a crucial role in
representing otherness, deploying power, and producing categories
through which individuals fashion their identities and organize their
ideologies and politics. As David Theo Goldberg and John Solomos
point out in a different context, film provides the pedagogical conditions through which race becomes a medium "by which difference is
represented and otherness produced, so that contingent attributes
such as skin color are transformed into supposedly essential bases for
identities, group belonging and exclusions, social privileges, and burdens, political rights and disfranchisements."[62] At the same time, if we
are to read films such as *Baby Boy* as social and political allegories articulating deeply rooted fears, desires, and visions, they have to be understood within a broader network of cultural spheres and institutions
rather than as isolated texts. The pedagogical and political character
of such films resides in the ways in which they align with broader social, sexual, economic, class, and institutional configurations. Rather
than being viewed as merely entertainment, films such as *Baby Boy*—
like all cultural texts—must be understood as part of a larger battle
over values, beliefs, and social relations and their potential for expanding or closing down democratic public life.

Needless to say, *Baby Boy* can be read differently by different audiences, and this suggests the necessity to take up such texts in the speci-
ficity of the contexts in which they are received. But at the same time,
educators, social critics, and others have an obligation to expose how

such texts legitimate some meanings, invite particular desires, and exclude others. Acknowledging the educational role of such films requires that educators and others find ways to make the political more pedagogical. One approach would be to develop a pedagogy of disruption that would raise questions regarding how certain meanings under particular historical conditions become more legitimate as representations than others, or how certain meanings take on the force of common sense assumptions and go relatively unchallenged in shaping broader discourses and social configurations. It would raise questions about how *Baby Boy*, for instance, resonates with the ongoing social conditions of racial fear that are mobilized through a wide variety of representations in the media and popular culture, as well as in a number of other institutional sites such as schools, churches, and advertising agencies. More specifically, a pedagogy of disruption would engage a film's attempts to shift the discourse of politics away from issues of justice and equality to a focus on violence and individual freedom as part of a broader neoliberal backlash against equity, social citizenship, and human rights. It would also examine *Baby Boy* within a network of wider cultural practices that mark the decline of the rhetoric of the social. Such an approach would not only critically address the dominant ideologies of black masculinity, violence, and dependency that give *Baby Boy* so much power in the public imagination, but also work to expose the ideological contradictions and political absences that characterize the film—challenging it as symptomatic of the growing reaction against civil rights, the right-wing assault on the welfare state, and the increasing use of violence to keep in check marginalized groups such as young black males and other youths of color (especially Arabs and Muslims) who are now viewed as a threat to order and national security.

Engaging the potential effects of films such as *Baby Boy* might mean discussing why this Hollywood film received such popular praise in a largely white-owned, dominant press, or equally important, why it did not receive much criticism given its extremely conservative message. Such a film also raises questions about how it functions as a public text that rationalizes both the demonization of minority youth and the reduction of funding for public and higher education, job training, and health care at a time when black youth are in desperate need of jobs, education, and resources to be able to participate in public life.

Pedagogically, this suggests that educators raise questions about a text that enables students to move from understanding it as a form of public pedagogy to using it as a resource to intervene in public life to transform social injustices. Analyzing any cultural text always runs the risk of elevating the cultural over the social, the textual over a publicly informed politics. By viewing film as a public pedagogy, it becomes possible, as Arif Dirlik points out, to develop a "language that is more cognizant of the historicity of the cultural, which in turn is premised on a politics driven not by questions of cultural identity but questions of social and public responsibility."[63] What Dirlik is rightly suggesting is that questions of identity and race can neither be transformed into static categories nor detached from the modalities of history, power, and politics.

The popularity of such films as *Baby Boy* in the heyday of the growing backlash against civil rights points to the need for educators and others to expand their understanding of racial politics and the politics of racial representation as part of a broader project designed to expand racial justice and economic democracy. Such a project refuses to seal off issues of identity, power, and cultural difference from their dialectical relationship to the historically constructed world of public politics. Moreover, this project must be understood within a wider critical tradition of defending the role of the intellectual as a citizen/scholar, while recognizing, as Toni Morrison observes, that the university may be one of the few public spheres we have left in the United States that is capable of protecting those values and civic freedoms that are crucial to a vibrant society.[64] In part, the challenge is to redefine the university's subversive role by providing opportunities for teachers, students, and others to engage in dialogue as the basis for challenging the underlying conditions that reproduce symbolic and institutional racism, especially as they bear down on youth of color. But the task of eliminating racism and human suffering, as part of the larger project of deepening a radical democracy, demands that the spaces for dissent and social activism both include and expand far beyond the reach of public and higher education. Critical scholarship at all levels of schooling is crucial to such a task but it is not enough. Such a task, given the ways in which race is entangled with entrenched forms of state power, ownership of resources, and privilege, demands a new understanding of how race works symbolically and institutionally to shape everyday life. The basis for this understanding resides in a politics that offers new forms of collective resistance, new visions, countervailing institutions, and new social movements. Collective resistance becomes meaningful and effective to the degree that it takes place across a variety of public spaces and spheres. For power to be generative as a way of exciting and enabling citizens to shape the conditions that govern their lives, it must be used to confront the reality of racial injustice and subordination in both those spaces and spheres traditionally marked by an imposed silence and in counter-public spheres where power becomes a visible resource for collective intervention. At the same time, it must be remembered that rebelling against injustice is crucial, but inadequate. Racial and economic justice in the service of a vibrant democracy also demands rebelling against the impoverishment of vision and imagination that seems so prevalent in the current climate of fear, racial profiling, and anti-terrorist hysteria. As Edward Said points out, resistance against racial and economic injustice can never be reconciled with the society that produced it. There is no comfort in the struggle against racism and the struggle for a fully realizable democracy except to recognize that such a struggle "will not allow conscience to look away or fall asleep."[65] When Claude Brown wrote *Manchild in the Promised Land* in 1965, he recognized clearly that the future and morality of any society is intimately connected to how it treats its children, and that such an insight becomes relevant to the degree that it generates a politics informed by the courage of conviction and moved by a public consciousness of compassion and justice.[66]

CHAPTER 7

Higher Education, Inc.

Training Students to Be Consumers

Neoliberalism is the defining political economic paradigm of our time—it refers to the policies and processes whereby a relative handful of private interests are permitted to control as much as possible of social life in order to maximize their personal profit. Associated initially with Reagan and Thatcher, for the past two decades neoliberalism has been the dominant global political economic trend adopted by political parties of the center and much of the traditional left as well as the right. These parties and the policies they enact represent the immediate interests of extremely wealthy investors and less than one thousand large corporations.

—Robert W. McChesney[1]

The task in theory no less than in practice is . . . to reilluminate public space for a civil society in collapse . . . Societies that pretend that market liberty is the same thing as civic liberty and depend on consumers to do the work of citizens are likely to achieve not unity but a plastic homogeneity—and . . . to give up democracy. . . . We seem fated to enter an era in which in the space where our public voice should be heard will be a raucous babble that leaves the civic souls of nations forever mute.

—Benjamin R. Barber[2]

The Dystopian Culture of Neoliberalism

As the forces of neoliberalism and corporate culture gain ascendancy in the United States, there is an increasing call for people to either surrender or narrow their capacities for engaged politics in exchange for market-based values, relationships, and identities. Market forces have radically altered the language we use in both representing and evaluating human behavior and action. Celebrities such as Martha Stewart, Jane Pratt, George Foreman, and Michael Jordan now market themselves as brand names. Management guru and best-selling author Tom Peters urges people to turn themselves into a brand name product, and has published a book entitled *The Brand You 50: Or: Fifty Ways to Transform Yourself From an 'Employee' Into a Brand that Shouts Distinction, Commitment and Passion!*[3] The widely read business magazine *Fast Company* devoted an entire issue to the theme, "The Brand Called You."[4] No longer defined as a form of self-development, individuality is reduced to the endless pursuit of mass-mediated interests and pleasures.

One egregious example of self-marketing can be observed in two recent high school graduates' successful attempt to secure corporate sponsorship to pay for their college tuition and expenses. Just before graduating from high school in June 2001, Chris Barrett and Luke Mc-Cabe created a website, ChrisandLuke.com, offering themselves up as "walking billboards for companies" willing to both sponsor them and pay for their college tuition, room, and board. Claiming that they "would put corporate logos on their clothes, wear a company's sunglasses, use their golf clubs, eat their pizza, drink their soda, listen to their music or drive their cars,"[5] these two young men appear impervious to the implications of defining themselves exclusively through market values, in which buying and selling define one's relationship to the larger social order. Eventually, First USA, a subsidiary of Bank One Corporation and a prominent leader in issuing Visa credit cards to students, agreed to sponsor Chris and Luke, thus providing them with the dubious distinction of becoming America's first fully corporate-sponsored university students.

Once the deal was sealed, Chris and Luke were featured in most of the major media, including *USA Today,* the *New York Times,* and *Teen Newsweek.* Hailed in the press as a heartwarming story about individual ingenuity, business acumen, and resourcefulness, there was very little criticism of the individual and social implications of what it meant for these young people both to define their identities as commodities and present themselves simply as objects to be appropriated and advertised. And, of course, nothing was said about spiraling tuition costs, which, coupled with evaporating financial aid, increasingly put higher education out of reach for working-class and middle-class youth. In a media-saturated society in which identities are marketed as brand names, it appears perfectly legitimate to assume that young people can define themselves almost exclusively through the aesthetic pleasures of consumerism and the dictates of commercialism, rather than through a notion of citizenship based on ethical norms and democratic values.[6] In short, it appears that a story in which students give up their identities to promote a corporate ideology is viewed in the pubic media less as a threat to democratic norms and civic courage than as an ode to the triumphant wisdom of market ingenuity. Equally disturbing is the assumption on the part of the two students that their identities as corporate logos is neither at odds with their role as university students nor incompatible with the role the university should play as a site of critical thinking, democratic leadership, and public engagement. Undaunted by blurring the line between their role as corporate pitchmen and their role as students, or for that matter about the encroachment of advertising into higher education, Chris and Luke defended their position by claiming, ironically, "We want to be role models for other kids to show that you don't have to wake up every day and be like everybody else."[7]

After Chris and Luke's story ran in the *New York Times*, a related incident, perhaps inspired by Chris and Luke's inventive entrepreneurialism, gained widespread public attention. A young couple in Mount Kisco, New York, attempted to auction off on E-bay and Yahoo the naming rights of their soon-to-be-born child to the highest corporate bidder. These are more than oddball stories. As William Powers, a writer for the *Atlantic Monthly* observes, these public narratives represent "dark fables about what we are becoming as a culture."[8] One wonders where this type of madness is going to end. But one thing is clear: as society is defined through the culture, values, and relations of neoliberalism, the relationship between a critical education, public morality, and civic responsibility as a condition for creating thoughtful and engaged citizens is sacrificed all too willingly to the interest of finance capital and the logic of profit-making.

This tragic narrative suggests that the individual choices we make as consumers are becoming increasingly difficult to differentiate from the "collective choices we make as citizens."[9] Under such circumstances, citizens lose their public voice as market liberties replace civic freedoms and society increasingly depends on "consumers to do the work of citizens."[10] Similarly, as corporate culture extends even deeper into the basic institutions of civil and political society, there is a simultaneous diminishing of non-commodified public spheres—those institutions such as public schools, churches, noncommercial public broadcasting, libraries, trade unions and various voluntary institutions engaged in dialogue, education, and learning—that address the relationship of the individual to public life, social responsibility, and the broader demands of citizenship, as well as provide a robust vehicle for public participation and democratic citizenship. As media theorists Edward Herman and Robert McChesney observe, non-commodified public spheres have played an invaluable role historically "as places and forums where issues of importance to a political community are discussed and debated, and where information is presented that is essential to citizen participation in community life."[11] Without these critical public spheres, corporate power often goes unchecked and politics becomes dull, cynical, and oppressive.[12] But more importantly, in the absence of such public spheres, it becomes more difficult for citizens to challenge the neoliberal myth that citizens are *merely* consumers and that "wholly unregulated markets are the sole means by which we can produce and distribute everything we care about, from durable goods to spiritual values, from capital development to social justice, from profitability to sustainable environments, from private wealth to essential commonweal."[13] As democratic values give way to commercial values, intellectual ambitions are often reduced to an instrument of the entrepreneurial self, and social visions are dismissed as hopelessly out of date.[14] Public space is portrayed exclusively as an investment opportunity, and any notion of the public becomes synonymous with disorder, disrepair, danger, and risk—for example, public schools, public transportation, public parks, and other public spaces. Within this discourse, anyone who does not believe that rapacious capitalism is the only road to freedom and the good life is dismissed as either a crank or worse. Hence it is not surprising that Joseph Kahn, writing in the *New York Times,* argues without irony: "These days, it seems, only wild-eyed anarchists and Third World dictators believe capitalism is not the high road to a better life."[15]

Neoliberalism has become the most dangerous ideology of our time.[16] It assaults all things public, mystifies the basic contradiction between democratic values and market fundamentalism, and weakens any viable consideration of political agency by offering no language capable of connecting private considerations to public issues. Similarly, as Jean and John Comaroff, distinguished professors of anthropology at the University of Chicago, argue, the animating force of neoliberalism undermines any concept of the social, society, and moral community. As they point out, neoliberalism in the age of millennial capitalism works to:

> displace political sovereignty with the sovereignty of "the market," as if the latter had a mind and morality of its own; to reorder the ontology of production and consumption . . . to encourage rapid movement of persons and goods, and sites of fabrication, thus calling into question existing forms of community; to equate freedom with choice, especially to consume, to fashion the self, to conjure with identities; to give free reign to the "forces" of hyperrationalization; to parse human beings into free-floating labor units, commodities, clients, stakeholders, strangers, their subjectivity distilled into ever more objectified ensembles of interests, entitlements, appetites, desires, purchasing "power."[17]

What becomes troubling under the rule of neoliberalism is not simply that ideas associated with freedom and agency are defined through the prevailing ideology and principles of the market, but that neoliberal ideology wraps itself in what appears to be an unassailable appeal to common sense. As Zygmunt Bauman notes, "What, however, makes the neo-liberal world-view sharply different from other ideologies—indeed, a phenomenon of a separate class—is precisely the absence of questioning; its surrender to what is seen as the implacable and irreversible logic of social reality."[18] More is lost here than neoliberalism's willingness to make its own assumptions problematic. Also lost is the very viability of politics itself. As the Comaroffs observe, "There is a strong argument to be made that neoliberal capitalism in its millennial moment portends the death of politics by hiding its own ideological underpinnings in the dictates of economic efficiency: in the fetishism of the free market, in the inexorable, expanding 'needs' of business, in the imperatives of science and technology. Or, if it does not conduce to the death of politics, it tends to reduce them to the pursuit of pure interest, individual or collective."[19]

Defined as the paragon of all social relations by Friedrich A. von Hayek, Milton Friedman, Robert Nozick, Francis Fukuyama and other market fundamentalists, neoliberalism attempts to eliminate an engaged critique about its most basic principles and social consequences by embracing the "market as the arbiter of social destiny."[20] Not only does neoliberalism, as I have stressed throughout this book, empty the public treasury, hollow out public services, limit the vocabulary and imagery available to recognize anti-democratic forms of power, and narrow models of individual agency, it also undermines the critical functions of any viable democracy by undercutting the ability of individuals to engage in the continuous translation between public considerations and private interests by collapsing the public into the realm of the private. As Bauman observes, "It is no longer true that the 'public' is set on colonizing the 'private.' The opposite is the case: it is the private that colonizes the public space, squeezing out and chasing away everything which cannot be fully, without residue, translated into the vocabulary of private interests and pursuits."[21] Divested of its political possibilities and social underpinnings, freedom offers few opportunities for people to translate private worries into public concerns and collective struggle.[22]

Within neoliberalism's market-driven discourse, corporate culture becomes both the model for the good life and the paradigmatic sphere for defining individual success and fulfillment. I use the term "corporate culture" to refer to an ensemble of ideological and institutional forces that functions politically and pedagogically to both govern organizational life through senior managerial control and to fashion compliant workers, depoliticized consumers, and passive citizens.[23] Within the language and images of corporate culture, citizenship is portrayed as an utterly solitary affair whose aim is to produce competitive, self-interested individuals vying for their own material and ideological gain.[24] Corporate culture largely cancels out or devalues social, class-specific, and racial injustices of the existing social order by absorbing the democratic impulses and practices of civil society within narrow economic relations (for example, some neoliberal advocates argue that the answer to states' staggering health care crises is the sale of public assets, such as land, to private interests). Corporate culture becomes an all-encompassing horizon for producing market identities, values, and practices. The good life, in this discourse, "is construed in terms of our identities as consumers—we are what we buy."[25] In addition, public spheres are replaced by commercial spheres, as the substance of critical democracy is emptied out and replaced by a democracy of goods and the increasing expansion of the cultural and political power of corporations throughout the world.

Accountable only to the bottom-line of profitability, corporate culture has signaled a radical shift in the notion of public culture, the meaning of citizenship, and the defense of the public good. For example, the rapid resurgence of corporate power in the last 20 years and the attendant reorientation of culture to the demands of commerce and deregulation have substituted the language of personal responsibility and private initiative for the discourses of social responsibility and public service. This can be seen in the enactment of government policies designed to dismantle state protections for the poor, the environment, working people, and people of color.[26] This includes not only President George W. Bush's proposed welfare bill, which imposes harsh working requirements on the poor without the benefits of child care subsidies, but also the dismantling of race-based programs such as the "California Civil Rights Initiative" and the landmark affirmative-action case, *Hopwood vs. Texas,* both designed to eliminate affirmative action in higher education; the reduction of federal monies for urban development, such as HUD's housing program; the weakening of federal legislation to protect the environment; and a massive increase in state funds for building prisons at the expense of funding for public higher education.[27] According to Terrance Ball, corporate culture rests on a dystopic notion of what he calls "marketopia" and is characterized by a massive violation of equity and justice. He argues that the main shortcoming of marketopia is its massive and systematic violation of a fundamental sense of fairness. Marketopians who cannot afford health care, education, police protection, and other of life's necessities are denied a fair (or even minimally sufficient) share of social goods. Indeed, they are destitute of every good, excluded from a just share of society's benefits and advantages, pushed to the margins, rendered invisible. They are excluded because they lack the resources to purchase goods and services that ought to be theirs by right.[28]

As a result of the corporate takeover of public life, the maintenance of democratic public spheres from which to launch a moral vision loses all relevance. State and civil society are limited in their ability to impose or make corporate power accountable. As a result, politics as an expression of democratic struggle is deflated, and it becomes more difficult, if not impossible, to address pressing social and moral issues in systemic and political terms. This is a hazardous turn in American society, one that both threatens our understanding of democracy as fundamental to our freedom and the ways in which we address the meaning and purpose of public and higher education.

Unchecked by traditional forms of state power and removed from any sense of place-based allegiance, neoliberal capitalism appears more detached than ever from traditional forms of political power and ethical considerations. Public-sector activities such as transportation (in spite of the recent Amtrak bailout, which is an exception to the rule), health care, and education are no longer safeguarded from incursions by the buying-and-selling logic of the market. The consequences are evident everywhere, as the language of the corporate commercial paradigm describes doctors and nurses as "selling" medical services, students as customers, admitting college students as "closing a deal," and university presidents as CEOs.[29] But there is more at stake here than simply the commodification of language. There is, as Pierre Bourdieu has argued, the emergence of a Darwinian world marked by the progressive removal of autonomous spheres of cultural production such as journalism, publishing, and film; the destruction of collective structures capable of counteracting the widespread imposition of commercial values and the effects of the pure market; the creation of a

global reserve army of the unemployed and the subordination of nation-states to the real masters of the economy. Bourdieu is worth quoting at length on the effects of this dystopian world of neoliberalism:

> First is the destruction of all the collective institutions capable of
> counteracting the effects of the infernal machine, primarily those of
> the state, repository of all of the universal values associated with the
> idea of the public realm. Second is the imposition everywhere, in the
> upper spheres of the economy . . . of that sort of moral Darwinism
> that, with the cult of the winner, schooled in higher mathematics and
> bungee jumping, institutes the struggle of all against all and cynicism
> as the norm of all action and behaviour.[30]

I am not suggesting that market institutions and investments cannot
at times serve the public good, but rather that in the absence of vibrant, democratic public spheres, corporate power, when left on its
own, appears to respect few boundaries based on self-restraint and the
public good, and is increasingly unresponsive to those broader
human values that are central to a democratic civic culture. I believe
that at this point in American history, neoliberal capitalism is not simply too overpowering, but that "democracy is too weak."[31] Hence, the
increasing influence of money over politics, corporate interests overriding public concerns, and the growing tyranny of unchecked corporate power and avarice. Increasing evidence of the shameless
greed-is-good mantra is not limited to films such as *Wall Street,* but can
also be found in the corruption and scandals that have rocked giant
corporations such as Enron, WorldCom, Xerox, Tyco, Wal-Mart, and
Adelphia. The fallout suggests a widening crisis of confidence in U. S.
economic leadership in the world, reflected in the comments of
Guido Rossi, a former Italian Telecom chairman, who points out that
"What is lacking in the U.S. is a culture of shame. No C.E.O. in the
U.S. is considered a thief if he does something wrong. It is a kind of
moral cancer."[32] Clearly, there is more at stake in this crisis than simply the greed of a few high-profile CEOs. More importantly, there is
the historic challenge of neoliberalism and market fundamentalism to
how we think about the meaning of democracy, citizenship, social justice, and civic education.

Struggling for democracy is both a political and educational task. Fundamental to the health of a vibrant democratic culture is the recognition that education must be treated as a public good—a crucial site where students gain a public voice and come to grips with their own power as individual and social agents. Public and higher education cannot be viewed merely as sites for commercial investment or for affirming a notion of the private good based exclusively on the fulfillment of individual needs. Reducing higher education to the handmaiden of corporate culture works against the critical social imperative of educating citizens who can sustain and develop inclusive democratic public spheres. A long tradition extending from Thomas Jefferson to John Dewey and C. Wright Mills extols the importance of education as essential for a democratic public life. For example, Sheila Slaughter has argued persuasively that at the close of the nineteenth century, "professors made it clear that they did not want to be part of a cutthroat capitalism. . . . Instead, they tried to create a space between capital and labor where [they] could support a common intellectual project directed toward the public good."[33] Amherst College president Alexander Meiklejohn echoed this sentiment in 1916 when he suggested:

> insofar as a society is dominated by the attitudes of competitive business enterprise, freedom in its proper American meaning cannot be known, and hence, cannot be taught. That is the basic reason why the schools and colleges, which are presumably commissioned to study and promote the ways of freedom, are so weak, so confused, so ineffectual.[34]

The legacy of public discourse appears to have faded as the American university reinvents itself by giving in to the demands of the marketplace. Venture capitalists now scour colleges and universities in search of ways to make big profits through licensing agreements, the control of intellectual property rights, and promoting and investing in university spinoff companies.[35] In the age of money and profit, academic disciplines gain stature almost exclusively through their exchange value on the market, and students now rush to take courses and receive professional credentials that provide them with the cache they need to sell themselves to the highest bidder. Michael M. Crow, president of Arizona State University, echoes this shift in the role of higher education by proclaiming, without irony, that professors should be labeled as "academic entrepreneurs." In light of his view of the role of academic labor, it is not surprising that he sees knowledge strictly as a form of financial capital. He states, "We are expanding what it means to be a knowledge enterprise. We use knowledge as a form of venture capital."[36]

As the line between for-profit and not-for-profit institutions of higher education collapses, educator John Palattela observes that many "schools now serve as personnel offices for corporations"[37] and quickly dispense with the historically burdened though important promise of creating vibrant forms of democratic higher education. Not surprisingly, students are now referred to as "customers," while faculty are defined less through their scholarship than through their ability to secure funds and grants from foundations, corporations, and other external sources. Instead of concentrating on critical teaching "that prepares citizens for active participation in a democratic society"[38] and research aimed at promoting the public good, faculty are now urged to focus on corporate largesse. Rather than being esteemed as engaged teachers and rigorous researchers, faculty are now valued as multinational operatives and increasingly reduced to contract employees.[39]

Such rhetoric reflects a fundamental shift in how we think about the relationship between corporate culture and democracy.[40] I want to argue that one of the most important indications of such a change can be seen in the ways in which educators are currently being asked to rethink the role of higher education. Underlying this analysis is the assumption that the struggle to reclaim higher education must be seen as part of a broader battle over the defense of public goods, and that at the heart of such a struggle is the need to challenge the ever-growing discourse and influence of neoliberalism, corporate power, and corporate politics. I also want to offer some suggestions as to what educators can do to reassert the primacy of higher education as an essential sphere for expanding and deepening the processes of democracy and civil society.

Incorporating Higher Education

The current debate over the reform of higher education appears indifferent both to the historic function of the American university and to the broader ideological, economic, and political issues that have shaped it. Against the encroaching demands of a market-driven logic, a number of educators have argued forcefully that higher education should be defended as both a public good and as an autonomous sphere for the development of a critical and productive democratic citizenry.[41] Higher education, for many educators, is a central site for keeping alive the tension between market values and those values representative of civil society that cannot be measured in narrow commercial terms but are crucial to an inclusive democracy. Key to defending the university as a public good and an institution of critical learning is the recognition that education must not be confused with training—suggesting all the more that educators prevent commercial values from shaping the purpose and mission of higher education. Richard Hofstadter, the renowned American historian, understood the threat that corporate values posed to education, and once argued that the best reason for supporting higher education "lies not in the services they perform . . . but in the values they represent."[42] For Hofstadter, it was the values of justice, freedom, equality, and the rights of citizens as equal and free human beings that were at the heart of higher education's role in educating students for the demands of leadership, social citizenship, and democratic public life.

The ascendancy of corporate culture in all facets of American life has tended to uproot the legacy of democratic concerns and rights that has historically defined the mission of higher education.[43] Moreover, the growing influence of corporate culture on university life in the United States has served largely to undermine the distinction between higher education and business that educators such as Hofstadter wanted to preserve. As universities become increasingly strapped for money, corporations are more than willing to provide the needed resources—but with strings attached. The consequences are troubling: Corporations increasingly dictate the very research they sponsor, and in some universities, such as the University of California at Berkeley, business representatives are actually appointed to sit on faculty committees that determine how research funds are to be spent and allocated. Equally disturbing is the emergence of a number of academics who either hold stocks or other financial incentives in the companies sponsoring their research. As the boundaries between public and commercial values become blurred, many academics appear less as disinterested truth seekers than as operatives for business interests.

But there is more at stake than academics selling out to the highest corporate bidder. In some cases, academic research is compromised, and corporations routinely censor research results that are at odds with their commercial interests. For instance, Eyal Press and Jennifer Washburn reported that in "a 1996 study published in the *Annals of Internal Medicine* . . . a senior research scholar at Stanford's Center for Biomedical Ethics, . . . Mildred Cho, found that 98 percent of papers based on industry-sponsored research reflected favorably on the drugs being examined, as compared with 79 percent of papers based on research not funded by the industry."[44] Press and Washburn also provide examples of companies that have censored corporate sponsored research papers by removing passages that highlighted unfavorable results or negative outcomes.[45] More recently, a study reported in *The New England Journal of Medicine* revealed that medical schools that conduct research sponsored by drug companies routinely disregard established guidelines intended to ensure that the research is unbiased, limit access to such research, and often suppress the publication of those studies whose data questions the effectiveness of the wares. For example, the drug company Apotex attempted to suppress the findings of a University of Toronto researcher, Dr. Nancy Olivieri, when she produced findings in which she argued that the "drug the company was manufacturing was ineffective, and could even be toxic."[46]

It gets worse. As large amounts of corporate capital flow into the universities, those areas of study that don't translate into substantial profits get marginalized, underfunded, or eliminated. Hence, we are witnessing both a downsizing in the humanities as well as the increasing refusal on the part of universities to fund research in academic fields such as public health or science that place a high priority on public service and largely affect people who can't pay for such services. The new corporate university appears to be indifferent to ideas, forms of learning, and modes of research that do not have any commercial value. For example, professor Patricia Brodsky tells the story of an enterprising dean at the University of Missouri at Kansas City who instructed the faculty of the department of foreign languages and literatures that he wanted them to offer a series of beginning language courses in German and Spanish. To save money, he proposed that the courses be taught by computer in the language laboratory rather than in a classroom by a traditional teacher. The word spread quickly among the students that the course was an easy way to get 10 hours' credit, and at one point over 500 students enrolled in first and second semester Spanish. There were only two part-time instructors to handle these students, and their role was limited to performing the technical task of assigning grades produced by computer-generated exams. It soon became clear that the computer-driven course was a disaster. As Brodsky points out:

> The method employed was totally passive. Students didn't speak at all and rarely wrote. They looked at pictures and listened to voices say words and sentences. Nor were any grammatical concepts presented. Exercises were not interactive, nor did they take advantage of other possibilities offered by computer technology. The only plus for the students was that they didn't have to show up for class at regularly scheduled times. The problems worsened when students attempted to transfer from these courses into the mainstream curriculum at the third semester level, for they had learned virtually nothing. This caused havoc for instructors in the third semester courses as well as hardship for the students. Their graduation dates sometimes had to be delayed, and they were justifiably angry at having wasted their time and money. It also necessitated our teaching additional remedial courses so that the students could fulfill their requirement.[47]

From the dean's perspective the course was a great success, in that he only had to pay the salaries of two part-time faculty to run the course while a huge number of students paid regular full tuition for each five-hour course. When the faculty voted to cancel the course because of its obvious problems and failures, the dean responded by claiming the faculty didn't know how to teach, and continued the courses by offering them under a different program. In this instance, profit, control, and efficiency—all hallmark values of the neoliberal corporate ethic—far outweighed any other consideration about the value of such a pedagogical approach and the role of the faculty in maintaining some control over how and what they teach.

In the neoliberal era of deregulation and the triumph of the market, many students and their families no longer believe that higher education is about higher learning, but about gaining a better foothold in the job market. Colleges and universities are perceived—and perceive themselves—as training grounds for corporate berths. Professor Jeff Williams goes even further by arguing that universities have become licensed storefronts for brand-name corporations. He writes:

> Universities are now being conscripted as a latter kind of franchise, directly as training grounds for the corporate workforce; this is most obvious in the growth of business departments but impacts English, too, in the proliferation of more "practical" degrees in technical writing and the like. In fact, not only has university work been redirected to serve corporate-profit agendas via its grant-supplicant status, but universities have become franchises in their own right, reconfigured according to corporate management, labor, and consumer models and delivering a name brand product. Related to this, many corporations have been getting into the education business for themselves, as evidenced by Motorola University or the University of Phoenix.[48]

The "brand naming" of the university is also evident in the increasing number of endowed chairs funded by major corporations and rich corporate donors. For example, at the University of Oregon, Nike CEO Phil Knight has donated $15 million to the creation of a number of endowed chairs across the campus, seven of which have been established, including the Knight Chair for University Librarian and a Knight Chair for the dean of the School of Law. The Knight Chair endowment, coupled with matching contributions, is "expected to eventually support at least 30 new endowed chairs."[49] In addition, the Knight family name will also appear on a new law school building, the William W. Knight Law Center, named after Phil Knight's father. The Lego company not only endowed a chair at the MIT Media Laboratory, it also funds a $5-million LEGO Learning Lab. Academic titles not only signal wealthy corporate donors' influence on universities; such titles also serve as billboards for corporations. Some of the more well known include: the General Mills Chair of Cereal Chemistry and Technology at the University of Minnesota; Stanford University's Yahoo! Chair of Information Management Systems; Wayne State University's Kmart's

Chair of Marketing; and the University of Memphis's FedEx Chair of Information-Management Systems.

But corporate funding of endowed chairs does more for corporations than provide them with academic billboards, it also provides an opportunity in some instances to play a significant role in selecting a faculty member to assume the position created in order to influence what kind of research actually takes place. For instance, Kmart approved the appointment of J. Patrick Kelly for its chair at Wayne State University. Kelly worked for years on joint projects with Kmart and, not surprisingly, once he occupied the chair, engaged in research projects that benefited Kmart by saving the company millions of dollars. In response to criticisms of his role as a Kmart researcher, Kelly argues in an article in *The Chronicle of Higher Education* that "Kmart's attitude always has been: What did we get from you this year? Some professors would say they don't like that position, but for me, it's kept me involved with a major retailer, and it's been a good thing." Kmart defends their influence over the chair by claiming "We continue to use Dr. Kelly for consulting as well as training. It's certainly an investment, and one that we do tap into."[50] The tragedy here is not simply that Kelly defines himself less as an independent researcher and critical educator than as a Kmart employee, but that he seems to have no clue whatsoever about the implications of this type of encroachment by corporate power and values upon academic freedom, responsible scholarly research, or faculty governance.

In the name of efficiency, educational consultants all over the United States advise their schools to act like corporations selling products and seek "market niches" to save themselves. The increased traffic between the world of venture capitalism and higher education is captured in an issue of *The Chronicle of Higher Education*.[51] Goldie Blumstyk, a *Chronicle* reporter, followed business consultant and venture capitalist Jonah Schnel of ITU Ventures for four days between southern California and Pittsburgh, Pennsylvania. In the course of his travels, Schnel met with deans and a number of promising professors at both UCLA and Carnegie-Mellon University in order to explore the possibility of creating spinoff companies capable of producing lucrative profits both for involved faculty and the university. Within this kind of commercialized education, the lure of profit is the only thing that seems to matter. Research projects are discussed not in terms of their contribution to the public good or for their potential intellectual break-throughs, but for what they produce and the potential profits they may make in the commercial sector.

The consequences of transforming university research into a com-mercially driven enterprise can be seen most clearly in the profitable bioscience and pharmaceutical industries. As educator David Trend points out, "the overwhelming majority of research investment [in the pharmaceutical industry] has gone not to saving the lives of millions of people in the developing world, but to what have been called 'lifestyle drugs' [which treat] such maladies as impotence, obesity, baldness and wrinkles. . . . [Even though] malaria, tuberculosis, and respiratory in-fections killed 6.1 million people last year,"[52] research investment for finding new drugs to combat these diseases is minuscule. While phar-maceutical companies will spend over $24 billion in research working with universities to develop high-profit drugs such as Viagra, only $2 billion will be spent on drugs used to combat deadly diseases such as malaria, even though the disease in the next 20 years is expected to kill over 40 million Africans alone.[53]

Within this corporatized regime, management models of decision-making replace faculty governance. Once constrained by the concept of "shared" governance, in the past decade administrations have taken more power and reduced faculty-controlled governance institutions to advisory status. Given the narrow nature of corporate concerns, it is not surprising that when matters of accountability become part of the language of school reform, they are divorced from broader considera-tions of social responsibility. As corporate culture and values shape uni-versity life, corporate planning replaces social planning, management becomes a substitute for leadership, and the private domain of indi-vidual achievement replaces the discourse of public politics and social responsibility. As the power of higher education is reduced in its abil-ity to make corporate power accountable, it becomes more difficult within the logic of the bottom line for faculty, students, and adminis-trators to address pressing social and ethical issues.[54] This suggests a perilous turn in American society, one that threatens our understand-ing of democracy as fundamental to our basic rights and freedoms, as well as the ways in which we can rethink and re-appropriate the mean-ing, purpose, and future of higher education.

Higher Education, Corporate Leadership, and the Rise of the Academic Manager

As corporate governance becomes a central feature of U.S. higher education, leadership is being transformed to model corporate culture. In a widely read article, "It's Lowly at the Top: What Became of the Great College Presidents," Jay Mathews argues that it has become increasingly difficult to find models of academic leadership in higher education that emulate the great college presidents of the past, many of whom played an esteemed and pronounced role in the drama of intellectual and political life. Pointing to such national luminaries as Charles Eliot, James Conant, Robert M. Hutchins, Theodore Hesburgh, Clark Kerr, and more recently Kingman Brewster, Mathews argues that the latter were powerful intellectuals whose ideas and publications provoked national debates, shaped public policy, and contributed to the intellectual culture of their respective universities and society as a whole. Leadership has taken a different turn under the model of the corporate university. Mathews argues, and rightly so, that today's college presidents are known less for their intellectual leadership than for their role "as fundraisers and ribbon cutters and coat holders, filling a slot rather than changing the world."[55]

Academic administrators today do not have to display intellectual reach and civic courage. Instead, they are expected to bridge the world of academe and business. Sought after by professional headhunters who want candidates who are both safe and "most likely to shine in corporate boardrooms,"[56] the new breed of university presidents is characterized less by their ability to take risks, think critically, engage important progressive social issues, and provoke national debates than they are for raising money, producing media-grabbing public relations, and looking good for photo shoots. As reported in *USA Today*, "more and more colleges and universities are hiring presidents straight from the business world."[57] To prove the point, the article provided three high profile examples: Babson College named a Wall Street veteran as its president; Bowdoin College gave the job to a corporate lawyer; and, in the most famous case of all, Harvard University picked as its president former treasury secretary Lawrence Summers. Though the neoliberal Summers seems to be equally concerned with engaging ideas and asking unsettling questions as with the more mundane task of fundraising,[58] the overt corporatization of university leadership makes clear that what was once part of the hidden curriculum of higher education—the creeping vocationalization and subordination of learning to the dictates of the market—has become an open and defining principle of education at all levels.[59]

With the U.S. recession and in the aftermath of the terrorist attacks of September 11, 2001, many colleges and universities are experiencing financial hard times. These events have exacerbated a downturn in economic conditions brought on by the end of the Cold War, coupled with a sharp reduction of state aid to higher education. As a result, many colleges and universities are all too happy to allow corporate leaders to run their institutions, form business partnerships, establish cushy relationships with business-oriented legislators, and develop curricular programs tailored to the needs of corporate interests.[60] Of course, I am not suggesting that corporate funding is any less reprehensible than military funding but I am noting how the changing nature of how universities finance themselves underscores their growing reliance on corporate models of leadership. One crucial example of this is the increasing willingness on the part of legislators, government representatives, and higher education officials to rely on corporate leaders to establish the terms of the debate in the media regarding the meaning and purpose of higher education. Bill Gates, Jack Welch, Michael Milken, Warren Buffet, and other members of the Fortune 500 "club" continue to be viewed as educational prophets—in spite of the smirched reputation of former CEOs such as Kenneth Lay of Enron, Al Dunlap of Sunbeam, and Dennis Kozlowski of Tyco.[61] And yet, the only qualifications they seem to have is that they have been successful in accumulating huge amounts of money for themselves and their shareholders, while at the same time laying off thousands of workers in order to cut costs and raise profits. While Gates, Milken, and others couch their statements about education in the rhetoric of public service, corporate organizations such as the Committee for Economic Development, an organization of about 250 corporations, have been more blunt about their interest in education.[62] Not only has the group argued that social goals and services get in the way of learning basic skills, but also that many employers in the business community feel dissatisfied because "a large majority of their new hires lack adequate writing and problem-solving skills."[63] Such skills are championed not because they form the basis of literacy itself, but because without them workers do not perform well.

Matters of leadership and accountability within neoliberalism and corporate culture in general rarely include broader considerations of ethics, equity, and justice, and it is precisely this element of market fundamentalism that corporate leaders often bring with them to academic leadership roles. Corporate culture lacks a vision beyond its own pragmatic interests and seldom is self-critical about its own ideology and its effects on society. It is difficult to imagine such concerns arising within corporations where questions of consequence begin and end with the bottom line. For instance, it is clear that neoliberalism, in it is drive to create wealth for a limited few, has no incentives for taking care of basic social needs. This is obvious not only in its attempts to render the welfare state obsolete, privatize all public goods, and destroy traditional state-provided safety nets, but also in its disregard for the environment, misallocation of resources between the private and public sectors, and relentless pursuit of profits. It is precisely this lack of emphasis on being a public servant and an academic citizen that is lacking from the leadership models that corporate executives transfer to their roles as academic administrators. Unfortunately, it often pays off—financially, that is.

As market-fund mogul George Soros has pointed out, neoliberalism represents a kind of market fundamentalism based on the untrammeled pursuit of self-interest—often wrapped up in the post–September 11 language of patriotism. The distinguishing feature of market fundamentalism are that "morality does not enter into [its] calculations" and it does not necessarily serve the common interest, nor is it capable of taking care of collective needs and ensuring social justice.[64] It is highly unlikely that corporations such as Disney, IBM, or General Motors will seriously address the political and social consequences of the policies they implement, which have resulted in downsizing, deindustrialization, and the "trend toward more low-paid, temporary, benefit-free, blue- and white-collar jobs and fewer decent permanent factory and office jobs."[65] Clearly, the interests served by such changes, as well as the consequences they have for working people, immigrants, and others, detract from those democratic arenas that business seeks to "restructure." Mega-corporations will say nothing about their profound role in promoting the flight of capital abroad; the widening gap between intellectual, technical, and manual labor; the growing class of those permanently under-employed in a mass of "de-skilled" jobs; the increasing inequality between the rich and the poor; or the scandalous use of child labor in Third World countries. Nor will they say anything critical about the control of the media by a handful of corporations and the effects of this concentration of power in undermining an effective system of political communication, which is crucial to creating an informed and engaged citizenry.[66] Rather, the onus of responsibility is placed on educated citizens to recognize that corporate principles of efficiency, accountability, and profit maximization have not created new jobs but in most cases have eliminated them.[67] It is their responsibility to recognize that the world presented to them through allegedly objective reporting is mediated—and manipulated by—a handful of global media industries run by moguls such as Rupert Murdoch and Michael Eisner. My point, of course, is that such omissions in public discourse constitute a defining principal of corporate ideology, which refuses to address—but must be made to address—the absence of moral vision in such calls for educational reform modeled after corporate management and ideology.

In the corporate model, knowledge is privileged as a form of investment in the economy, but appears to have little value in terms of self-definition, social responsibility, or the capacities of individuals to expand the scope of freedom, justice, and democracy.[68] Stripped of ethical and political considerations, knowledge offers limited, if any, insights into how schools should educate students to push against the oppressive boundaries of gender, class, race, and age domination. Nor does such a corporate language provide the pedagogical conditions for students to critically engage school knowledge as an ideology deeply implicated in issues and struggles concerning the production of identities, culture, power, and history. Education is a moral and political practice, and always presupposes an introduction to and preparation for particular forms of social life, a particular rendering of what community is, and an idea of what the future might hold.

If higher education is, in part, about the production of knowledge, values, and identities, then curricula modeled after corporate culture have been enormously successful in preparing students for low-skilled service jobs in a society that has little to offer in the way of meaningful employment for the vast majority of its graduates. If CEOs are going to provide some insight into how education should be reformed, they will have to reverse their tendency to collapse the boundaries between corporate culture and civic culture, between a society that defines itself by the interests of corporate power and one that defines itself through more democratic considerations, such as substantive citizenship and social responsibility. Moreover, they will have to recognize that the problems with American schools cannot be reduced to matters of accountability or cost-effectiveness. Nor can the solution to such problems be reduced to the spheres of management, economics, and technological quick fixes such as Distance Education, which offers academic courses on-line. The problems of higher education must be addressed in terms of values and politics, while engaging critically the most fundamental beliefs Americans have as a nation regarding the meaning and purpose of education and its relationship to democracy.

Corporate Culture's Threat to Faculty and Students

As universities increasingly model themselves after corporations, it becomes crucial to understand how the principles of corporate culture have altered the meaning and purpose of the university, the role of knowledge production in the twenty-first century, and the social practices inscribed within teacher-student relationships. The signs are not encouraging. In many ways, the cost accounting principles of efficiency, calculability, predictability, and control of the corporate order have restructured the meaning and purpose of education. With the never-ending search for new sources of revenue, the intense competition for more students, and the ongoing need to cut costs, many colleges and university presidents are actively pursuing ways to establish closer ties between their institutions and the business community. For example, *USA Today* approvingly reports that Brian Barefoot, the new president of Babson College, has 30 years of experience at PaineWebber and Merrill Lynch and will "use his business contacts to get graduates jobs, and he'll make sure the curriculum reflects employer needs."[69] The message here is clear. Knowledge with a high market value is what counts, while those fields, such as the liberal arts and humanities, that cannot be quantified in such terms will either be underfunded or allowed to become largely irrelevant in the hierarchy of academic knowledge. Moreover, those professors who are rewarded for bringing in outside money will be more heavily represented in fields such as science and engineering, which attract corporate and government research funding. As Sheila Slaughter observes, "Professors in fields other than science and engineering who attract funds usually do so from foundations which account for a relatively small proportion of overall research funding."[70]

In other quarters of higher education, the results of the emergence of the corporate university appear even more ominous. One telling example took place in 1998 when James Carlin, a multimillionaire and former successful insurance executive who had been appointed as the chairman of the Massachusetts State Board of Education, gave a speech to the Greater Boston Chamber of Commerce.[71] Signaling corporate culture's dislike of organized labor and its obsession with cost cutting, Carlin launched a four-fold attack against the academic professoriate. First, he argued that higher education has to model itself after successful corporations, and this means that colleges and universities have to be downsized. Second, he echoed the now familiar call on the part of corporate culture to abolish tenure. Third, he made it clear that democratic governance was not in keeping with the corporate model of the university and that faculty have too much power in shaping decisions in the university. Finally, he explicitly condemned those forms of knowledge whose value lie outside of their practical application in the marketplace. More specifically, Carlin argued that "at least 50 percent of all non-hard sciences research on American campuses is a lot of foolishness" and should be banned.[72] He further predicted that "there's going to be a revolution in higher education. Whether you like it or not, it's going to be broken apart and put back together differently. It won't be the same. Why should it be? Why should everything change except for higher education?"[73] Carlin's "revolution" was spelled out in his call for increasing the workload of professors to four three-credit courses a semester, effectively reducing the time educators might have to do research or shape institutional power.

There is more at stake in university reform than the principles of profit-making and the harsh realities of cost cutting. Neoliberalism, fueled by its unwavering belief in market values and the unyielding logic of corporate profit-making, has little patience with non-commodified knowledge or with the more lofty ideals that have defined higher education as a public service. Carlin's anti-intellectualism and animosity toward educators and students alike is simply a more extreme example of the forces at work in the corporate world that would like to take advantage of the profits to be made in higher education, while simultaneously refashioning colleges and universities in the image of the new multinational conglomerate landscape. Missing from the corporate model is the recognition that academic freedom implies that knowledge has a critical function; that intellectual inquiry that is unpopular and critical should be safeguarded and treated as an important social asset; and that faculty in higher education are more than merely functionaries of the corporate order. Such ideals are at odds with the vocational function that corporate culture wants to assign to higher education.

While the idea of downsizing higher education appears to have caught the public's imagination at the moment, it belies the fact that such "reorganization" has been going on for some time. In fact, more professors are working part-time and at two-year community colleges than at any other time in the country's recent history. A 2001 report by the National Study of Postsecondary Faculty recently pointed out that "in 1998–1999, less than one-third of all faculty members were tenured . . . [and that] in 1992–1993, 40 percent of the faculty was classified as part-time and in 1998–99, the share had risen to 45 percent."[74] Creating a permanent underclass of part-time professional workers in higher education is not only demoralizing and exploitative for many faculty who have such jobs, it also increasingly de-skills both part- and full-time faculty by increasing the amount of work they have to do. With less time to prepare, larger class loads, almost no time for research, and excessive grading demands, many adjuncts run the risk of becoming either demoralized, ineffective, or both. Michael Dubson, writing as an adjunct, captures the situation in the following comments:

I am an adjunct. . . . I bought the bag of lies we call the American Dream. I was intoxicated on the Nitrous Oxide idealism forced upon me in graduate school. I believed caring, working hard, doing a good job mattered and would add up to something concrete. Instead, I find myself on a wheel that turns but goes nowhere. I don't expect this situation to change. I know I have joined the huge group of teachers who become permanent adjuncts, who do a good job only to get one more chance to do it again. . . . I have watched my self-esteem drop, drop, drop from doing work that is, theoretically, enhancing the self-esteem of my students. I have seen the tired eyes, the worn clothes, the ancient eyes of long-term adjuncts. I have looked into their eyes as they have failed to look back into mine. . . . I have known thirty-year-old men living at home with their parents, forty-year-old women teaching college and going hungry, uninsured fifty-year-olds with serious illnesses. I have known adjunct teachers who hand out As and Bs like vitamins and help students cheat on their exams so they'll get good course evaluations. . . . I am a dreamer. I am an idealist. I am a victim. I am a whore. I am a fool. I am an adjunct.[75]

There is more at work here than despair; there are the harsh lessons of financial deprivation, overburdened work loads, and powerlessness. As power shifts away from the faculty to the managerial sectors of the university, adjunct faculty increase in number while effectively being removed from the faculty governance process. In short, the hiring of part-time faculty to minimize costs simultaneously maximizes managerial control over faculty and the educational process itself. As their ranks are depleted, full-time faculty live under the constant threat of being either given heavier work loads or of simply having their tenure contracts eliminated or drastically redefined through "post-tenure reviews." These structural and ideological factors send a chill through higher education faculty and undermine the collective power faculty need to challenge the increasing corporate-based, top-down administrative structures that are becoming commonplace in many colleges and universities.

The turn to downsizing and de-skilling faculty is also exacerbated by the attempts on the part of many universities to expand into the profitable market of distance education, whose on-line courses now reach thousands of students. Such a market is all the more lucrative since it is being underwritten by the combined armed services, which in August of 2000 pledged almost $1 billion to "provide taxpayer-subsidized university-based distance education for active-duty personnel and their families."[76] David Noble has written extensively on the restructuring of higher education under the imperatives of the new digital technologies and the move into distance education. If he is correct, the news is not good. According to Noble, on-line learning largely functions through pedagogical models and methods of delivery that not only rely on standardized, pre-packaged curricula and methodological efficiency, they also reinforce the commercial penchant towards training, de-skilling, and de-professionalization. With the de-skilling of the professoriate, there will also be a rise in the use of part-time faculty, who will be "perfectly suited to the investor-imagined university of the future."[77] According to Noble, the growing influence of these ideological and methodological tendencies in higher education will be exacerbated by the powerful influence of the military.[78] As Noble observes, an education subsidized by the military

> is likely to entail familiar patterns of command, control, and precisely specified performance, in accordance with the hallmark military procurement principles of uniformity, standardization, modularization, capital intensiveness, system compatibility, interchangeability, measurability, and accountability—in short, *a model of education as a machine,* with standardized products and prescribed processes.[79] [my emphasis]

Columbia University's Teacher College President Arthur Levine has predicted that the new information technology may soon make the traditional college and university obsolete. He is hardly alone in believing that on-line education will either radically alter or replace traditional education. As journalists Eyal Press and Jennifer Washburn point out, "In recent years academic institutions and a growing number of Internet companies have been racing to tap into the booming market in virtual learning, which financial analysts like Merrill Lynch estimate will reach $7 billion by 2003."[80] The marriage of corporate culture, higher education, and the new high-speed technologies also offers universities big opportunities to cut back on maintenance expenses, eliminate entire buildings such as libraries and classrooms, and trim labor costs. Education scholars William Massy and Robert Zemsky make the latter point clear in their claim that universities must take advantage of the new technologies to cut back on teaching expenditures. As they put it, "With labor accounting for 70 percent or more of current operating cost, there is simply no other way."[81]

Reporting on the coming restructuring of the university around on-line and distance education, the *Chronicle of Higher Education* claims that this new type of education will produce a new breed of faculty, "who hails not from academia but from the corporate world." Hired more for their "business savvy than their degree, a focus on the bottom line is normal; tenure isn't." This alleged celebration of faculty as social entrepreneurs appears to offer no apologies for turning education into a commercial enterprise and teaching into a sales pitch for profits. As one enthusiastic distance educator put it for the *Chronicle,* "I love not only the teaching but the selling of it."[82]

Universities and colleges across the country are flocking to the on-line bandwagon. As Press and Washburn point out, "more than half of the nation's colleges and universities deliver some courses over the Internet."[83] Mass-marketed degrees and courses are not only being offered by prestigious universities such as Seton Hall, Stanford, Harvard, New School University, and the University of Chicago, they are also giving rise to cyber-backed colleges such as the Western Governors University, and for-profit, stand-alone virtual institutions such as the University of Phoenix. This is not to suggest that on-line distance education is the most important or only way in which computer-based technologies can be used in higher education, or that the new electronic technologies by default produce oppressive modes of pedagogy. Many educators use e-mail, networking, and the Internet in very productive ways for their classes. The real issue is whether such technology in its various pedagogical uses is narrowly appropriated as a mode of technocratic rationality that undermines human freedom and development. As Herbert Marcuse has argued, when the rationality that drives technology is instrumentalized and "transformed into standardized efficiency, . . . liberty is confined to the selection of the most adequate means for reaching a goal which [the individual] did not set."[84] The consequence of the substitution of technology for pedagogy is that instrumental goals replace ethical and political considerations, to the detriment of classroom control by teachers, and to the advantage of standardization and rationalization of course materials. Zygmunt Bauman underscores such a danger by arguing that when technology is coupled with calls for efficiency, modeled on instrumental rationality, it almost always leads to forms of social engineering that authorize actions that become increasingly "reasonable" and dehumanizing at the same time.[85] In other words, when the new computer technologies are tied to narrow forms of instrumental rationality, they serve as "moral sleeping pills" which are increasingly made available by corporate power and the modern bureaucracy of higher education.

The issue here is not only that the new computer technologies promote on-line pedagogical approaches such as distance education, and replace place-based, "real" education with limited forms of simulated and virtual exchanges, but that such technologies—when not shaped by ethical considerations, collective dialogue, and dialogical approaches—lose whatever possibilities they might have for linking education to critical thinking, and learning to democratic social change.[86] Under such conditions, the new technologies run the risk of contributing to an educational future marked by the increasing de-skilling of teachers, the growth in a reserve army of part-time instructors, and a dehumanizing pedagogy for students. In fact, when business values replace the imperatives of critical learning, a division based on social class begins to appear, in which poor and marginalized students will get low-cost, low-skilled knowledge and second-rate degrees from on-line sources, while those students being educated for leadership positions in the elite schools will be versed in personalized instruction and socially interactive pedagogies in which high-powered knowledge, critical thinking, and problem-solving will be a priority—coupled with a high status degree. Under such circumstances, traditional modes of class and racial tracking will be reinforced and updated in what David Noble calls "digital diploma mills."[87] Noble underemphasizes, in his otherwise excellent analysis, indications that the drive towards corporatizing the university will take its biggest toll on those second- and third-tier institutions that are increasingly defined as serving no other function than to train semi-skilled and obedient workers for the new post-industrialized order. The role slotted for these institutions is driven less by the imperatives of the new digital technologies than by the need to reproduce gender, racial, and class divisions of labor that support the neoliberal global market revolution and its relentless search for bigger profits.

Held up to the profit standard, universities and colleges will increasingly calibrate supply to demand, and the results look ominous with regard to what forms of knowledge, pedagogy, and research will be rewarded and legitimated. As colleges and corporations collaborate over the content of degree programs, particularly with regard to on-line graduate degree programs, college curricula run the risk of being narrowly tailored to the needs of specific businesses. For example, Babson College developed a master's degree program in business administration specifically for Intel workers. Similarly, the University of Texas at Austin is developing an on-line master of science degree in science, technology, and commercialization that caters only to students who work at IBM. Moreover, the program will orient its knowledge, skills, and research to focus exclusively on IBM projects.[88] Not only do such courses run the risk of becoming company training workshops, they also open up higher education to powerful corporate interests who have little regard for education as the cultivation of an informed, critical citizenry capable of actively participating in and governing a democratic society.

At the same time, while it is crucial to recognize the dangers inherent in on-line learning and the instructional use of information technology, it is also important to recognize that there are many thoughtful and intelligent people who harness such technologies in ways that can be progressively useful. Moreover, not everyone who uses these technologies can be simply dismissed as living in a middle-class world of techno-euphoria in which computers are viewed as the panacea for everything. Andrew Feenberg, a professor at San Diego State University and a former disciple of Herbert Marcuse, rejects the essentialist view that technology reduces everything to functions, efficiency, and raw materials, "while threatening both spiritual and material survival."[89] Feenberg argues that the use of technology in both higher education and other spheres has to be taken up as part of a larger project to expand democracy, and that under such conditions it can be used "to open up new possibilities for intervention."[90] By implication, many educators use e-mail, web resources, on-line discussion groups, and computer-based interaction to provide invaluable opportunities for students to gain access to new knowledge and enhance communication, dialogue, and learning. But with this caveat in mind, there is still the important question of how technology might be used to threaten the integrity of democratic education, identities, values, and institutions. This question returns us to some more critical considerations.

On-line courses also raise important issues about intellectual property—who owns the rights for course materials developed for on-line use. Because of the market potential of on-line lectures and course materials, various universities have attempted to lay ownership claims to such knowledge. The passing of the 1980 Bayh-Dole Act and the 1984 Public Law 98–620 by the United States Congress enabled "universities and professors to own patents on discoveries or inventions made as a result of federally supported research."[91] These laws accorded universities intellectual property rights, with specific rights to own, license, and sell their patents to firms for commercial profits. The results have been far from unproblematic.[92] Julia Porter Liebeskind, a professor at the Marshall School of Business, points to three specific areas of concern that are worth mentioning.

First, the growth of patenting by universities has provided a strong incentive "for researchers to pursue commercial projects," especially in light of the large profits that can be made by faculty.[93] For instance, five faculty members at the University of California system and an equal number at Stanford University in 1995 earned a total of $69 million in licensing income (fees and royalties). And while it is true that the probability for large profits for faculty is small, the possibility for high-powered financial rewards cannot be discounted in the shaping of the production of knowledge and research at the university.

Second, patenting agreements can place undue restraints on faculty, especially with respect to keeping their research secret and delaying publication, or even prohibiting "publication of research altogether if it is found to have commercial value."[94] Such secrecy not only undermines faculty collegiality and limits a faculty member's willingness to work with others; it can also damage faculty careers, and most importantly, prevent significant research from becoming part of the public intellectual commons.

Finally, the ongoing commercialization of research puts pressure on faculty to pursue research that can raise revenue, and poses a threat to faculty intellectual property rights. For example, at the University of California Los Angeles, an agreement was signed in 1994 that allowed an outside vender, on-lineLearning.net, to create and copyright on-line versions of UCLA courses. The agreement was eventually "amended in 1999 to allow professors' rights to the basic content of their courses . . . [but] under the amended contract, on-line Learning retain[ed] their right to market and distribute those courses on-line, which is the crux of the copyright dispute."[95]

The debate over intellectual property rights calls into question not only the increasing influence of neoliberal and corporate values on the university, but also the vital issue of academic freedom. As universities make more and more claims on owning the content of faculty notes, lectures, books, computer files, and media for classroom use, the first casualty is, as Ed Condren, a UCLA professor points out, "the legal protection that enables faculty to freely express their views without fear of censorship or appropriation of their ideas."[96] At the same time, by selling course property rights for a fee, universities infringe on the ownership rights of faculty members by removing them from any control over how their courses might be used in the public domain.

As globalization and corporate mergers increase, new technologies develop, and cost-effective practices expand, there will be fewer jobs for certain professionals—resulting in the inevitable elevation of admission standards, restriction of student loans, and the reduction of student access to higher education, particularly for those groups who are marginalized because of their class and race.[97] Fewer jobs in higher education means fewer students will be enrolled, but it also means that the processes of vocationalization—fueled by corporate values that mimic "flexibility," "competition," or "lean production," and rationalized through the application of accounting principles—threatens to gut many academic departments and programs that cannot translate their subject matter into commercial gains. Programs and courses that focus on areas such as critical theory, literature, feminism, ethics, environmentalism, post-colonialism, philosophy, and sociology involve an intellectual cosmopolitanism or a concern with social issues that will be either eliminated or cut back because their role in the market will be judged as ornamental. Similarly, those working conditions that allow professors and graduate assistants to comment extensively on student work, provide small seminars, spend time advising students, conduct independent studies, and do collaborative research with both faculty colleagues and students do not appear consistent with the imperatives of downsizing, efficiency, and cost accounting.[98]

Corporate culture's threat to students will include privatization as higher education joins hands with the corporate banking world. Lacking adequate financial aid, students, especially poor students, will increasingly finance the high costs of their education through private corporations such as Citibank, Chase Manhattan, Marine Midland, and other lenders. Given the huge debt such students accumulate, it is reasonable to assume, as Jeff Williams points out, that such loans "effectively indenture students for ten to twenty years after graduation and intractably [reduce] their career choices, funneling them into the corporate workforce in order to pay their loans."[99]

Of course, for many young people caught in the margins of poverty, low-paying jobs, and the recession, the potential costs of going on to higher education, regardless of its status or availability, will dissuade them from even thinking about the possibilities of going to college. Unfortunately, as state and federal agencies and university systems direct more and more of their resources (such as state tax credits and scholarship programs) towards middle- and upper-income students, the growing gap in college enrollments between high income students (95 percent enrollment rate) and low income students (75 percent enrollment rate) with comparable academic abilities will widen even further.[100] In fact, a recent report by a federal advisory committee claimed that nearly 48 percent of qualified students from low-income families will not be attending college in the fall of 2002 because of rising tuition charges and a shortfall in federal and state grants for low- and moderate-income students. The report claims that "Nearly 170,000 of the top high-school graduates from low- and moderate-income families are not enrolling in college this year because they cannot afford to do so."[101]

Those students who do go on to higher education will often find themselves in courses being taught by an increasing army of part-time and adjunct faculty. Given that personnel costs, "of which salaries and benefits for tenured faculty . . . typically account for 90 percent of operating budgets,"[102] university administrators are hiring more part-time faculty and depleting the ranks of tenured faculty. Applying rules taken directly from the cost-effective, downsizing strategies of industry, universities continuously attempt to cut costs, maximize their efficiency, and reduce the power of the professoriate by keeping salaries as low as possible, substituting part-time teaching positions for full-time posts, chipping away at or eliminating employee benefits, and threatening to restructure or get rid of tenure. Not only do such policies demoralize the full-time faculty, exploit part-time workers, and overwork teaching assistants, they also cheat students. Too many undergraduates find themselves in oversized classes taught by faculty who are overburdened by heavy teaching loads. Understandably, such faculty have little loyalty to the departments or universities in which they teach, rarely have the time to work collaboratively with other faculty or students, have almost no control over what they teach, and barely have the time to do the writing and research necessary to keep up with their fields of study. The result often demeans teachers' roles as intellectuals, proletarianizes their labor, and shortchanges the quality of education that students deserve.[103] Professor David L. Kirp suggests that hiring part-time workers is a form of outsourcing, "the academic equivalent of temp agency fill-ins," and as a practice undermines the intellectual culture and the academic energy of higher education.[104] He supports this charge by claiming:

> From a purely financial perspective, it's a no-brainer to outsource teaching, because it saves so much money. . . . But the true costs to higher education—even if hard to quantify—are very high. To rely on contract labor in the classroom creates a cadre of interchangeable instructors with no sustained responsibility for their students, scholars with no attachment to the intellectual life of the institution through which they are passing.[105]

Unfortunately, Kirp seems to suggest that the part-time workers are as deficient as the conditions that create them. It is one thing to be the victim of a system built on greed and scandalous labor practices, and another thing to take the heat for trying to make a living under such conditions—as if the quality of one's teaching can be measured simply by what takes place in the classroom. The real issue here is that such conditions are exploitative and that the solutions to fixing the problem lie not simply in hiring more full-time faculty, but, as Cary Nelson points out, in reforming "the entire complex of economic, social and political forces operating on higher education."[106]

Neoliberalism's obsession with spreading the gospel of the market and the values of corporate culture through privatization and commercialization has not only transformed the nature of educational leadership, the purpose of higher education, the work relations of faculty, the nature of what counts as legitimate knowledge, and the quality of pedagogy itself, it has also restructured those spaces and places in which students spend a great deal of time outside of classrooms. Increasingly, corporations are joining up with universities to privatize a seemingly endless array of services that universities handled by themselves at one time. University bookstores are now run by big corporate conglomerates such as Barnes & Noble, while companies such as Sodexho-Marriott (also a large investor in the U.S. private prison industry) run a large percentage of college dining halls, and McDonald's and Starbucks occupy prominent locations on the student commons. In addition, housing, alumni relations, health care, and a vast array of other services are now being leased out to private interests to manage and run. One consequence is that spaces once marked as public and non-commodified now have the appearance of shopping malls, as David Trend points out:

> student union buildings and cafeterias took on the appearance—or were conceptualized from the beginning—as shopping malls or food courts, as vendors competed to place university logos on caps, mugs, and credit cards. This is a larger pattern in what has been termed the "Disneyfication" of college life, . . . a pervasive impulse toward infotainment . . . where learning is "fun," the staff "perky," where consumer considerations dictate the curriculum, where presentation takes precedence over substance, and where students become "consumers."[107]

Commercial logos, billboards, and advertisements now plaster the walls of student centers, dining halls, cafeterias, and bookstores. Everywhere students turn outside of the university classroom, they are confronted with vendors and commercial sponsors who are hawking credit cards, athletic goods, Pepsi, and other commodities that one associates with the local shopping mall. Universities and colleges compound this marriage of commercial and educational values by signing exclusive contracts with Pepsi, Nike, Starbucks, and other contractors, further blurring the distinction between student and consumer. The message to students is clear: customer satisfaction is offered as a surrogate for learning and "to be a citizen is to be a consumer, and nothing more. Freedom means freedom to purchase."[108]

Colleges and universities do not simply produce knowledge and values for students, they also play an influential role in shaping their identities. If colleges and universities are to define themselves as centers of teaching and learning vital to the democratic life of the nation, they are going to have to acknowledge the real danger of becoming corporate, mere adjuncts to big business. At the very least, this demands that they exercise the political, civic, and ethical courage needed to refuse the commercial rewards that would reduce them to being simply another brand name or corporate logo.

Higher Education as a Democratic Public Sphere

Pierre Bourdieu has written that "What I defend above all is the possibility and the necessity of the critical intellectual. . . . There is no genuine democracy without genuine opposing critical powers."[109] Higher education should be viewed as a resource vital to the democratic and civic life of the nation against the current onslaught to corporatize higher education. But more importantly, higher education needs to be safeguarded as a public good against these ongoing attempts because, as Ellen Willis points out, the university "is the only institution of any size that still provides cultural dissidents with a platform."[110] Rather than being viewed as a source of profits in which curriculum becomes a product, students are treated as consumers, and faculty relegated to the status of contract employees,[111] higher education must be embraced as a democratic sphere because it is one of the few public spaces left where students can learn the power of questioning authority, recover the ideals of engaged citizenship, reaffirm the importance of the public good, and expand their capacities to make a difference.

188 / THE ABANDONED GENERATION

Central to such a task is the challenge to resist the university becoming what literary theorist Bill Readings has called a consumer-oriented corporation more concerned about accounting than accountability, and whose mission, defined largely through an appeal to excellence, is comprehended almost exclusively in terms of a purely instrumental efficiency.[112]

Higher education can be removed from its narrow instrumental justification by encouraging students to think beyond what its means simply to get a job or be an adroit consumer. Moreover, the crisis of higher education needs to be analyzed in terms of wider configurations of economic, political, and social forces that exacerbate tensions between those who value such institutions as public goods and those advocates of neoliberalism who see market culture as a master design for all human affairs. Educators must challenge all attempts on the part of conservatives and liberals to evacuate democracy of its substantive ideals by reducing it to the imperatives of hyper-capitalism and the glorification of financial markets. Moreover, as Jeff Williams points out, educators must "distinguish the university as a not-for-profit institution, which serves a public interest, from for-profit organizations, which by definition serve private interests and often conflict with public interests"; he goes on to suggest that they propose "new images or fictions of the university, to reclaim the ground of the public interest, and to promote a higher education operating in that public interest."[113]

Challenging the encroachment of corporate power is essential if democracy is to remain a defining principle of education and everyday life. Educators, students, and others must create organizations capable of mobilizing civic dialogue, provide an alternative conception of the meaning and purpose of higher education, and develop political organizations that can influence legislation to challenge corporate power's ascendancy over the institutions and mechanisms of civil society. In strategic terms, revitalizing public dialogue suggests that faculty, students, and administrators need to take seriously the importance of defending higher education as an institution of civic culture whose purpose is to educate students for active and critical citizenship.[114] To do so, educators, students, and others will have to provide the rationale and mobilize efforts toward creating enclaves of resistance, new public spaces to counter official forms of public pedagogy, and institutional spaces that highlight, nourish, and evaluate the tension between civil society and corporate power, while simultaneously struggling to prioritize citizen rights over consumer rights.

Situated within a broader context of issues concerned with social responsibility, politics, and the dignity of human life, higher education should be an institution that offers students the opportunity to involve themselves in the deepest problems of society and to acquire the knowledge, skills, and ethical vocabulary necessary for critical dialogue and broadened civic participation. This suggests developing pedagogical conditions for students to come to terms with their own sense of power and public voice as individual and social agents by enabling them to examine and frame critically what they learn in the classroom "within a more political or social or intellectual understanding of what's going on" in their lives and the world at large.[115] At the very least, students need to learn how to take responsibility for their own ideas, take intellectual risks, develop a sense of respect for others, and learn how to think critically in order to function in a wider democratic culture. At issue here is providing students with an education that allows them to recognize the dream and promise of a substantive democracy, particularly the idea that as citizens they are "entitled to public services, decent housing, safety, security, support during hard times, and most importantly, some power over decision making."[116]

But more is needed than defending higher education as a vital sphere in which to develop and nourish the proper balance between democratic values and market fundamentalism, between identities founded on democratic principles and identities steeped in forms of competitive, self-interested individualism that celebrate their own material and ideological advantages. Given the current assault by politicians, conservative foundations, and the right-wing media on educators who spoke critically about U.S. foreign policy in light of the tragic events of September 11, it is politically crucial that educators at all levels of involvement in the academy be defended as public intellectuals who provide an indispensable service to the nation. Such an appeal cannot be made in the name of professionalism, but in terms of the civic good such intellectuals provide. Too many academics have retreated into narrow specialties that serve largely to consolidate authority rather than critique its abuses. Refusing to take positions on controversial issues or to examine the role they might play in lessening human suffering, such academics become models of moral indifference and unfortunate examples of what it means to disconnect learning from public life. On the other hand, many left and liberal academics have retreated into arcane discourses that offer them mostly the safe ground of the professional recluse. Making almost no connections to audiences outside of the academy or to the issues that bear down on their lives, such academics have become largely irrelevant. This is not to suggest that they do not publish or speak at symposiums, but that they often do so to very limited audiences and in a language that is often overly abstract, highly aestheticized, rarely takes an overt political position, and seems quite indifferent to broader public issues. I am reminded of the story of one rising "left-wing" public relations intellectual, who berated one of his colleagues for raising some political concerns about an author that the esteemed left-oriented professor had read. His argument was that political discourse was not "cool," thus affirming the separation of scholarship from commitment while justifying a form of anti-intellectualism that parades under the banner of cleverness that threatens no one. This is a sign of more than academic fluff or the mark of an impoverished imagination; it is irrelevance by design. Engaged intellectuals such as Arundhati Roy, Noam Chomsky, Edward Said, and the late Pierre Bourdieu have offered a different and more committed role for academics. Arguing that those for whom irony and cleverness appear to be the last refuge are academic scoundrels who disdain any form of commitment, Roy defends the link between scholarship and commitment because it is precisely "uncool"—as if being fashionable is the most important factor for shaping the identity and work of engaged intellectuals. She writes,

> I take sides. I take a position. I have a point of view. What's worse, I make it clear that I think it's right and moral to take that position, and what's even worse, I use everything in my power to flagrantly solicit support for that position. Now, for a writer of the twenty-first century, that's considered a pretty uncool, unsophisticated thing to do. . . . Isn't it true, or at least theoretically possible, that there are times in the life of a people or a nation when the political climate demands that we—even the most sophisticated of us—overtly take sides?[117]

Noam Chomsky claims that "the social and intellectual role of the university should be subversive in a healthy society. . . . Individuals and society at large benefit to the extent that these liberatory ideals extend throughout the educational system—in fact, far beyond."[118] Postcolonial and literary critic Edward Said takes a similar position and argues that academics should engage in ongoing forms of permanent critique of all abuses of power and authority, "to enter into sustained and vigorous exchange with the outside world," as part of a larger project of helping "to create the social conditions for the collective production of realist utopias."[119]

Following Bourdieu and others, I believe that intellectuals who work in our nation's universities should represent the conscience of this society because they not only shape the conditions under which future generations learn about themselves and their relations to others and the outside world, but also because they engage pedagogical practices that are by their very nature moral and political, rather than simply cost-effective and technical. At its best, such pedagogy bears witness to the ethical and political dilemmas that animate the broader social landscape; these approaches are important because they provide spaces that are both comforting and unsettling, spaces that both disturb and enlighten. Pedagogy in this instance not only works to shift how students think about the issues affecting their lives and the world at large, but potentially energizes them to seize such moments as possibilities for acting on the world and engaging it as a matter of politics, power, and social justice. The appeal here is not merely ethical; it also addresses the materiality of resources, access, and politics, while viewing power as generative and crucial to any viable notion of individual and social agency.

Organizing against the corporate takeover of higher education also means fighting to protect the jobs of full-time faculty, turning adjunct jobs into full-time positions, expanding benefits to part-time workers, and putting power into the hands of faculty and students. Moreover, such struggles must address the exploitative conditions under which many graduate students work, constituting a de facto army of service workers who are underpaid, overworked, and shorn of any real power or benefits.[120] Similarly, programs in many universities that offer remedial programs, affirmative action, and other crucial pedagogical resources are under massive assault, often by conservative trustees who want to eliminate from the university any attempt to address the deep inequities in the society, while simultaneously denying a decent education to minorities of color and class. For example, City University of New York, as a result of a decision made by a board of trustees, has decided to end " its commitment to provide remedial courses for academically unprepared students, many of whom are immigrants requiring language training before or concurrent with entering the ordinary academic discipline. . . . Consequently . . . a growing number of prospective college students are forced on an already overburdened job market."[121] Both teachers and students increasingly bear the burden of overcrowded classes, limited resources, and hostile legislators.

But resistance to neoliberalism and its ongoing onslaught against public goods, services, and civic freedoms cannot be limited either to the sphere of higher education or to outraged faculty. Educators and students need to join with community people and social movements around a common platform that resists the corporatizing of schools, the roll back in basic services, and the exploitation of teaching assistants and adjunct faculty. There are several important lessons that faculty can learn from the growing number of broad-based student movements that are protesting neoliberal global policies and the ongoing commercialization of the university and everyday life. As far back as 1998, students from about 100 colleges across the United States and Canada "held a series of 'teach-ins' challenging the increasing involvement of corporations in higher education."[122] Students from Yale, Harvard, Florida State University, and the University of Minnesota, among other schools, organized debates, lectures, films, and speakers to examine the multifaceted ways in which corporations are affecting all aspects of higher education. Within the last few years, the pace of such protests on and off campuses has picked up and spawned a number of student protest groups, including the United Students Against Sweatshops (USAS), with over180 North American campus groups,[123] the nationwide 180/Movement for Democracy and Education, and a multitude of groups protesting the policies of the World Trade Organization and the International Monetary Fund.[124]

Students have occupied the offices of university presidents, held hunger strikes, blocked traffic in protests of the brand-name society, conducted mass demonstrations against the WTO in Seattle, and protested the working conditions and use of child labor in the $2.5-billion-dollar collegiate apparel industry. In January 2000, students from the conservative Virginia Commonwealth University joined the rising tide of anti-corporate protest by organizing a sleep-in "outside of the vice president's office for two nights to protest the university's contract with McDonald's (the school promised the fast-food behemoth a twenty-year monopoly over the Student Commons)."[125] As diverse as these struggles might appear, what seems to be one of the common threads that ties them together is their resistance to the increasing incursion of corporate power over higher education. As journalist Liza Featherstone observes:

> But almost all of the current student struggles—whether over tuition increases, apparel licenses, socially responsible investing, McDonald's in the student union, the rights of university laundry workers, a dining-hall contractor's investment in private prisons or solidarity with striking students in Mexico—focus on the reality of the university as corporate actor.[126]

Many students reject the model of the university as a business. Students recognize that the corporate model of leadership shaping higher education fosters a narrow sense of responsibility, agency, and public values because it lacks a vocabulary for providing guidance on matters of justice, equality, fairness, equity, and freedom—values that are crucial to the functioning of a vibrant, democratic culture. Students are refusing to be treated as consumers rather than as members of a university community in which they have a voice, help shape the conditions under which they learn, and have some say in how the university is organized and run. The alienation and powerlessness that ignited student resistance in the 1960s appears to be alive and well today on college campuses across the country. Featherstone, once again, captures this rising anti-corporate sentiment. She writes:

> "Campus democracy" is an increasingly common rallying cry (just as, at major off campus protests, demonstrators chant "this is what democracy looks like").... Like the idealists who wrote the Port Huron Statement, students are being politicized by disappointment:

Academia, they believe, is supposed to provide a space in which humane values at least compete with the bottom line. Many are shocked to find out that their administrators, many of whom now like to be called CEOs, think like businesspeople.[127]

Student resistance to corporate power has also manifested itself outside of the campus in struggles for global justice that have taken place in cities such as Seattle, Prague, Washington, D.C., Davos, Porto Alegre, Melbourne, Quebec, Gothenburg, Genoa, and New York. These anti-corporate struggles not only include students, but also labor unions, community activists, environmental groups, and other social movements. The importance of these struggles, in part, is that they offer students alliances with non-student groups both within and outside the United States, and point to the promise of linking a public pedagogy of resistance that is university-based to broader pedagogical struggles and social movements that can collectively fight to change neoliberal policies. Equally important is that these movements link learning to social change by making visible alternative models of radical democratic relations in a wide variety of sites, from the art gallery to alternative media to the university. Such movements offer instances of collective resistance to the glaring material inequities and the growing cynical belief that today's culture of investment and finance makes it *impossible* to address many of the major social problems facing both the United States and the world. These new forms of politics perform an important theoretical service by recognizing the link between civic education, critical pedagogy, and oppositional politics as pivotal to challenging the depoliticization of politics and opening up the possibilities for promoting autonomy and democratic social transformation.

Students protesting the corporatization of the university and neoliberalism's assault on public institutions and civil society both understand how dominant pedagogies work within the various formations and sites of capital—particularly corporate capital's use of the global media and the schools—and refuse to rely on dominant sources of information. Such strategies point to an alternative form of politics outside of the party machines, a politics that astutely recognizes both the world of material inequality and the landscape of symbolic inequality.[128] In part, this has resulted in what Imre Szeman calls "a new public space of pedagogy" that employs a variety of old and new media, including computers, theater, digital video, magazines, the Internet, and photography, as tools for both learning and organizing designed to link learning to social change, while creating networks that challenge the often hierarchical relations that characterize more orthodox political organizations and cultural institutions.[129]

Both higher education and the larger culture are too corporatized to be the only sites of learning and struggle. New forms of resistance have to be developed, and this demands new forms of pedagogy and new sites in which to conduct it, while not abandoning traditional spheres of learning. The challenge for faculty in higher education is, in part, to find ways to contribute their knowledge and skills to understand how neoliberalism creates the conditions for devaluing critical learning and undermining viable forms of political agency. Academics, as Imre Szeman puts it, need to figure out how neoliberalism and corporate culture "constitute a problem of and for pedagogy."[130] Academics need to be attentive to the oppositional pedagogies put into place by various student movements in order to judge their "significance . . . for the shape and function of the university curricula today."[131]

The challenge here is for faculty to learn as much as possible from student movements about what it means to deepen and expand the struggle for establishing pedagogical approaches and movements that can be used to mediate the fundamental tension between the public values of higher education and the commercial values of corporate culture, on the one hand, and fight against the devastating assaults waged against the welfare state and other public goods on the other. If the forces of corporate culture are to be challenged, educators must also enlist the help of diverse communities, interests, foundations, social movements, and other forces to ensure that public institutions of higher learning are adequately funded so that they will not have to rely on corporate sponsorship and advertising revenues.

Jacques Derrida has suggested in another context that any viable notion of higher education should be grounded in a vibrant politics, which makes the promise of democracy a matter of concrete urgency. For Derrida, making visible a democracy that is to come, as opposed to that which presents itself in its name, provides a referent for both criticizing everywhere what parades as democracy—"the current state of all so-called democracy"[132]—and critically assessing the conditions and possibilities for democratic transformation. Derrida sees the promise of democracy as the proper articulation of a political ethics, and by implication suggests that when higher education is engaged and articulated through the project of democratic social transformation it can function as a vital public sphere for critical learning, ethical deliberation, and civic engagement. Toni Morrison rightly emphasizes the fragile nature of the relationship between higher education and democratic public life, and she suggests, given the urgency of the times, the necessity for all members of academia to rethink the meaning and purpose of higher education. She writes:

> If the university does not take seriously and rigorously its role as a guardian of wider civic freedoms, as interrogator of more and more complex ethical problems, as servant and preserver of deeper democratic practices, then some other regime or menage of regimes will do it for us, in spite of us, and without us.[133]

Both Derrida and Morrison recognize that the present crisis represents a historical opportunity to refuse the common sense assumption that democracy is synonymous with capitalism and critical citizenship is limited to being an unquestioning consumer. Markets need to be questioned not simply as a matter of economic considerations but also on the grounds of ethical and political concerns. The language of neoliberalism and the emerging corporate university radically alter the vocabulary available for appraising the meaning of citizenship, agency, and civic virtue. Within this discourse everything is for sale, and what is not has no value as a public good or practice. It is in the spirit of such a critique and act of resistance that educators need to break with the "new faith in the historical inevitability professed by the theorists of [neo]liberalism [in order] to invent new forms of collective political work capable of" confronting the march of corporate power.[134] This will not be an easy task, but it is a necessary one if democracy is to be won back from the reign of financial markets and the Darwinian values of an unbridled capitalism. Academics can contribute to such a struggle by, among other things, defending higher education for the contribution it makes to the quality of public life, fighting for the crucial role it plays pedagogically in asserting the primacy of democratic values over commercial interests, and struggling collectively to preserve its political responsibility in providing students with the capacities they need for civic courage and engaged critical citizenship.

The current regime of neoliberalism and the incursion of corporate power into higher education present difficult problems and demand a profoundly committed sense of collective resistance. Unfortunately, it is no exaggeration to suggest that we live in a culture in which a growing sense of fear and powerlessness feed into a collective cynicism that has become a powerful fixture of everyday life. But rather than make despair convincing, I think it is all the more crucial to take seriously Meghan Morris's argument that "Things are too urgent now to be giving up on our imagination."[135] More specifically, we must take up the challenge of Jacques Derrida's recent provocation that "We must do and think the impossible. If only the possible happened, nothing more would happen. If I only did what I can do, I wouldn't do anything."[136]

NOTES

Introduction

1. Jean Baudrillard, "The Dark Continent of Childhood," in *Screened Out*, trans. Chris Turner (London: Verso Press, 2002), 102, 104.

2. The link between neoliberal ideology and state terrorism is not new, as Noam Chomsky has courageously and brilliantly been reminding readers for over 30 years. See, for example, Noam Chomsky, *Profits over People* (New York: Seven Stories, 1999).

3. Cited in "Criminalizing Youth," *CounterPunch* (December 20, 2000), 2. Available online at www.counterpunch.org/youth.html

4. Barbara Kantrowitz and Pat Wingert, "How Well Do You Know Our Kid?" *Newsweek* (May 10, 1998), 39. I have used this example before, but it seems even more relevant today as a marker of how the dominant media represents children. See Henry A. Giroux, *Stealing Innocence: Corporate Culture's War On Children* (New York: Palgrave, 2000), 20.

5. Lawrence Grossberg, "Why Does Neo-Liberalism Hate Kids? The War on Youth and the Culture of Politics," *The Review of Education/Pedagogy/Cultural Studies* 23:2 (2001), 133.

6. I have taken up a similar argument in *Stealing Innocence*, 20.

7. For a classic example of this position, see Milton Friedman, "The Market Can Transform Our Schools," *New York Times* (Tuesday, July 2, 2002), A19. According to Friedman, the market alone makes progress possible in "every other area of economic and civic life." One wonders if Friedman lives on the same planet as I do along with billions of others. From my perspective, the market also generates vast inequalities in wealth, floods the globe with needless goods, commercializes and cheapens public space, corrupts politics by turning it over to the power of money and finance capital, turns the media into a vehicle for advertisers to create audiences, damages the environment, and offers no insight whatsoever for addressing a host of issues that cannot be resolved through an appeal to market relations and values—i.e., questions like what is the meaning of a substantive democracy, how can we imagine a

good life outside of the nexus of buying and selling, or how do we address the tension between democratic values and market fundamentalism? Most importantly, market values provide no guidance for defending vital social institutions as a public good and no guidance whatsoever on matters of justice, equity, fairness, equality and freedom, which are crucial to any inclusive democracy.

8. Manuel Castells, *The Information Age: Economy, Society, and Culture-End of Millennium, Volume III* (Malden, Mass.: Blackwell, 1998), 159.

9. Comaroff, 307.

10. Heather Wokusch, "Leaving Our Children Behind," *Common Dreams News Center* (July 8, 2002), available online at www.commondreams. org/views02/0708–08.htm, 1.

11. These figures are taken from Child Research Briefs, "Poverty, Welfare, and Children: A Summary of the Data." Available online at www.childtrends.org

12. These figures are taken from Childhood Poverty Research Brief 2, "Child Poverty in the States: Levels and Trends From 1979 to 1998." Available online at www.nccp.org.

13. These figures largely come from Children's Defense Fund, *The State of Children in America's Union: A 2002 Action Guide to Leave No Child Behind* (Washington, D.C.: Children's Defense Fund Publication, 2002), iv-v, 13.

14. Jennifer Egan, "To Be Young and Homeless," *The New York Times Magazine* (March 24, 2002), 35.

15. Heather Wokusch, 1.

16. Noreena Hertz, *The Silent Takeover: Global Capitalism and the Death of Democracy* (New York: The Free Press, 2001), 11.

17. The term "inclusive democracy" comes from Takis Fotopoulos, *Towards an Inclusive Democracy,* (New York: Cassell, 1997).

18. Richard Swift, *The No-Nonsense Guide to Democracy* (London: Verso Press, 2002), 109.

Chapter 1

1. Barnor Hesse and S. Sayyid, "A War Against Politics," *Open Democracy* (November 28, 2001), 3, available at openDemocracy@opendemocracy.net.

2. Anatole Anton, "Public Goods as Commonstock: Notes on the Receding Commons," In Anatole Anton, Milton Fisk, and Nancy Holmstrom, eds., *Not for Sale: In Defense of Public Goods* (Boulder: Westview Press, 2000), 29.

3. Edward Said, "Thoughts About America," *Counterpunch*, March 5, 2002, 5. Available at www.counterpunch.org/saidamerica.html.

4. Ellen Willis, "Dreaming of War," *The Nation*, October 15, 2001, 12.

5. Zygmunt Bauman, *Community: Seeking Safety in an Insecure World* (Cambridge, U.K.: Polity, 2001), 4.

6. Cited in Lewis H. Lapham, "American Jihad," *Harper's Magazine*, January 2002, 7.

7. Jerry L. Martin and Anne D. Neal, *Defending Civilization: How Our Universities are Failing America and What Can Be Done about It*, May 7, 2002. Available at www.goatca.org/reportsframeset.htm.

8. Frank Rich, "The Wimps of War," *New York Times*, March 30, 2002, A27.

9. Cited in Rich, A27.

10. Ibid.

11. Eric Hobsbawm, *The Age of Extremes* (London: Michael Joseph, 1994), 428.

12. Lapham, "American Jihad," 8.

13. Susan George, "Another World is Possible," *The Nation*, February 18, 2002, 12.

14. Judith Butler, "Explanation and Exoneration, or What We Can Hear," *Theory & Event* 5:4 (2002), 8, 16.

15. Lewis H. Lapham, "Innocents Abroad," *Harper's Magazine*, June 2002, 7.

16. Ledeen cited in Douglas Valentine, "Homeland Insecurity," *Counterpunch*, November 8, 2001. Available online at www.counterpunch.org/homeland1.html.

17. Anthony Lewis, "Taking Our Liberties," *New York Times*, March 9, 2002, A27.

18. Dan Van Natta, Jr., "Government Will Ease Limits on Domestic Spying by F.B.I." *New York Times*, May 20, 2002, A1.

19. Cited in Elaine Monaghan and Tim Reid, "U.S. to Set Up 'Big Brother' Citizen Database." Available online from Common Dreams News Center at www.commondreams.org/headlines02/1122–05.htm.

20. Bob Herbert, "Isn't Democracy Worth It?," *New York Times*, June 7, 2002, A21.

21. Jonathan Turley, "Camps for Citizens: Ashcroft's Hellish Vision," *Los Angeles Times*, August 14, 2002, 1.

22. See www.citizencorps.gov/tips.html.

23. Jerome Binde, "Toward an Ethic of the Future," *Public Culture* 12:1 (2000), 52.

24. Ibid., 52.

25. Hesse and Sayyid, p/ 3. Available at openDemocracy@opendemocracy.net.

26. Steven Lukes and Nadia Urbinati, "Words Matter," *Open Democracy* November 27, 2001, 1.

27. Cornelius Castoriadis, "The Greek Polis and the Creation of Democracy," *Philosophy, Politics, Autonomy: Essays in Political Philosophy* (New York: Oxford University Press, 1991), 113–14.

28. Roger I. Simon, "On Public Time," Ontario Institute for Studies in Education. Unpublished paper, 4.

29. Simon Critchley, "Ethics, Politics, and Radical Democracy—The History of a Disagreement," *Culture Machine*. Available at www.culturemachine.tees.ac.uk/frm_f1.htm.

30. Cornelius Castoriadis, "The Crisis of the Identification Process," *Thesis Eleven* 49 (May 1997), 85–98.

31. Critical reactions to the Bush administration's holding of secret hearings for immigrants detained in the weeks after September 11 are not limited to unpatriotic dissenters. A federal judge in New Jersey recently rejected the government's blanket suppression of the rights of immigrant detainees. See Susan Sachs, "Judge Rejects U. S. Policy of Secret Hearings," *New York Times*, May 30, 2002, A21.

32. Said, "Thoughts About America," 2.

33. Hesse and Sayyid, "A War Against Politics," 3.

34. These figures are taken from Thomas W. Pogge, "The Moral Demands of Global Justice," *Dissent* (Fall 2000), 37–43.

35. Butler, 19.

36. John Edgar Wideman, "Whose War," *Harper's Magazine* (March 2002), 33–38.

37. Benjamin R. Barber, "Beyond Jihad vs. Mcworld: On Terrorism and the New Democratic Realism," *The Nation*, January 21, 2002, 17.

38. I want to thank Jane Gordon for helping me think through the relationship between politics and purity, which cuts across ideological boundaries.

39. Children's Defense Fund, *The State of Children in America's Union: A 2002 Action Guide to Leave No Child Behind* (Washington, D.C.: Children's Defense Fund Publication, 2002), xix.

Chapter 2

1. Zygmunt Bauman captures this sentiment well in his observation that "Although it has been unnoticed, ignored, or played down by most of us, the truth is that the world is full. The great dream of the West, the dream that there is always a new place to discover, a new land to colonize, has dissolved. The great hope that a nation could wall itself off from the others is likewise over." Zygmunt Bauman, "Global Solidarity," *Tikkun* 17:1 (January/February 2002), 12.

2. On this issue, see Lewis Lapham, "Drums Along the Potomac," *Harper's Magazine*, November 2001, 35–41; Steve Rendall, "The Op-Ed Echo Chamber, *Extra* (November/December 2001), 14–15; Seth Ackerman, "Network of Insiders," *Extra* (November/December 2001), 11–12.

3. Eric Alterman, "Patriot Games," *The Nation*, October 29, 2001, 10.

4. Cited in the National Public Radio/Kaiser Family foundation/ Kennedy School of Government Civil Liberties Poll. Available on line at wsiwyg:5http://www.npr.org/news . . . civillibertiespll/011130.poll. html (November 30, 2001), 3.

5. Carl Boggs argues that in the 1990s, "American society had become more depoliticized, more lacking in the spirit of civic engagement and public obligation, than at any other time in recent history, with the vast majority of the population increasingly alienated from a political system that is commonly viewed as corrupt, authoritarian, and simply irrelevant to the most important challenges of our time." Carl Boggs, *The End of Politics* (New York: Guilford Press, 2000), vii. I also take up this theme in *Public Spaces, Private Lives: Beyond the Culture of Cynicism* (Lanham, Md.: Rowman and Littlefield, 2001).

6. On the growing culture of surveillance, see William G. Staples, *The Culture of Surveillance: Discipline and Social Control in the United States* (New York: St. Martin's Press, 1997).

7. For some excellent sources on the growing repression in American life, see Marc Mauer, *Race to Incarcerate* (New York: The New Press, 1999); David Garland, *The Culture of Control: Crime and Social Order in Contemporary Society* (Chicago: University of Chicago Press, 2001); Jill Nelson, *Police Brutality* (New York: Norton, 2000); and David Cole, *No Equal Justice: Race and Class in the American Criminal Justice System* (New York: The New Press, 1999); Marc Mauer and Meda Chesney-Lind, eds., *Invisible Punishment: The Collateral Consequences of Mass Imprisonment* (New York: The New Press, 2002).

8. Mike Davis, "The Flames of New York," *New Left Review* 12 (November/ December 2001), 48. Davis points out that of the 11,000 that were held initially, only 4 had direct connections to bin Laden (p. 49).

9. Ibid., 49. See also Edward Said, "Thoughts about America." Available online at www.counterpunch.org/saidamerica.html

10. Ibid., 50.

11. Both quotes are from David Cole, "National Security State," *The Nation,* December 17, 2001, 4–5.

12. Mike Weisbrot, "The F.B.I.'s Dirty Secrets," *Counterpunch* (June 5, 2002), 1. Available online at www.counterpunch.org/. See also Don Van Natta, Jr., "Government Will Ease Limits On Domestic Spying by F.B.I.," *New York Times,* May 30, 2002, A1, A21.

13. William Safire, "J. Edgar Mueller," *New York Times,* June 3, 2002, A19.

14. Jonathan Schell, "Seven Million at Risk," *The Nation,* November 5, 2001, 8.

15. Homi Bhabha, "A Narrative of Divided Civilizations," *The Chronicle Review,* section 2 of the *Chronicle of Higher Education* (September 28, 2001), B12.

16. For some excellent examples of such teaching practices, see the special issue of *Rethinking Schools*, 16:2 (Winter 2001/2002), titled "War, Terrorism, and America's Classrooms."

17. Richard Reeves, "Patriotism Calls Out the Censor," *The New York Times On the Web* www.nytimes.com, October 1, 2001, 1.

18. Robin Wilson, "CUNY Chancellor, Trustees Denounce Professors Who Criticized U.S. Policy After Attacks," *The Chronicle of Higher Education* http://chronicle.com/free/2001/10/2001100502n.htm (October 5, 2001), 1.

19. Cited in Richard Rothstein, "Terror, Excuses and Explanations," *New York Times*, October 17, 2001, 20.

20. Cited in David Glenn, "The War on Campus: Will Academic Freedom Survive," *The Nation*, December 3, 2001, 11.

21. Lieberman has since denounced the report and his role in founding the American Council of Trustees and Alumni. A report in the December 21, 2001 on-line version of the *Chronicle of Higher Education* counters Lieberman's claim and argues that he was a founding member of the organization. See Thomas Bartlett, "Sen. Lieberman Distances Himself from Report Decrying Campuses' 'Blame America' Attitude," available at http://chronicle.com/daily/2001/12/2001122105n.htm.

22. Goldie Blumenstyk, "Group Denounces "Blame America First' Response to September 11 Attacks," *The Chronicle of Higher Education* at http://chronicle.com/free/2001/11/2001111202n.htm (November 12, 2001), 1. For the full report, see Jerry L. Martin's and Anne D. Neal's self-righteously titled book, *Defending Civilization: How Our Universities Are Failing America and What We Can Do About It* (Washington, D.C.: The American Council of Trustees and Alumni, 2001).

23. As part of her ongoing attacks on leftist scholarship, which she argues is politically biased and partisan, Lynne Cheney has presented herself for years as a paragon of Arnoldian objectivity and an innocent advocate of traditional truths that transcend time, ideology, and power. For a brilliant rebuttal of Cheney's alleged disinterested scholarship and political biases, see Donald Lazere, "Ground Rules for Polemicists: the Case of Lynne Cheney's Truths," *College English* 59:6 (October 1997), 661–685.

24. For a critical analysis of this report and its political implications for higher education, see Eric Scigliano, "Naming—and Un-Naming—Names," *The Nation*, December 31, 2001, 16.

25. Lewis H. Lapham, "Mythography," *Harper's Magazine*, February 2002, 6.

26. Jerome Binde, "Toward an Ethic of the Future," *Public Culture* 12:1 (2000), 52.

27. David Glenn, "The War on Campus: Will Academic Freedom Survive," *The Nation*, December 3, 2001, 11–14.

28. Rothstein, 20.

29. One telling sign of the creeping suppression of dissent can be found in an article by Maria Puente in *USA Today*. Puente defines the current public outcry against dissent as simply a matter of confusion that has its roots in the political correctness movement of the last decade. Hence, she suggests that the suppression of dissenting opinions is nothing more than an overly sensitive response to language, and that we have now entered a period that demands that Americans not only be politically correct, but also emotionally correct. Implicit in this embarrassing commentary is the assumption that the left is responsible for the current attack on freedom of speech, and that the defense of the latter has nothing to do with either ethical or legal principles. This is the same logic that the Reverend Jerry Falwell used in his remarks in which he blamed liberals, homosexuals, abortion supporters, and Hollywood for the terrorist acts of September 11. See Maria Puente, "Potentially Confusing," *USA Today*, October 8, 2001, 6D.

    Another notable example of collapsing the distinction between justifying and explaining an event was evident in a public exchange on CNN on May 30, 2002, between William Bennett, former Secretary of Education in the Reagan administration, and social critic Noam Chomsky. Paula Zahn, the show's anchor, began by reading the follow except from Chomsky's book, *9–11:* "Nothing can justify crimes such as those of September 11, but we can think of the United States as an innocent victim only if we adopt the convenient path of ignoring the record of its actions and those of its allies, which are, after all, hardly a secret." Bennett responded to this quote with the comment: "it is grossly irresponsible to talk about this country as a terrorist nation, and to suggest, as do you in your book, that there is justification, moral justification, for what happened on 9/11." Oblivious to the distinction made by Chomsky between condemning the terrorist acts of September 11, and the call for trying to establish a context for understanding them, Bennett follows up on his misrepresentation by suggesting that Chomsky should leave the country because he is critical of U.S. foreign policy. This exchange and the above quotes can be found in the published transcript of the debate at "CNN Debate on 'Terrorism': Chomsky v. Bennett," available online at www.counterpunch.org/.

30. Judith Butler, "Explanation and Exoneration, or What We Can Hear," *Theory and Event*, 5:4 (2002), 5. Available on line at http://muse.jhu.edu/jounals/theory_and_event/v005/5.4butlerhtml.

31. Robin Wilson and Ana Marie Cox, "Terrorist Attacks Put Academic Freedom to the Test," *The Chronicle of Higher Education* (October 5, 2001), A12.

32. Cited in "49 % of Americans Want Arabs to carry 'Special ID's'," *The Online Newspaper Gazette*, available at http://thamus.org/News/us/arab_IDs.html, 1.

33. Cited in Edward Said, "Backlash and Backtrack," on line at L-commdialogue&Lists@psu.edu, 1.

34. The notion of addressing the meaning of patriotism through the connection between national identity and public citizenship is developed in Michael Berube, *The Employment of English: Theory, Jobs, and the Future of Literary Studies* (New York: New York University Press, 1998), 238.

35. Cited in Bauman, 14.

36. Matthew Rothschild, "The New McCarthyism," *The Progressive,* January 2002, 18–23.

37. Frank Rich, "Patriotism on the Cheap," *New York Times,* January 5, 2002, A31.

38. This issue was also explored brilliantly by Doug Kellner with respect to the war against Iraq under the senior Bush presidency. See Douglas Kellner, *Media Culture: Cultural Studies, Identity, and Politics Between the Modern and the Postmodern* (New York: Routledge, 1995), especially 213–14.

39. David Barstow and Diana B. Henriques, "Lines of Profit and Charity Blur for Companies with 9/11 Tie-Ins," *New York Times,* February 2, 2002, A15.

40. Ibid.

41. Ibid.

42. Ibid.

43. Boggs, vii.

44. Davis, 44.

45. Ibid., 45.

46. Figures cited in "The Pentagon Spending Spree," *New York Times,* February 6, 2002, A26.

47. See Bob Herbert's commentary on the Padilla case in "Isn't Democracy Worth It?," *New York Times,* June 17, 2002, A21.

48. Children's Defense Fund, *The State of Children in America's Union: A 2002 Action Guide to Leave No Child Behind* (Washington, D.C.: Children's Defense Fund Publication, 2002), xvii.

49. Ellen Willis, "Dreaming of War," *The Nation,* October 15, 2001, 12. I am not suggesting that all of the media is behind the war or simply presenting the standard government line. On the contrary, there has been an enormous amount of dissent in a wide variety of media, especially on the Internet. At the same time, while critical and dissenting voices have been aired even in the dominant print and visual media, this in no way suggests that there is any reasonable notion of balance in the

media, nor should we underestimate the power of the dominant media to shape public consciousness.

50. Friedman spells this out clearly in *Capitalism and Freedom* (Chicago: University of Chicago Press, 1963).

51. Edward W. Said, "The Public Role of Writers and Intellectuals," *The Nation*, October 1, 2001, 31.

52. Editorial, "Bush's Domestic War," *The Nation*, December 31, 2001, 3.

53. Ibid.

54. Sheldon Wolin, "Political Theory: From Vocation to Invocation," in Jason Frank and John Tambornino, eds., *Vocations of Political Theory* (Minneapolis: University of Minnesota Press, 2000), 4.

55. Giroux, *Public Spaces, Private Lives*.

56. Lewis Lapham, "Res Publica," *Harper's Magazine*, December 2001, 10.

57. Even Maureen Dowd, a columnist for the New York Times, recently claimed that she couldn't take increasing control of American society by corporate interests, that George W. Bush continues "to give away the store to Big Business . . . [and that] His White House has become a holding company for Big Money and Media Oligarchy—Murdoch, Gates, Case, Eisner, Redstone." See Maureen Dowd, "I Can't Take It Anymore," *New York Times* Week In Review, September 9, 2001, 19.

58. A more recent analysis of the corporatization of schooling can be found in Kenneth J. Saltman, *Collateral Damage: Corporatizing Public Schools—A Threat to Democracy* (Lanham, Md.: Rowman and Littlefield, 2000). See also, Henry A. Giroux, *Stealing Innocence: Corporate Culture's War on Children* (New York: Palgrave, 2001).

59. See Peter Kilborn, "Rural Towns Turn to Prisons to Reignite Their Economies," *New York Times*, August 1, 2001, A1.

60. Paul Street, "Prisons and the New American Racism," *Dissent* (Summer 2001), 49–50.

61. Consider that "in the last twenty years the Justice Department's budget grew by 900 percent; over 60 percent of all prisoners are in for non-violent drug crimes; an estimated one-in-three black men between the ages of twenty and twenty-nine are under some type of criminal justice control or sought on a warrant; nationwide some 6.5 million people are in prison, on parole, or probation. [This suggests] that the United States is an over-policed, surveillance society that uses prison as one of its central institutions." Given the current talk about limiting civil liberties, these figures make such a demand all the more problematic. See Christian Parenti, "The 'New' Criminal Justice System," *Monthly Review* 53:3 (2001), 19.

62. Betsy Hartman, "The Return of Relevance" (October 29). Reproduced from sysop@zmag.org.

63. Zygmunt Bauman, *The Individualized Society* (London: Polity Press, 2001).

64. Boggs, ix.

65. Zygmunt Bauman, *Globalization: The Human Consequences* (New York: Columbia University Press, 1998), 82.

66. Cited in Anna Greenberg, "What Young Voters Want," *The Nation*, February 11, 2001, 15.

67. For an excellent commentary on how the current discourse of security undermines some basic civil liberties, see Bruce Shapiro, "All in the Name of Security," *The Nation*, October 21, 2001, 20–21.

68. Frank Rich, "The End of the Beginning," *New York Times*, September 29, 2001, A23.

69. For one excellent analysis of this issue, see Ralph Nader, "Corporate Patriotism," available on line at www.citizenworks.org (November 10, 2001).

70. Cornelius Castoriadis, "Institution and Autonomy," in Peter Osborne, *A Critical Sense: Interviews with Intellectuals* (New York: Routledge, 1996), 8.

71. See. Giroux, *Public Spaces, Private Lives*.

72. I am referring to work that extends from John Dewey to some of the more prominent contemporary critical educational theorists such as Paulo Freire and Jonathan Kozol.

73. Pierre Bourdieu, *Acts of Resistance* (New York: Free Press, 1998).

74. Samin Amin, "Imperialization and Globalization," *Monthly Review* (June 2001), 12.

75. Alain Badiou, *Ethics: An Essay on the Understanding of Evil* (London: Verso, 1998), 115–116.

76. George Lipsitz, "Academic Politics and Social Change," in Jodi Dean, ed., *Cultural Studies and Political Theory* (Ithaca: Cornell University Press, 2000), 81.

77. Gary Olson and Lynn Worsham, "Staging the Politics of Difference: Homi Bhabha's Critical Literacy," *Journal of Advanced Composition* 18:3 (1999), 11.

78. Stuart Hall cited in Les Terry, "Traveling 'The Hard Road to Renewal," *Arena Journal* 8 (1997), 55.

79. Theodor W. Adorno, *Critical Models* (New York: Columbia University Press, 1993), 290.

80. Robert Jensen, "Against Dissent: Why Free Speech is Important as the U.S. Drops Cluster Bombs," Counterpunch, available at www.counterpuncy.org/jensen11.html, 3.

81. Paul Krugman, "For Richer: How the Permissive Capitalism Has Destroyed American Equality," *New York Times Magazine* (November 20, 20002), 142.

82. Patricia Williams cited in "Civil Wrongs," Maya Jaggi, *The Guardian,* June 22, 2002, 2. Online at www.guardian.co.uk/print/ 0,3858,4444779,00.html; see also Bob Herbert's commentary on the Padilla case in Bob Herbert, "Isn't Democracy Worth It?," *New York Times,* June 17, 2002, A21.

Chapter 3

1. Cited in Richard Swift, *No-Nonsense Guide to Democracy* (London: Verso Press, 2002), 79.
2. For one collection that brings many articles together on this issue, see Frank J. Lechner and John Boli, eds., *The Globalization Reader* (Malden, Mass.: Basil Blackwell, 2000); see also a collection of educational work in Henry A. Giroux and Peter McLaren, eds., *Between Borders* (New York: Routledge, 1994).
3. See, for instance, Immanuel Wallerstein, *The End of the World as We Know It: Social Science for the Twenty-First Century* (Minneapolis: University of Minnesota Press, 2001).
4. Zygmunt Bauman, *Work, Consumerism and the New Poor* (Philadelphia: Open University Press, 1998), especially chapter 2, "From the Work Ethic to the Aesthetic of Consumption," 23–41.
5. Walter LaFeber, *Michael Jordan and the New Global Capitalism* (New York: W.W. Norton &Company, 1999), 102.
6. There are many sources that take this issue up, but one exceptionally lucid analysis can be found in Zygmunt Bauman, *The Individualized Society* (London: Polity Press, 2001).
7. One of the more brilliant expositions on this theme can be found in the work of Manual Castells, especially his *The Information Age: Economy, Society and Culture, Volume III: End of Millennium* (Malden, Mass.: Basil Blackwell, 1998).
8. Zygmunt Bauman, *In Search of Politics* (Stanford: Stanford University Press, 1999), 170.
9. See Manuel Castells, *The Information Age: Economy, Society, and Culture* (3 vols., Malden, Mass.: Blackwell, 1998); Ulrich Beck, *What is Globalization?* (London: Polity Press); Zygmunt Bauman, *In Search of Politics* (Stanford: Stanford University Press, 1999).
10. LeFeber, 57.
11. Bauman, *Work, Consumerism and the New Poor.*
12. This theme is taken up in too many sources to repeat here, but see for example Zygmunt Bauman, *Globalization: The Human Condition* (New York: Columbia University Press, 1998); Pierre Bourdieu, *Acts of Resistance* (New York: The New Press, 1998).

13. Evelyn Nieves, "In Famously Tolerant City, Impatience With Homeless," *New York Times*, January 18, 2002, A14.
14. State repression has a long history in both American foreign and domestic policy. What is new is that under neoliberalism, it is imposed less through an appeal to spread the ideals of a bogus democracy than through the brutal necessity of accumulating capital and profits for the multinational corporations. See, for example, Noam Chomsky, *Profits over People: Neoliberalism and the Global Order* (Boston: South End Press, 1999).
15. On the culture of control, see David Garland, *The Culture of Control: Crime and Social Order in Contemporary Society* (Chicago: University of Chicago Press, 2001).
16. Anatole Anton, "Public Goods as Commonstock: Notes on the Receding Commons," in Anatole Anton, Milton Fisk, and Nancy Holmstrom, eds., *Not for Sale: In Defense of Public Goods* (Boulder: Westview Press, 2000), 24.
17. Ibid., 29.
18. Bauman, *In Search of Politics*, 50.
19. Mike Davis, "The Flames of New York," *New Left Review* 12 (November-December, 2001), 48.
20. Ibid., 45.
21. See the work of Manual Castells, Zygmunt Bauman, Immanuel Wallerstein, Arif Dirlik, William Grieder, Arjun Apadurai, Ulrich Beck and others.
22. See, for example, Edward S. Herman and Robert W. McChesney, *The Global Media: The New Missionaries of Global Capitalism* (Washington: Cassell, 1997).
23. Christian Parenti, *Lockdown America: Police and Prisons in the Age of Crisis* (London: Verso, 1999).
24. This issue is taken up in Stanley Aronowitz, *The Last Good Job in America* (Lanham, Md.: Rowman and Littlefield, 2001).
25. Leerom Medovoi, "Globalization as Narrative and Its Three Critiques," *The Review of Education/Pedagogy/Cultural Studies* 24 (2002), 63.
26. Fredric Jameson, *The Cultural Turn* (London: Verso, 1998), 1–2.
27. Thomas Friedman, The Lexus and the Olive Tree (New York: Anchor Books, 1999). See also Kenichi Ohmei's *A Borderless World* (New York: HarperBusiness, 1990), and the most vulgar example of this position can be found in John Micklethwait and Adrian Wooldridge, *A Future Perfect: The Challenge and Hidden Promise of Globalization* (New York: Crown Business, 2000).
28. Samin Amin, "Imperialism and Globalization," *Monthly Review* 53:2 (June 2001), 9.
29. I take up this issue in *Public Spaces, Private Lives: Beyond the Culture of Cynicism* (Lanham, Md.: Rowman and Littlefield, 2001). The notion of culture as a form of permanent education comes directly from Raymond Williams,

"Preface to the Second Edition," *Communications* (New York: Barnes and Noble, 1967), 15–16.

30. Leerom Medovoi, "Globalization as Narrative and Its Three Critiques," *The Review of Education/Pedagogy/Cultural Studies* 24 (2002), 66.

31. John Brenkman, "Extreme Criticism," in Judith Butler, John Guillary, and Kendal Thomas, eds., *What's Left of Theory* (New York: Routledge, 2000), 123.

32. This is a position long advocated by Chantal Mouffe, *The Return of the Political* (London: Verso, 1993).

33. Peter Marcuse, "The Language of Globalization," in Monthly Review 52:3 (www.monthlyreview.org: July-August 2000), 2.

34. Stuart Hall, "Subjects in History: Making Diasporic Identities," in Wahneema Lubiano, *The House that Race Built* (New York: Pantheon, 1997), 295.

35. This idea comes from George Lipsitz, who argues that "Taking a position is not the same as waging a war of position; changing your mind is not the same as changing society." See George Lipsitz, "Academic Politics and Social Change," in Jodi Dean ed., *Cultural Studies and Political Theory* (Ithaca: Cornell University Press, 2000), 81.

36. Arundhati Roy, *Power Politics* (Cambridge, Mass.: Sound End Press, 2001), 5.

37. Robert W. McChesney, "Global Media, Neoliberalism, and Imperialism," *Monthly Review* (March 2001), 1–19.

38. Jack Lang, cited in Walter LaFeber, *Michael Jordan and the New Global Capitalism,* 110.

39. *United Nations Human Development Report 1999* (New York: Oxford University Press, 1999), 3; see also Robert w. McChesney, "Global Media, Neoliberalism, and Imperialism," *Monthly Review* (March 2001), 18.

40. Thomas W. Pogge, "The Moral Demands of Global Justice," *Dissent* (Fall 2000), 37–38.

41. Pogge, 38.

42. Doug Henwood, "Debts Everywhere," *The Nation* (July 19, 1999), 2. On income inequality in the United States, see Kevin Phillips, *Wealth and Democracy: A Political History of the American Rich* (New York: Broadway Books, 2002).

43. Cited in "Ownership Statistics," The Shared Capitalism Institute, available online at www.sharedcapitalism.org/scfacts.html, 5.

44. One such example can be found in Michael Hardt and Antonio Negri, *Empire* (Cambridge: Harvard University Press, 2000); for a clear and precise example of their position, see Michael Hardt, "Folly of Our Masters of the Universe." Available online at www.commondreams.org/views02/1218–02.htm. Also, see the thinly veiled apology for a U.S. driven global empire in Michael Ignatieff, "The American Empire," *New York Times Magazine* (January 5, 2003), 22–27, 50–54.

45. Ernst Bloch, "Something's Missing: A Discussion Between Ernst Bloch and Theodor W. Adorno on the Contradictions of Utopian Longing," in Ernst Bloch, *The Utopian Function of Art and Literature: Selected Essays* (Cambridge: MIT Press, 1988), 3.

46. Alain Badiou, *Ethics: An Essay on the Understanding of Evil* (London: Verso, 2001), 115.

47. Thomas L. Dunn, "Political Theory for Losers," in Jason A. Frank and John Tambornino, eds., *Vocations of Political Theory* (Minneapolis: University of Minnesota Press, 2000), 160.

48. Bauman, *The Individualized Society*.

49. Russell Jacoby, "A Brave Old World," *Harper's Magazine* (December 2000), 72–80. Geras, "Minimum Utopia: Ten Theses," 41–42; Leo Panitch and Sam Gindin, "Transcending Pessimism: Rekindling Socialist Imagination," in Leo Panitch and Sam Gindin, eds., *Necessary and Unnecessary Utopias* (New York: Monthly Review Press, 1999), 1–29; David Harvey, *Spaces of Hope* (University of California Press, 2000); Russell Jacoby, *The End of Utopia: Politics and Culture in an Age of Apathy* (New York: Basic Books, 1999).

50. Jacoby, "A Brave Old World," 80.

51. Norman Podhoretz cited in Ellen Willis, "Buy American," *Dissent* (Fall 2000), 110.

52. For a critique of entrepreneurial populism of this diverse group, see Thomas Frank, *One Market under God: Extreme Capitalism, Market Populism and the End of Economic Democracy* (New York: Doubleday, 2000).

53. Ron Aronson, "Hope After Hope," *Social Research* 66:2 (Summer 1999), 489.

54. Ruth Levitas, "The Future of Thinking About the Future," in Jon Bird, Barry Curtis, Tim Putnam, George Robertson, eds., *Mapping Futures: Local Cultures, Global Change* (New York: Routledge, 1993), 265.

55. Houston A. Baker, Jr., "Critical Memory and the Black Public Sphere," *Public Culture* 7:1 (1994), 3–33.

56. Chantal Mouffe cited in Gary Olson and Lynn Worsham, "Rethinking Political Community: Chantal Mouffe's Liberal Socialism," *JAC* 18:3 (1999), 178.

57. Cornelius Castoriadis, "Culture in a Democratic Society, " in *The Castoriadis Reader*, ed. David Ames Curtis (Malden, Mass.: Blackwell, 1997), 347.

58. Stuart Hall, "Democracy, Globalization, and Difference," unpublished manuscript, (2000), 1.

59. Ibid., 2.

60. For an example of how the language of critique, absent any sense of possibility, can degenerate into a totalizing dismissal, if not cynical indifference, of the multiple spheres at which politics and social struggle takes place, see Carol Stabile, "Pedagogues, Pedagogy, and Political Struggle,"

in Amitava Kumar, ed., *Class Issues* (New York: New York University Press, 1997), 208–220. For an extensive critique of this type of pedagogy, see "Stuart Hall, Public Pedagogy and the Crisis of Cultural Politics," *Cultural Studies* 14:2 (2000), 341–360; Henry A. Giroux, *Pedagogy and the Politics of Hope: Theory, Culture, and Schooling* (Boulder: Westview Press, 1997); Henry A. Giroux, "Pedagogy of the Depressed: Beyond the New Politics of Cynicism," *College Literature* 28:3 (Fall 2001), 1–32.

61. Cornelius Castoriadis, "Power, Politics, and Autonomy," *Philosophy, Politics Autonomy: Essays in Political Philosophy* (New York: Oxford University Press, 1991), 143–76.

62. Antonio Gramsci, *Selections from the Prison Notebooks* (New York: International Press, 1971), 350.

63. Pierre Bourdieu, *Acts of Resistance* (New York: Free Press, 1998), 66.

64. Simon Critchley, "Ethics, Politics, and Radical Democracy—The History of a Disagreement," Culture Machine, available at www.culturemachine.tees.ac.uk/frm_f1.htm.

65. Immanuel Wallerstein, "A Left Politics for An Age of Transition," *Monthly Review* 53:8 (January 2002), 17–23.

66. Ibid., 19.

67. Imre Szeman, "Introduction: Learning to Learn from Seattle," *The Review of Education/Pedagogy/Cultural Studies* 24:1–2 (2002), 3–4.

68. Ibid., 4.

69. Cited in "Project Hip-Hop," available on line at www.aclu-mass.org/youth/hiphop.html, 1.

70. Liza Featherstone, "Sweatshops, Students and the Corporate University,' *Croonenbergh's Fly* 2 (Spring/Summer 2002), 113.

71. Jonathan Rutherford, "After Seattle," *The Review of Education/Pedagogy/Cultural Studies* 24 (1–2) (January–June, 2002), 14.

72. Zygmunt Bauman, Global Solidarity," *Tikkun* 17:1 (2002), 12.

73. Homi Bhabha, "A Narrative of Divided Civilizations," *The Chronicle Review*, section 2, *The Chronicle of Higher Education* (September 28, 2001), B12.

74. David Held and Mary Kaldor, "New War, New Justice," *Open Democracy* (September 21, 2001), 3.

75. On the politics of place, see the brilliant work by Arif Dirlik, especially "Placed-Based Imagination: Globalism and the Politics of Place," in Roxann Prazniak and Arif Dirlik, eds., *Places and Politics in an Age of Globalization* (Lanham, Md.: Rowman and Littlefield, 2001), 15–52.

Chapter 4

1. Children's Defense Fund, *The State of Children in America's Union: A 2002 Action Guide to Leave No Child Behind* (Washington, D.C.: Children's Defense Fund Publication, 2002), v.

2. Even Bush's touted call for increased spending for education is duplicitous since his alleged $6 billion dollar-increase includes $2.1 billion that the previous Congress had appropriated in advance for the current school year. Hence, Bush's increase for education is a meager $2.5 billion. By comparison, Congress in 2001 increased education spending by $6.5 billion. Representative George Miller of California has attacked Bush's latest budget request for the new education bill claiming that it "failed to provide money for many initiatives in that law . . . and calls for the smallest spending increase in education in seven years." Cited in Robert Pear, "Democrats Criticizing Bush budget on Education," *New York Times,* February 13, 2002, A21.

3. For a summary of some of the studies invalidating Edison's claims to improve achievement, see Barbara Miner, "For-Profits Target Education," *Rethinking Schools* 16:3 (Spring 2002), 16–17. For a mainstream analysis of the problems faced by Edison and its head, Chris Whittle, see Diana B. Henriques, "A Learning Curve for Whittle Venture," *New York Times,* May 25, 2002, B1, B3.

4. Patricia J. Williams, "Tests, Tracking and Derailment," *The Nation,* April 22, 2002, 9.

5. Derrick Jackson, "The Wild, Wild Bush Boyz." Available online at wysiwyg://http://www.commondreams.org.views02/1101–01/htm.

6. Children's Defense Fund, vii.

7. Marion Wright Edelman, "President Bush's Welfare Reform Plan Leaves Millions of Children Behind," (March 14, 2002), 2, available online at www.childrendefense.org/fs_bushwelfplan.htm.

8. Cited in Alfie Kohn, "The Real Threat to American Schools," *Tikkun* (March-April 2001), 25.

9. Children's Defense Fund, *Leave No Child Behind,* xv.

10. On this issue, see Bob Herbert, "Fewer Students, Greater Gains," *New York Times,* March 12, 2001, A19. Also see Paul Wellstone and Jonathan Kozol, "What Tests Can't Fix," *New York Times,* March 13, 2001, A25.

11. Barbara Miner, "Who's Vouching for Vouchers?" *The Nation,* June 5, 2000, 23–24.

12. Stephen Metcalf, "Reading Between the Lines," *The Nation,* January 28, 2002, 18.

13. These ideas are taken from David F. Labaree, "No Exit: You Can Run But You Can't Hide From Public Education as a Public Good," Michigan State University, July 2, 2000, unpublished manuscript, 11.

14. Carol Ascher, Norm Fruchter, and Robert Berne, *Hard Lessons: Public Schools and Privatization* (New York: The Twentieth Century Fund, 1996).

15. Mark Walsh, "Businesses Flock to Charter Schools," *Education Week* 21:37 (May 22, 2002), 1. This same issue of *Education Week* is filled with a number of articles on charter schools in which it celebrates various

entrepreneurial efforts to turn them into lucrative markets for various corporate interests.

16. Deborah W. Meier, "Choice Can Save Public Education," *The Nation,* March 4, 1991, 253.

17. Gerald W. Bracey, "Poison Bill," *Disinformation,* June 20, 2002; available online at www.america-tomorrow.com/bracey/EDDRA25.htm. As has been widely reported, the prison industry has become big business, with many states spending more on prison construction than on university construction. See Anthony Lewis, "Punishing the Country," *New York Times,* December 2, 1999, A1-A2. This is well documented in Nicholas Lemann, *The Big Test: The Secret History of the American Meritocracy* (New York: Farrar, Straus & Giroux, 2000); see also Marc Mauer and Meda Chesney-Lind, eds., *Invisible Punishment: The Collateral Consequences of Mass Imprisonment* (New York: The New Press, 2002).

18. Bracey, 1.

19. Ibid., 2.

20. "Bad for Business," *The Nation,* July 1, 2002, 6.

21. This is particularly evident as schools engage in market-sponsored contests in which teachers spend valuable teaching time coaching kids how to collect cash receipts, sell goods to their friends and neighbors, or learn the rules for bringing in profits for companies who then offer prizes to schools. See Alex Molnar, *Giving Kids the Business* (Boulder: Westview, 1996), especially chapter 3.

22. David F. Labaree, "Are Students 'Consumers'?" *Education Week,* September 17, 1997, 48.

23. Stanley Aronowitz and Henry A. Giroux, *Education Still Under Siege* (Westport: Bergin and Garvey Press, 1993); Jeffrey R. Henig, *Rethinking School Choice: Limits of the Market Metaphor* (Princeton: Princeton University Press, 1994); Karen A. McClafferty, Carlos Alberto Torres, and Theodore R. Mitchell, eds., *Challenges of Urban Education* (Albany: SUNY Press, 2000).

24. I take up this issue in *Stealing Innocence: Corporate Culture's War on Children* (New York: Palgrave, 2001). See also Molnar, *Giving Kids the Business.*

25. Jeffrey Henig, "The Danger of Market Rhetoric," in Rethinking Schools Publication, eds., *Selling out Our Schools* (Milwaukee: Rethinking Schools, Ltd., 1996), 11.

26. Amy Gutman, "What Does 'School Choice' Mean? *Dissent,* Summer 2000, 23.

27. Barbara Miner, "Making the Grade," *The Progressive,* August 2000, 40.

28. Stan Karp, "Let Them Eat Tests," *Rethinking Schools,* Summer 2002, 3.

29. See Linda McNeil, *Contradictions of School Reform: Educational Costs of Standardized Testing* (New York: Routledge, 2000). It is worth noting that the Mexican American Legal Defense and Education Fund re-

ported in 1997 that "although white students have passed the [TAAS] test at a rate of approximately 70%, Mexican Americans and African Americans have passed at rates of around only 40% . . . and that they represent 85% of the 7,650 students who fail the final administration of the TAAS each year." Cited in Rebecca Gordon, Libero Della Piana, and Terry Keleher, *No Exit: Testing, Tracking and Students of Color in U.S. Public Schools* (Oakland: Applied Research Center, March 1999), 4.

30. John Mintz, "In Bush's Texas, An Educational Miracle or Mirage?" *The Detroit News*, April 22, 2000. Available at http:detnews.com/2000/politic/0004/24/politics–41188.htm, 2.

31. Greg Winter, "More Schools Rely on Tests, But Big Study Raises Doubts," *New York Times* (December 28, 2002), A1, A13.

32. E. Wayne Ross and Sandra Mathison, "No Child Left Untested," *Z Magazine* (March 2002), 14.

33. The U. S. Department of Education reported that in 1993–1994, the difference in per capita pubic school expenditures ranged from $3,100 to $42,000, depending upon the school district. Cited in Gordon, Della Piana, and Keleher, *No Exit*, 5.

34. Gary Orfield and Johanna Wald, "Testing, Testing," *The Nation*, June 5, 2000, 38- 40. For a representative sample of some of the excellent critiques of standardized testing, see Peter Sacks, *Standardized Minds : The High Price of America's Testing Culture and What We Can Do to Change It* (New York: Perseus Press, 2000); Alfie Kohn, *The Case Against Standardized Testing: Raising the Scores, Ruining the Schools* (Portsmouth: Heinemann, 2000); Linda McNeil, *Contradictions of School Reform: Educational Costs of Standardized Testing* (New York: Routledge, 2000).

35. Williams, "Tests, Tracking and Derailment, 9.

36. I take this issue up in great detail in *Public Spaces, Private Lives: Beyond the Culture of Cynicism* (Lanham, Md.: Rowman and Littlefield, 2001). See especially the chapter, "Youth, Domestic Militarization, and the Politics of Zero Tolerance."

37. Linda McNeil, "Creating New Inequalities: Contradictions of Reform," *Phi Delta Kappan* (June 2000), 730.

38. Lani Guinier, "Race, Testing, and the Miner's Canary," *Rethinking Schools* (Summer 2002), 13, 23.

39. Kohn, "The Real Threat to American Schools," 26–27.

40. See for instance, Jean Anyon, *Ghetto Schooling* (New York: Teachers College Press, 1997).

41. This is well documented in Nicholas Lemann, *The Big Test.*

42. Cited in Barbara Miner, "Bush's Plan is Shallow and Ignores Critical Details," Rethinking Schools On line 51:2 (Winter 2000/2001), www.rethinkingschools.org, p.2.

43. Deborah W. Meier, "Saving Public Education," *The Nation*, February 17, 1997, 24.

44. Alan O' Shea, "A Special Relationship? Cultural Studies, Academia and Pedagogy," *Cultural Studies* 12:4 (1998), 521–22.

45. Both quotes are taken from Stephen Metcalf, "Reading Between the Lines," *The Nation*, January 28, 2002, 18.

46. Ibid., 20.

47. Richard Rothstein, "The Weird Science of the Education Law," *New York Times*, January 16, 2002, A18.

48. Peter Dreier and Dick Flacks, "Patriotism's Secret History," *The Nation*, June 3, 2002, 42.

49. Rothstein, "The Weird Science of the Education Law," A18.

50. Both quotes are from President George W. Bush, *No Child Left Behind* (Washington, D.C.: U.S. Government Printing Office, 2001), 20.

51. For example, see Richard Rothstein, "Schools, Crime and Gross Exaggeration," *New York Times*, February 7, 2001, A16.

52. Ibid.

53. I take up this issue in *Public Spaces, Private Lives;* see also, Franklin E. Zimring, Gordon Hawkins, and Sam Kamin, *Punishment and Democracy: Three Strikes and You're Out in California* (New York: Oxford University Press, 2001).

54. For an extensive analysis of racial discrimination in the public schools, see the report by Rebecca Gordon, Libero Della Piana, and Terry Keleher, *Facing the Consequences: An Examination of Racial Discrimination in U.S. Public Schools* (Oakland: Applied Research Center, March 2000).

55. David Trend, *Welcome to Cyberschool: Education at the Crossroads in the Information Age* (Boulder: Rowman and Littlefield, 2001), 58.

56. Children's Defense Fund, "Children or Tax Cuts: The Nation Must Decide," available online at http://www.childrensdefense.org/release020508.php.

57. See, for example, Stan Karp, "Bush Plan Fails Schools," *Z Magazine* (April 2001), 40–44.

58. Cornelius Castoriadis, "Democracy as Procedure and Democracy as Regime," *Constellations* 4:1 (1997), 4.

59. Donna Gaines, "How Schools Teach Our Kids to Hate," *Newsday* (April 25, 1999), B5.

60. As has been widely reported, the prison industry has become big business, with many states spending more on prison construction than on university construction. See Anthony Lewis, "Punishing the Country," *New York Times*, December 2, 1999, A1.

61. Most of these figures are taken from Jeff Madrick, "Economic Scene," *New York Times*, June 13, 2002, C2.

62. Children's Defense Fund, *Leave No Child Behind*, v.

Chapter 5

1. Ngugi Wa Thiong' O, *Moving the Centre: The Struggle for Cultural Freedom* (London: James Currey, 1993), 76.
2. Zygmunt Bauman, *Work, Consumerism and the New Poor* (Philadelphia: Open University Press, 1998), 73.
3. John Binde, "Toward an Ethic of the Future," *Public Culture* 12:1 (2000), 51–72.
4. See Manuel Castells, *The Information Age: Economy, Society, and Culture*, 3 vols. (Malden, Mass.: Blackwell, 1998); Ulrich Beck, *What is Globalization?* (London: Polity Press, 2000); and Zygmunt Bauman, *In Search of Politics* (Stanford: Stanford University Press, 1999).
5. Zygmunt Bauman, *The Individualized Society* (London: Polity Press, 2001), 149.
6. This issue is taken up in detail in a number of sources; see Stanley Aronowitz, "Globalization and the State," in *The Last Good Job in America* (Lanham, Md.: Rowman and Littlefield, 2001), 159–75. See also Christian Parenti, *Lockdown America: Police and Prisons in the Age of Crisis* (London: Verso Press, 1999) and David Garland, *The Culture of Control* (Chicago: University of Chicago Press, 2001).
7. Bauman, *Work, Consumerism and the New Poor,* 65.
8. Ulrich Beck, *Risk Society,* trans. M. Ritter (Thousand Oaks: Sage, 1992), 137.
9. Bauman, *In Search of Politics.*
10. Lewis H. Lapham, "Res publica," *Harper's Magazine,* December 2001, 10.
11. Zygmunt Bauman, *In Search of Politics,* 2.
12. Herbert Marcuse, *Technology, War and Fascism: The Collected Papers of Herbert Marcuse,* vol. 1, ed. Douglas Kellner (London Routledge, 1998), 80.
13. Lewis H. Lapham, "Res publica," 8.
14. Bauman, *Work, Consumerism and the New Poor.*
15. Henry A. Giroux, *Stealing Innocence: Corporate Culture's War on Children* (New York: Palgrave, 2001).
16. Lawrence Grossberg, "Why Does Neo-Liberalism Hate Kids? The War on Youth and the Culture of Politics," *The Review of Education/Pedagogy/Cultural Studies* 23:2 (2001), 117.
17. Ibid., 133.
18. A conversation between Lani Guinier and Anna Deavere Smith, "Rethinking Power, Rethinking Theater," *Theater* 31:3 (Winter 2002), 31.
19. Jeff Gates, "Modern Fashion or Global Fascism?" *Tikkun* 17:1 (2001), 30.
20. Doug Henwood, "Debts Everywhere," *The Nation,* July 19, 1999, 12.
21. Charles Handy, *The Hungry Spirit* (New York: Broadway, 1998), 17.
22. Mike Clark, "'Ghost World' Charms, 'Freddy' Fizzles," *USA Today,* December 28, 2001, 13D.
23. Grossberg, "Why Does Neo-Liberalism Hate Kids?," 112–113.

24. See Znet Commentary/Cynthia Peters/Teens, 2.
25. These figures are taken from the Children's Defense Fund web site, and are available at www.childrensdefense.org/factsfigures_moments.htm. Also, see Grossberg, "Why Does Neo-Liberalism Hate Kids?," 114–115.
26. Grossberg, "Why Does Neo-Liberalism Hate Kids?," 127–128.
27. Guinier and Smith, "Rethinking Power," 40.
28. Grossberg, "Why Does Neo-Liberalism Hate Kids?," 133.
29. Arif Dirlik, "Literature/Identity: Transnationalism, Narrative and Representation," *Review of Education/Pedagogy/Cultural Studies* (in press), 7.
30. Margaret Miles, *Seeing and Believing: Religion and Values in the Movies* (Boston: Beacon Press, 1996), 14.
31. Gary Olson and Lynn Worsham, "Staging the Politics of Difference: Homi Bhabha's Critical Literacy," *JAC* 18:3 (1999), 11.

Chapter 6

1. Claude Brown, *Manchild in the Promised Land* (New York: Signet, 1965), 295.
2. Ibid., 419.
3. Frantz Fanon, *Black Skin, White Masks*, trans. Charles Lam Markman (New York: Grove Press, 1967), 27.
4. Robin D. G. Kelley, "Confessions of a Nice Negro, or Why I Shaved my Head," in Don Belton, *(Speak My Name): Black Men on Masculinity and the American Dream* (Boston: Beacon Press, 1997), 2.
5. Ibid.
6. Ellen Willis argues that the two major upheavals to America's racial hierarchy have been the destruction of the Southern caste system and the subversion of whiteness as an unquestioned norm. She also argues rightly that to dismiss these achievements as having done little to change racist power relations insults people who have engaged in these struggles. See Ellen Willis, "The Up and Up: On the Limits of Optimism," *Transition* 7:2 (1998), 44–61.
7. For a compilation of figures suggesting the ongoing presence of racism in American society, see Ronald Walters, "The Criticality of Racism," *Black Scholar* 26:1 (Winter 1996), 2–8; Children's Defense Fund, *The State of Children in America's Union: A 2002 Action Guide to Leave No Child Behind* (Washington, D.C.: Children's Defense Fund Publication, 2002), xvii.
8. Ginsburg cited in "Race On Screen and Off," *The Nation*, December 29, 1997, 6.
9. Jeff Madrick, "Economic Scene," *New York Times,* June 13, 2002, C2.
10. Shipler summarized in Jack H. Geiger, "The Real World of Race," *The Nation*, December 1, 1998, 27. See also David Shipler, "Reflections on

Race," *Tikkun* 13:1 (1998), 59, 78, and *A Country of Strangers: Blacks and Whites in America* (New York: Vintage, 1998).

11. For a devastating critique of Randall Kennedy's move to the right, see Derrick Bell, "The Strange Career of Randall Kennedy," *New Politics* 7:1 (Summer 1998), 55–69.

12. David Theo Goldberg, *Racist Culture* (Malden, Mass.: Basil Blackwell, 1993), 105.

13. Katya Gibel Azoulay, "Experience, Empathy and Strategic Essentialism," *Cultural Studies* 11:1 (1997), 91.

14. Robin D. G. Kelley, "Integration: What's Left," *The Nation*, December 14, 1998, 18.

15. Cited in Randall Johnson, "Editor's Introduction: Pierre Bourdieu on Art, Literature and Culture," in Pierre Bourdieu, *The Field of Cultural Production* (New York: Columbia University Press, 1993), 19.

16. Ibid., 17.

17. Gary Olson and Lynn Worsham, "Staging the Politics of Difference: Homi Bhabha's Critical Literacy," *JAC* 18:3 (1999), 29.

18. Susan Bordo, *Twilight Zones: The Hidden Life of Cultural Images from Plato to O.J.* (Stanford: University of California Press, 1997), 2.

19. Herman Gray, *Watching Race: Television and the Struggle for "Blackness"* (Minneapolis: University of Minnesota Press, 1995), 132.

20. Robin D. G. Kelley, *Yo'Mama's Disfunktional!: Fighting the Culture Wars in Urban America* (Boston: Beacon Press, 1997).

21. What is strange about this discourse is that in the name of emancipation, it reproduces the very kind of infantilization that post-colonial theorists such as Frantz Fanon identified as central to anti-black racism. See Fanon, *Black Skin, White Masks,* especially chapter one: "The Negro and Language," and chapter six, "The Negro and Psychopathology." For a brilliant analysis of Fanon's refusal to see blacks as the problem, see Lewis Gordon, "Through the Zone of Nonbeing: Reading Fanon's *Black Skin, White Masks* Fifty Years Later," in *The C. L. R. James Journal* (forthcoming).

22. Stanley Crouch, "A Lost Generation and its Exploiters," *New York Times*, August 26, 2001, AR, 8.

23. Roger Ebert, "Baby Boy," *Chicago Sun-Times*, June 27, 2001, 1.

24. David Theo Goldberg, *The Racial State* (Malden, Mass.: Blackwell, 2002), 206, 217.

25. For example, see Loic Wacquant, "From Slavery to Mass Incarceration: Rethinking the 'race question' in the US," *New Left Review* (January-February, 2002), 41–60.

26. S. Craig Watkins, *Representing: Hip Hop Culture and the Production of Black Cinema* (Chicago: University of Chicago Press, 1998), 1.

27. Paul Street, "Prisons and the New American Racism," *Dissent* (Summer 2001), 49.

28. Catherine Campbell cited in *Counterpunch* editorial, "Criminalizing Youth," (December 20, 2000), 3, 4; available on line at www.counterpunch.org/youth.html.

29. Cindy Fuchs, "All Grown Up: John Singleton on the Mature Baby Boy," www.citypaper.net/articles/062801/mov.singleton.shtml (June 28-July 5, 2001), 2.

30. Michael Eric Dyson, *Holler If You Hear Me: Searching for Tupac Shakur* (New York: Basic Books, 2001), 125.

31. Marilyn Elias, "Disparity in Black and White?" *USA Today*, December 11, 2000, 9D.

32. Cited in David Barsamian, "Interview with Angela Davis," *The Progressive*, February 2001, 35.

33. David Cole, *No Equal Justice: Race and Class in the American Criminal Justice System* (New York: The New Press, 1999), 144.

34. Steven R. Donziger, *The Real War on Crime: The Report of the National Criminal Justice Commission* (New York: Harper, 1996), 101.

35. Cited in Eyal Press, "The Color Test," *Lingua Franca* (October 2000), 55.

36. David Theo Goldberg, *The Racial State* (Malden, Mass.: Basil Blackwell, 2002), 4.

37. S. Craig Watkins, 4.

38. Robin D. G. Kelley, "Neo-Cons of the Black Nation," *Black Renaissance Noire* 1:2 (Summer/Fall 1997), 142.

39. David Theo Goldberg and John Solomos, "General Introduction," in David Theo Goldberg and John Solomos, eds., *A Companion to Ethic and Racial Studies* (Malden, Mass.: Blackwell, 2002), 5–6.

40. I take up this issue in great detail throughout this book, but also in *Public Spaces, Private Lives: Beyond the Culture of Cynicism* (Boulder: Rowman and Littlefield, 2001). See also Zygmunt Bauman, *The Individualized Society* (London: Polity Press, 2001).

41. Goldberg, *The Racial State*, 112.

42. These ideas are taken from ibid., 233.

43. Bauman, *The Individualized Society*, 73.

44. Armond White, "A Child at the Oscars," *First of the Month* 4:1 (2002), 5.

45. Lawrence Grossberg, "Identity and Cultural Studies; Is That All there Is," in Stuart Hall and Paul Du Gay, eds., *Questions of Cultural Identity* (Thousand Oaks: Sage, 1996), 99–100.

46. This theme is extensively explored in Paul Gilroy, *Against Race* (Cambridge: Harvard University Press, 2000).

47. Ibid., 230.

48. Ibid., 231.

49. Goldberg, *The Racial State*, 131.

50. Ellen Willis, *Don't Think, Smile: Notes on a Decade of Denial* (Boston: Beacon Press, 1999), 74.

51. bell hooks, *Yearning: Race, Gender, and Cultural Politics* (Boston: South End Press, 1990), 59.

52. Dyson, *Holler If You Hear Me*, 185.

53. Dave Kehr, "Mother Love, Too Little Or Too Much," *New York Times* late edition, July 29, 2001, 2.

54. Dyson, 184–185.

55. Willis, *Don't Think, Smile*, 157.

56. bell hooks, *Black Looks* (Boston: South End Press, 1992), 89.

57. Zygmunt Bauman, *In Search of Politics* (Stanford: Stanford University Press, 1999), 185.

58. John Brenkman, "Extreme Criticism," in Judith Butler, John Guillary, and Kendal Thomas, eds., *What's Left of Theory* (New York: Routledge, 2000), 119.

59. These figures are taken from Paul Street, "Race, Prison, and Poverty: The Race to Incarcerate in the Age of Correctional Keynesianism," *Z Magazine* (May 2001), 25–31.

60. These issues are taken up in David Theo Goldberg, "Surplus Value: The Political Economy of Prisons," in Joy James, ed., *Police, Detention, Prisons* (New York: St. Martin's Press, forthcoming), 3–25.

61. Cited in Lawrence Grossberg, "The Victory of Culture, Part I," University of North Carolina at Chapel Hill, unpublished manuscript, February 1998, 27.

62. Goldberg and Solomos, "General Introduction, 3.

63. Arif Dirlik, "Literature/Identity: Transnationalism, Narrative, and Representation," *Review of Education/Pedagogy/Cultural Studies* (in press), 20.

64. Toni Morrison, "How Can Values Be Taught in the University?," *Michigan Quarterly Review* (Spring 2001), 278.

65. Edward W. Said, "The Public Role of Writers and Intellectuals," *The Nation*, October 1, 2001, 36.

66. Robin D. G. Kelley brilliantly captures this combination of imagination and compassion as central to any viable politics in *Freedom Dreams: The Black Radical ImagiNation*, Boston: Beacon Press, 2002).

Chapter 7

1. Robert W. McChesney, "Introduction," to Noam Chomsky, *Profit Over People* (New York: Seven Stories Press, 1999), 7.

2. Benjamin R. Barber, "Blood Brothers, Consumers, or Citizens? Three Models of Identity—Ethnic, Commercial, and Civic," in Carol Gould

and Pasquale Pasquino, eds., *Cultural Identity and the Nation State* (Lanham, Md.: Rowman and Littlefield, 2001), 65.

3. Some critical commentaries on this phenomenon can be found in Alex Kuczynski, "Hold Me! Squeeze Me! Buy a 6-Pack!," *New York Times,* Sunday styles section, November 10, 1997, 1, 4; Rob Walker, "Me, My Brand and I," *New York Times Magazine,* May 14, 2000, 19–20.

4. See Tom Peters, "The Brand Called You," *Fast Company* (August / September 1997), 83–94.

5. This quote is taken from the ChrisandLuke.com website. Available at www.ChrisandLuke.com/a html.

6. For a classic critique of the brand-name society, see Naomi Klein, *No Logo: Taking Aim at the Brand Bullies* (New York: Picador, 1999).

7. Cited in Dawn Kessler, "What Would you Do for A Free Ride to College?" Available at www.collegeboundmag.com/side/quickconnect.html.

8. William Powers, "The Art of Exploitation," *The Atlantic Monthly,* available on-line at www.theatlantic.... om/politic/nj/powers2001–08–08.html.

9. Terrance Ball, "Imagining Marketopia," *Dissent* (Summer 2001), 80.

10. These ideas are taken from Barber, "Blood Brothers, Consumers, or Citizens?" in *Cultural Identity and the Nation State,* 65.

11. Edward S. Herman and Robert W. McChesney, *The Global Media: The New Missionaries of Global Capitalism* (Washington and London: Cassell, 1997), 3.

12. I address this issue in *Public Spaces, Private Lives: Beyond the Culture of Cynicism* (Lanham, Md.: Rowman and Littlefield, 2001).

13. Barber, "Blood Brothers, Consumers, or Citizens?," in *Cultural Identity and the Nation State,* 59.

14. I take up this issue of cynicism in great detail in *Public Spaces, Private Lives.*

15. Joseph Kahn, "Redrawing the Map," *New York Times,* Section 4, June 25, 2000, 5.

16. This is a position shared by a number of influential social and political theorists. For example, see Robert W. McChesney, *Corporate Media and the Threat the Democracy* (New York: Seven Stories Press, 1997); Pierre Bourdieu, *Acts of Resistance: Against the Tyranny of the Market* (New York: The New Press, 1998); Noam Chomsky, *Profit Over People: Neoliberalism and Global Order* (New York: Seven Stories Press), 1999; Colin Leys, *Market Driven Politics* (London: Verso, 2001).

17. Jean Comaroff and John L. Comaroff, "Millennial Capitalism: First Thoughts on a Second Coming," *Public Culture* 12(2), 333.

18. Zygmunt Bauman, *In Search of Politics* (Stanford: Stanford University Press, 1999), 127.

19. Comaroff and Comaroff, "Millennial Capitalism," 322.
20. James Rule, "Markets, in Their Place," *Dissent* (Winter 1998), 31.
21. Zygmunt Bauman, *The Individualized Society* (London: Polity Press, 2001), 107.
22. Ibid.
23. The classic dominant texts on corporate culture are Terrance Deal and Alan Kennedy, *Corporate Culture: The Rites and Rituals of Corporate Life* (Reading, Mass.: Addison-Wesley, 1982), and Thomas Peterson and Robert Waterman, *In Search of Excellence* (New York: Harper and Row, 1982). I also want to point out that corporate culture is a dynamic, ever-changing force. But in spite of its innovations and changes, it rarely if ever challenges the centrality of the profit motive, or fails to prioritize commercial considerations over a set of values that would call the class-based system of capitalism into question. For an informative discussion of the changing nature of corporate culture in light of the cultural revolution of the 1960s, see Thomas Frank, *The Conquest of Cool* (Chicago: University of Chicago Press, 1997).
24. Gary Becker captures this sentiment in his book, *The Economic Approach to Human Behavior.* He argues "We not only ought to think and act as self-interested agents, but we are already acting (if not yet thinking) in precisely those ways. We are each of us self-interested calculators of our own advantage, however much we might wish to hide that fact from others and even (or perhaps especially) from ourselves." Cited in Terrance Ball, 78.
25. Alan Bryman, *Disney and His Worlds* (New York: Routledge, 1995), 154.
26. Robin D. G. Kelley, *Yo' Mama's Disfunktional: Fighting the Culture Wars in Urban America* (Boston: Beacon Press, 1997).
27. For a context from which to judge the effects of such cuts on the poor and children of America, see Children's Defense Fund, *The State of America's Children—A Report from the Children's Defense Fund* (Boston: Beacon Press, 2002). On the emergence of the prison-industrial complex and how it diverts money from higher education, see my *Public Spaces, Private Lives;* Christian Parenti, *Lockdown America: Police and Prisons in the Age of Crisis* (London: Verso Press, 1999).
28. Ball, 78.
29. This example is taken from Leys, *Market Driven Politics,* 212–13.
30. Pierre Bourdieu, "The Essence of Neoliberalism," *Le Monde Diplomatique* (December 1998). Available on-line at www.en.monde diplomatique.fr/1998/12/08bourdieu), 4.
31. Benjamin R. Barber, "A Failure of Democracy, Not Capitalism," *New York Times,* July 29, 2002, A23.
32. Cited in Tom Turnipseed, "Crime in the Suites Enabled by Political Corruption Causes a Crisis in the Credibility of US Capitalism," *Common*

Dreams, June 29, 2002, 1. Available on-line at www.commondreams.org/views02/0629–01.htm.

33. Sheila Slaughter, "Professional Values and the Allure of the Market," *Academe* (September-October, 2001), 1.

34. Cited in Beth Huber, "Homogenizing the Curriculum: Manufacturing the Standardized Student." Available on-line at www.louisville.edu/journal/workplace/huber.html, 1.

35. An example of how cozy the relationship between venture capitalism and the university has become can be seen in the story uncritically reported in *The Chronicle of Higher Education.* See Goldie Blumenstyk, "Chasing the Rainbow: A Venture Capitalist on the Trail of University-Based Companies," *The Chronicle of Higher Education* (March 15, 2002), A28-A32.

36. Goldie Blumenstyk, "Knowledge is a form of Venture Capital for a Top Columbia Administrator," *The Chronicle of Higher Education* (February 8, 2001), A29.

37. John Palattella, "Ivory Towers in the Marketplace," *Dissent* (Summer 2001), 73.

38. See Ronald Strickland, "Gender, Class and the Humanities in the Corporate University," Genders 35 (2002), 2; available on-line at www.genders.org/g35/g35_stricland.html.

39. The percentage of part-time faculty in higher education continues to grow from 33 percent in 1987 to 43 percent in 1998. Moreover, 53 percent of such institutions offered no benefits to part-time faculty. See Mary Beth Marklein, "Part-time instructors march for better pay," *USA Today,* October 30, 2001, 11D.

40. Critical educators have provided a rich history of how both public and higher education have been shaped by the politics, ideologies, and images of industry. For example, see Samuel Bowles and Herbert Gintis, *Schooling in Capitalist America* (New York: Basic Books, 1976); Martin Carnoy and Henry Levin, *Schooling and Work in the Democratic State* (Stanford: Stanford University Press, 1985); Stanley Aronowitz and Henry A. Giroux, *Education Still Under Siege* (Westport: Bergin and Garvey, 1993); Stanley Aronowitz and William DiFazio, *The Jobless Future* (Minneapolis: University of Minnesota Press, 1994); Cary Nelson, *Will Teach for Food: Academic Labor in Crisis* (Minneapolis: University of Minnesota Press, 1997); D.W. Livingstone, *The Education-Jobs Gap* (Boulder: Westview, 1998).

41. Some recent examples include: Aronowitz and Giroux, *Education Still Under Siege;* Randy Martin, *Chalk Lines* (Minneapolis: University of Minnesota Press, 1998); Stanley Aronowitz, *The Knowledge Factory* (Boston: Beacon Press, 2000); and Henry A. Giroux, *Impure Acts: The Practical Politics of Cultural Studies* (New York: Routledge, 2000).

42. Richard Hoftstadter cited in Eyal Press and Jennifer Washburn, "The Kept University," *The Atlantic Monthly*, March 20, 2000, 54. Hofstadter expands on these views in *The Development and Scope of Higher Education in the United States* (with C. De Witt Hardy) (New York: Columbia University Press, 1952); *The Development of Academic Freedom in the United States* (with Walter Metzger) (New York: Columbia University Press, 1955); and *Anti-Intellectualism in American Life* (New York: Vintage Books, 1963). A more complicated, though ultimately distorting critique appears in Stephen Brier and Roy Rosenzweig, "The Keyboard Campus," *The Nation*, April 22, 2002, 29–32.
43. See Sheila Slaughter and Larry L. Leslie, *Academic Capitalism: Politics, Policies, and the Entrepreneurial University* (Baltimore: Johns Hopkins University, 1997).
44. Press and Washburn, "The Kept University," 42.
45. Ibid., 39–54.
46. Cited in Katherine S. Mangan, "Medical Schools Routinely Ignore Guidelines on Company-Sponsored Research, Study Finds," *The Chronicle of Higher Education*, available on-line at http://chronicle.com/daily/2002/10/2002102050ln.htm.
47. Patricia Brodsky, "Shrunken Heads: The Humanities Under the Corporate Model," available on-line at www.louisville.edu/journal/workplace/patbrodsky.html., 5.
48. Jeff Williams, "Brave New University," *College English* 61:6 (July 1999), 744.
49. Maureen Shine, "Knight, Matching Gifts Endow Record Number of UO Chairs," University of Oregon news release. Available on-line at http://comm.uoregon.edu/newsreleses/latest/june98/0o61198.html . It should be noted that "the Gates Foundation Minority Fellowship Program spends more on advertising than it does on the scholarships themselves." Cited in Jennifer L. Croissant, "Can This Campus be Bought," Academe (September-October 2001), available on-line at www.aau org/publications/Academe01SO/so01cro.html, 3.
50. Both quotes are cited in Julianne Basinger, "Increase in Number of Chairs Endowed by Corporations Prompt New Concerns," *The Chronicle of Higher Education*, April 24, 1998, A53.
51. Blumenstyk, "Chasing the Rainbow," A28-A32.
52. David Trend, *Welcome to Cyberschool: Education at the Crossroads in the Information Age* (Lanham, Md.: Rowman and Littlefield, 2001), 59.
53. Ibid.
54. On this issue, see Bauman, *In Search of Politics*.
55. Jay Mathews, "Its Lowly at the Top: What Became of the Great College Presidents?" *The Washington Post*, June 10, 2001, B01.
56. Clara M. Lovett, "The Dumbing Down of College Presidents," *The Chronicle of Higher Education: The Chronicle Review*, April 5, 2002, B20.

57. Jim Hopkins, "Universities Hire More Executives to Lead," *USA Today,* April 22, 2002, 1B.

58. Ibid., 1B. See, for instance, the story on Summers by Martin Van Der Werf, "Lawrence Summers and His Tough Questions," *The Chronicle of Higher Education,* April 26, 2002, A29-A32.

59. There are a number of texts that touch on this issue. Some of these include: Aronowitz and Giroux, *Education Still Under Siege;* Michael Berube and Cary Nelson, eds., *Higher Education Under Fire* (New York: Routledge, 1995); Bill Readings, *The University in Ruins* (Cambridge: Harvard University Press, 1996); Slaughter and Leslie, *Academic Capitalism;* Aronowitz, *The Knowledge Factory;* Geoffrey D. White, ed., *Campus, Inc.: Corporate Power in the Ivory Tower* (Amherst, New York: Prometheus Books, 2000).

60. Stanley Aronowitz, "The New Corporate University," *Dollars and Sense,* March / April, 1998, 32–35.

61. The many books extolling corporate CEO's as a model for leadership in any field are too extensive to cite, but one typical example can be found in Robert Heller, *Roads to Success: Put Into Practice the Best Business Ideas of Eight Leading Gurus* (New York: Dorling Kindersley, 2001).

62. For an excellent analysis of Michael Milken's role in various education projects, see Robin Truth Goodman and Kenneth Saltman, *Strange Love: Or How We Learn to Stop Worrying and Love the Market* (Lanham, Md.: Rowman and Littlefield, 2002).

63. Catherine. S. Manegold, "Study Says Schools Must Stress Academics," *New York Times,* September 23, 1998, A22. It is difficult to understand how any school system could have subjected students to such a crude lesson in commercial pedagogy.

64. George Soros, *On Globalization* (New York: Public Affairs, 2002), 164, 6.

65. Stanley Aronowitz and William Difazio, "The New Knowledge Work," in A. H. Halsey, Hugh Lauder, Phillip Brown, Amy Stuart Wells, eds., *Education: Culture, Economy, Society* (New York: Oxford, 1997), 193.

66. This issue is explored in great detail in Robert W. McChesney, *Rich Media, Poor Democracy: Communication Politic in Dubious Times* (New York: The New Press, 1999).

67. This is amply documented in Jeremy Rifkin, *The End of Work* (New York: G. Putnam Book, 1995); William Wolman and Anne Colamosca, *The Judas Economy: The Triumph of Capital and the Betrayal of Work* (Reading: Addison-Weslsey Publishing, 1997); Stanley Aronowitz and William Difazio, *The Jobless Future* (Minneapolis: University of Minnesota Press, 1994; *The New York Times Report: The Downsizing of America* (New York: Times Books, 1996); and Stanley Aronowitz and Jonathan Cutler, *Post-Work* (New York: Routledge, 1998).

68. Cornel West, "The New Cultural Politics of Difference," *October* 53 (Summer 1990), 35.

69. Jim Hopkins, "Universities Hire More Executives to Lead," *USA Today,* April 22, 2002, 1B.

70. Sheila Slaughter, "Professional Values and the Allure of the Market," *Academe* (September-October, 2001), 3–4.

71. I also take up Carlin's position in much greater detail in *Impure Acts* (New York: Routledge, 2000), 51–54.

72. Carlin cited in William H. Honan, "The Ivory Tower Under Siege," *New York Times,* section 4A, January 4, 1998, 33.

73. Ibid.

74. Cited in NEA Higher Education Research Center, *Update* 7:3 (June 2001), 1.

75. Michael Dubson, "Introduction," *Ghosts in the Classroom: Stories of College Adjunct Faculty—and the Price We All Pay* (Boston: Camel's Back Books, 2001), 9–10.

76. David F. Noble, "The Future of the Digital Diploma Mill," *Academe* 87:5 (September-October 2001), 29.These arguments are spelled out in greater detail in David F. Noble, *Digital Diploma Mills: The Automation of Higher Education* (New York: Monthly Review Press, 2002).

77. Noble, "The Future of the Digital Diploma Mill," 31.

78. For an extensive commentary on the Army's distance-education program, see Michael Arnone, "Army's Huge Distance-Education Effort Wins Many Supporters in Its First Year," *The Chronicle of Higher Education,* February 8, 2002, A33-A35. This highly favorable, if not flattering piece of reporting, is accompanied by another commentary on David Noble in which his views are badly simplified and his professional integrity called into question. See Jeffrey R. Young, "Distance-Education Critic's Book Takes Aim at Army's Efforts," *The Chronicle of Higher Education,* February 8, 2002, A34.

79. Noble, "The Future of the Digital Diploma Mill," 29–30.

80. Both Levine's statement and the following quote can be found in Eyal Press and Jennifer Washburn, "Digital Diplomas," *Mother Jones,* January / February 2001. Available on-line at www.motherjones.com/ mother_jones/JF01/toc.html, 1.

81. Massy and Zemsky cited in Press and Washburn, "Digital Diplomas," 8.

82. Cited in Noble, op. cit., 31.

83. Press and Washburn, "Digital Diplomas," 2.

84. Herbert Marcuse, "Some Social Implications of Modern Technology," *Technology, War, and Fascism,* ed. Douglas Kellner (New York: Routledge, 1998), 45.

85. Zygmunt Bauman, *Modernity and the Holocaust* (Ithaca: Cornell University Press, 1989).

86. For a critical analysis of the flaws and possibilities of such approaches in higher education, see: Trend, *Welcome to Cyberschool;* Andrew Feenberg,

228 / THE ABANDONED GENERATION

Questioning Technology (New York: Routledge, 1999); Hubert L. Dreyfus, *On the Internet* (New York: Routledge, 2001; Mark Poster, *What is the Matter with the Internet?* (Minneapolis: University of Minnesota Press, 2001).

87. Noble, *Digital Diploma Mills.*

88. For more details on the creation of on-line degrees for corporations, see Dan Carnevale, "Colleges Tailor on-line Degrees for Individual Companies," *The Chronicle of Higher Education,* January 28, 2002; available on-line at http://chronicle.com/cgi2-bin/printable.cgi.

89. Feenberg, *Questioning Technology,* viii.

90. Ibid., xv.

91. Slaughter, "Professional Values and the Allure of the Market," 3.

92. For an extensive analysis of the issue of intellectual property rights and the control over academic work in the university, see Corynne McSherry, *Who Owns Academic Work?: Battling for Control of Intellectual Property* (Cambridge: Harvard University Press, 2002).

93. Julia Porter Liebeskind, "Risky Business: Universities and Intellectual Property," *Academe,* (September-October, 2001), available on-line at www.aaup.org/publications/Academe/01SO/so01lie.htm, 2.

94. Ibid.

95. Press and Washburn, "Digital Diplomas," 8.

96. Condren cited in Press and Washburn, "Digital Diplomas," 8.

97. Stanley Aronowitz, "The New Corporate University," *Dollars and Sense* (March/April, 1998), 34–35.

98. This issue is taken up in Michael Berube, "Why Inefficiency is Good for Universities," *The Chronicle of Higher Education,* March 27, 1998, B4-B5.

99. Jeff Williams, "Brave New University," *College English* 61:6 (July 1999), 740.

100. This information is taken from "Pricing the Poor Out of College," *New York Times,* March 27, 2002, A27.

101. Stephen Burd, "Lack of Aid Will Keep 170,000 Qualified, Needy Students Out of College This Year, Report Warns," *The Chronicle of Higher Education,* June 27, 2002, 1. Available on-line at http://chronicle.com/daily/2002/06/2002062701n.html. For a robust argument for making college free for all students, see Adolph L. Reed, Jr., "Free College for All," *The Progressive,* April 2002, 12–14.

102. Michael Margolis, "Brave New Universities," *FirstMonday* (January 2002), 2, available on-line at www.firstmonday.dk/issues3_5/margolis/.

103. For a variety of critical commentaries on this issue, see Nelson, *Will Teach for Food;* Martin, ed., *Chalk Lines;* Cary Nelson and Stephen Watt, *Academic Keywords: A Devil's Dictionary for Higher Education* (New York: Routledge, 1999); Stanley Aronowitz, *The Knowledge Factory* (Boston: Beacon Press, 2000).

104. David L. Kirp, "Higher Ed Inc.: Avoiding the Perils of Outsourcing," *The Chronicle Review*, March 15, 2002, B14.
105. Ibid.
106. Cary Nelson, *Manifesto of a Tenured Radical* (New York: New York University Press, 1997), 169.
107. Trend, *Welcome to Cyberschool*, 55.
108. Jennifer L. Croissant, "Can This Campus be Bought," 2.
109. Bourdieu, *Acts of Resistance*, 8.
110. Ellen Willis, *Don't Think, Smile: Notes on a Decade of Denial* (Boston: Beacon Press, 1999), 27.
111. Peter Euben, "Reforming the Liberal Arts," *The Civic Arts Review*, No. 2 (Summer-Fall 2000), 10.
112. Bill Readings, *The University in Ruins* (Cambridge: Harvard University Press, 1996). As Ronald Strickland points out, Readings has almost nothing to say about how the corporate university reproduces the academic and social division of labor between elite and second-tier universities that is so central to changing the economic landscape. See Ronald Strickland, "Gender, Class and the Humanities in the Corporate University," *Genders* 35 (2002), 1–16; available on-line at www.genders.org/g35/g35_strickland.html.
113. Williams, "Brave New University," 750.
114. There are a number of books that take up the relationship between schooling and democracy. Some of the more important recent critical contributions include: Elizabeth A. Kelly, *Education, Democracy, & Public Knowledge* (Boulder: Westview, 1995); Wilfred Carr and Anthony Hartnett, *Education and the Struggle for Democracy* (Philadelphia: Open University Press,1996); Henry A. Giroux, *Schooling and the Struggle for Public Life* (Minneapolis: University of Minnesota Press, 1988); Stanley Aronowitz and Henry A. Giroux, *Postmodern Education* (Minneapolis: University of Minnesota Press, 1991); Aronowitz and Giroux, *Education Still Under Siege;* and Henry A. Giroux, *Pedagogy and the Politics of Hope* (Boulder: Westview, 1997).
115. A conversation between Lani Guinier and Anna Deavere Smith, "Rethinking Power, Rethinking Theater," *Theater* 31:1 (Winter 2002), 36.
116. Robin D. G. Kelley, "Neo-Cons of the Black Nation," *Black Renaissance Noire* 1:2 (Summer/Fall 1997), 146.
117. Arundhati Roy, *Power Politics* (Cambridge: South End Press, 2001), 11–12.
118. Noam Chomsky, "Paths Taken, Tasks Ahead," *Profession* (2000), 35.
119. Pierre Bourdieu, "For a Scholarship of Commitment," *Profession* (2000), 45, 42–43.
120. See Nelson, *Will Teach For Food*.

121. Aronowitz, *The Knowledge Factory,* 63, 109–110.
122. Short Subjects, "Students Hold 'Teach-Ins' to Protest Corporate Influence in Higher Education," *The Chronicle of Higher Education,* March 13, 1998, A11. Also note Peter Dreier's commentary on the student activism emerging in 1998, in "The Myth of Student Apathy," *The Nation,* April 13, 1998, 19–22.
123. Liza Featherstone, "Sweatshops, Students, and the Corporate University," *Croonenbergh's Fly* No. 2 (Summer 2002), 108.
124. For a commentary on Students Against Sweatshops, see Featherstone, 107–117.
125. Liza Featherstone, "The New Student Movement," *The Nation,* May 15, 2000, 12.
126. Ibid.
127. Featherstone, "Sweatshops, Students, and the Corporate University," 112.
128. I have taken this idea from Nick Couldry, "A Way Out of the (Televised) Endgame?" *OpenDemocracy,* available on-line at www.opendemocracy. net/forum/strands_home.asp, 1.
129. Imre Szeman, "Introduction: Learning to Learn from Seattle," in Imre Szeman, ed., special double issue, *The Review of Education, Pedagogy, and Cultural Studies* 24:1–2 (January-June, 2002), 5.
130. Ibid., 4.
131. Ibid., 5.
132. Jacques Derrida, "Intellectual Courage: An Interview," *Culture Machine* vol. 2 (2000), 9; available at http://culturemachine.tees.ac.uk/articles/art_derr.htm.
133. Toni Morrison, "How Can Values Be Taught in This University," *Michigan Quarterly Review* (Spring 2001), 278.
134. Bourdieu, *Acts of Resistance,* 26.
135. Meghan Morris cited in "Why Does Neo-Liberalism Hate Kids? The War on Youth and the Culture of Politics," *The Review of Education/Pedagogy/Cultural Studies* 23:2 (2001), 114.
136. Jacques Derrida, "No One is Innocent: A Discussion with Jacques Derrida About Philosophy in the Face of Terror," *The Information Technology, War and Peace Project,* 2. Available at www.watsoninstitute.org/infopeace/911/derrida_innocence.html.

INDEX